How To
Do Your Best
On Law School
Exams

By Professor John Delaney

Drawings by Anne Burgess

Second Revised Edition	November 1988
Third Revised Edition	April 2001
Fourth Revised Edition	October 2006
Fifth Revised Edition	February 2012

Published by
John Delaney Publications
119 Greenpoint Road
Catskill, NY 12414
518-943-9507
www.johndelaneypub.com
www.facebook.com/johndelaneypublications

For My Sparkling Daughters

Jacqueline, Joan Colette and Clare

Children of the Dream

ABOUT THE AUTHOR

A law professor for thirty years, John Delaney taught Criminal Law, Advanced Criminal Law, Comparative Criminal Law, International Criminal Law and other subjects to law school students and students in masters and doctoral degree programs at the New York University School of Law. He then taught Criminal Law, Advanced Criminal Law, the First Amendment, the Fourteenth Amendment, Jurisprudence, a First-Year Seminar and other subjects at the City University of New York Law School. *How To Do Your Best on Law School Exams* emerged from these many years of teaching and reflecting.

Now retired, Professor Delaney is also the author of law review articles. His First Amendment article, "Police Power Absolutism and Nullifying the Free Exercise Clause: A Critique of Oregon v. Smith," 25 Ind. L. Rev. 71 (1991), has been cited in more than thirty-five law-review articles and by thirty-nine federal and state courts including the Supreme Court of California and the Supreme Court of Texas. His books additionally include *Learning Legal Reasoning, Briefing, Analysis and Theory;* and *Learning Criminal Law as Advocacy Argument: Complete with Exam Problems and Answers.* He was also the General Editor of nine other books, mostly about comparative law, in the *American Series of Foreign Penal Codes.*

Prior to teaching, Professor Delaney conducted approximately one thousand trials and he prepared more than one hundred and fifty appeals. He lives with his wife Pat and daughter Clare mostly in the beautiful Catskill region of New York and communicates with students by e-mail.

Composite Preface

This latest Revision incorporates new insights from my internet-based coaching of first-year students, and perfects the Book in other ways. The coaching of students from law schools throughout the country enables me to keep current with apparent exam trends and this Fifth Revision reflects such trends. It also clarifies the three issue-spotting methods detailed in Chapter Four, and it strengthens emphasis on the holistic nature of learning, outlining, issue spotting, and diverse exam argument-making. It adds a section on multiple-choice questions and it also adds an important new problem, "Books, Books and Books," that models a popular back-and-forth pattern of exam contract issues. And it merges Chapter Six and Seven. But I have resisted the temptation to embody the "On Looking Back" comments at the end of most Chapters into the new chapter contents, believing that their current location tells the story of the Book's evolution over decades, along with our more recent website, as I have deepened my insight. While a few other law-exam books that I have seen have clear value, they also suffer from a misleading reductionism, ignoring the variety of types of exams that most law students actually confront.

Despite improvements in law school pedagogy in recent years, the following quotations from the 1988 and 2001 Revisions still reflects my belief as to the need for this book. This Revision, too, is

> implicitly a critique of the obscurity that permeates too much of legal pedagogy. The challenge in law teaching is to empower students, not to add obscurity and mystification, a now [seemingly] waning "hide-the-ball" type of teaching often performed by a bullying professor who was hiding out from the real challenge. That real challenge is to illuminate the complex understanding, insight and method that students must learn. This multi-dimensional reality includes history, jurisprudence, doctrine and modes of legal [argument]. It also includes critical perspectives relating to the diverse realms of law, practice and public life as a lawyer. It is this understanding, insight and method — not an artificially added professorial complexity — that enables students to make sense of this form of the human enterprise. The challenge of legal culture demands that teachers be illuminators, not obfuscators [1988].

> The very survival of first-year, in-class, and closed-book exams requiring hurried first-draft writing with intense time pressure as the sole basis for grading at a graduate school is indefensible. And disgraceful is the fact that [many] of these exams still concentrate on a grossly reductive, two-note theme: Slotting key facts into the right categories [and explaining the choices] while implicitly pretending that law is not deeply historical, political, cultural and value-saturated [2001].

There is a better way: a first-year exam that mirrors a typical task one sees in legal practice. I refer to take-home exams where students have six, eight, or ten hours to complete the exam with full access to their notes, outlines and any other materials. In various kinds of practice, lawyers are sometimes asked by legal supervisors to produce a memorandum by the "end of the day" or asked by judges to submit a memorandum by "the next morning." Such a take-home exam eliminates the high-school-type reliance on memory[1] and instead poses a challenge to marshal core lawyerly skills and understanding in apt framing and cogent argument making. Enabling student access to all materials exactly matches what conscientious lawyers do in practice: they check and verify everything, including case-specific evidentiary rules. They do not rely on memory. Rather, they make sure everything is immediately accessible as they litigate the case. Adding a maximum word limit discourages inapt responses that simply regurgitate all that seems to be relevant. Such a take-home exam also roughly responds to the comment of a colleague at the NYULS who said to me, "I've never been asked in practice to respond to three questions in three hours — and without use of the library." The increased use of this simple change in law exams would be a major step towards fairness, legitimacy and sense.

---

[1] Some professors have additional expectations for a standout 'A' exam argument that will be illustrated in Chapter Five.

The scourge of elitism and the need for humility

Justice Antonin Scalia consecrates "the best and the brightest" law-school graduates as coming from Harvard and Yale. Yes, indeed, they have triumphed on these predominantly reductive "two-note theme" law exams. But I wonder how Socrates, Aristotle, Aquinas, Kant, Maimonides and Einstein would perform on the LSAT or first-year, in-class, time-pressured, memory-based exams. Edmund Burke's eloquent comment is relevant: "The law sharpens the mind, by narrowing it," and Oliver Wendell Holmes echoed, "whilst it sharpens the edge it narrows the blade." We all need more modesty about law exams and legal education, their strengths and weaknesses. Success in law test taking surely involves an acute (but narrow) intelligence and a set of related skills, but is hardly the measure of the diverse intelligences, skills and qualities needed to be an outstanding lawyer — and person. Indeed, brilliant, deep thinkers who habitually reflect in a multi-perspective manner before responding can be penalized and even lost to the profession by time-pressured exams that favor quick, but not necessarily the best, thinking. A more robust emphasis on both ethical and emotional intelligence, and the role of the lawyer as counselor, is needed.

Meanwhile, back at school you have to cope with what exists, and you can be comforted with the prospect that becoming a lawyer can transform your opportunities and your life. I am pleased that I did what I wanted — initially, intensive trial and appellate experience followed by public policy practice (especially analysis and writing for governmental "blue ribbon" commissions), and then decades of full-time law teaching, studying and authoring of books and articles.

I wish to acknowledge the legion of professors over the years who have helped to shape and sharpen the book. Any deficiencies in it are, of course, solely their responsibility. I especially wish to express my gratitude to former NYULS students Professors Robert Pugsley of the Southwestern University School of Law in Los Angeles and Jesse Kasowitz, formerly of the NYULS. Other NYULS Professors who aided include Oscar Chase, Eleanor Fox, Charles Knapp, Jack Slain and Harry Subin. At CUNYLS and many other law schools, they include: Jane Aiken, Dean Kristin Booth, Dean Bridget McCormack, Ellen Mosen James, the late Luis DeGraffe, Eric Lane, Dean Mary Lu Bilek, Cheryl Meyer, Liaquat Nax and Susan Stabile.

Another legion of friends, former students (at both NYULS and CUNYLS) as well as lawyers, editors, artists and other accomplices over the years, include: Larry Abramson, Lea Bernstein, Anne Burgess, Edgar Campbell, Ann and Jim Chamberlain, Lewis Creekmore, Patricia Crown, Theresa Delaney, Johanna deNiet, Michael de Leeuw, Nancy Feldman, Mary Jane Graves, Howard Klumpp, Irruska Kocka, Gloria Macri, Susan Martin, Chris McAliley, Jerry McElroy, Sheryl Michaelson, Kathy Morahan, Eleanor Nigretti, Catherine Park, Mordechai Pelta, Angel Recchia, Nitin Savur, and Betty Tabor.

I wish again to thank my wife, Patricia Ruck, Esq., and our sparkling twenty-two-year-old, Clare, for the continuing love and support that sustain all my writing projects. I also thank my older daughters, Jacqueline and Joan and their seven children, for their continuing love and support. Jackie's children are Devin, Michael, Jack, and Grace; Joan's children are Jack, Julia, and Liam. I thank Pat for her brilliant ideas, inspiration, insights, editing, and remarkable overall performance in accomplishing this 2012 Revision. I wish also to express my appreciation again to Christine Bush who ably and conscientiously carried out the prior Revision in 2006, and to Nina Sklansky who expertly and impressively edited this new Revision. And I appreciate the many valuable insights and suggestions of Christopher Byck, a recent law-school graduate; they have materially improved the Book in recent years.

Professor John Delaney (retired)
February, 2012

SUMMARY
TABLE OF CONTENTS

DETAILED TABLE OF CONTENTS

CHAPTER THREE—MASTERY OUTLINING OF YOUR COURSES FOR EXAMS

Chapter Four—Spotting Issues on Law Essay Exams

CHAPTER FIVE—OUTLINING AND WRITING 'A' EXAM ARGUMENTS

CHAPTER SIX—SAMPLE EXAM PROBLEMS AND ARGUMENTS

CHAPTER SEVEN: AVOIDING COMMON PITFALLS

APPENDICES

INTRODUCTION

The funny thing about law school is that we have you come to class and read cases, but you aren't tested over that. You need to learn how to take exams. The best way to do it is to take old exams, and talk about them with other students, and play with hypotheticals.

Harvard Law School Professor

THE NEED FOR THIS BOOK IS FOUNDED ON THREE REALITIES

- You can be smart, go to class, know the cases well, and still do poorly on law school exams.

- To excel on these exams, you must not only study hard—you must study smart. You must understand, practice, and master a set of lawyerly skills to apply what you know on the exams by spotting issues and then resolving them with lawyerly arguments.

- If at first you did not do your best, you can do better. Many students who initially did not do well have substantially improved their grades over time. They learned how to do better by painful "trial and error learning." From decades of law school teaching, I know you can learn these exam skills without the suffering and disadvantage inherent in unguided, trial and error learning.

The exam skills you need to do well are not genetically acquired, nor are they mysterious or exotic. These skills can be identified, understood, practiced, and refined. These performance skills apply to every subject and to each law exam you take, with important customizing for individual courses and professors. Once internalized, these skills enable you to do your best on the exams.

THE GOOD NEWS

You need not be a Holmes or Cardozo to master and apply these performance skills. The challenge is formidable, but in no sense Herculean. Remember that battalions of law students have annually mastered these skills. Many were not as able as you. In the past, it was an easy matter to be admitted to law school and not too difficult to be admitted to the "best schools." Today, it is far more difficult; it is therefore an achievement, one in which you should take a measure of pride. You are privileged to have this opportunity to transform yourself into a lawyer, a powerful position in our society that opens up vistas of opportunity and service.

What exactly are these exam performance skills? What exactly are the criteria by which you will be graded by your professors? How can you go about developing and perfecting these skills so that you can do your best on the exams? This book answers these questions in a systematic and integrated way. It is designed to present you with a holistic approach so that you can most effectively utilize the limited time available to equip yourself to do your best on the exams.

If you learn and apply the approaches and methods detailed in this book, it may mean the difference between 'Cs' and 'Bs' or 'Bs' and 'As'. Remember that no student can write model arguments. Indeed, no professor can write model arguments in the allotted exam time. You can make mistakes on exams and still do very well. Don't be discouraged by initial mistakes; be kind to yourself. With persistent practice over the semester, you can master these skills and perform well.

FAILURE OF LAW SCHOOLS TO PREPARE STUDENTS FOR EXAMS

Regrettably, while law schools can sometimes be impressive in what they do, most fail to systematically prepare students to take law exams. Many first-year students are painfully surprised by their first law-school exam grades. The exam format and your professors' expectations about your performance are radically different from what is expected in class, what you have faced in college, and in most other exams. Even worse, the elaborated, even discursive, reasoning in many of the appellate cases you decode in class is the very opposite of the concise, cogent argument making required for most exams. In addition, you do not routinely have your exams returned to you with specific comments about your exam strengths and weaknesses, so that you can identify your strengths and weaknesses and struggle to improve.

This routine failure by most law schools is an atrocious, even scandalous, pedagogy. It is axiomatic that taking exams should be a form of learning, and not only a performance measure. The fact that many law professors allow students to review their exams, and that a limited number have a model argument available, or that students can sometimes compare their responses with 'A' arguments ameliorates the harm. But it is no substitute for the professorial comment and review that is routine in most schooling and mandated by fundamental pedagogic principle.

Present law-school exam practice still reeks of mystification and obfuscation. I take pleasure in helping to demystify the exam process, to dispel the secrecy that surrounds it, and to make familiar what is unfamiliar.

Many students who compare their responses to excellent arguments of others having 'A' grades, or with a model argument, are puzzled. They have often told me that they made all or most of the points set forth in the 'A' argument, or the model argument, but that the 'A' response, "said them differently." Sometimes, these statements are accurate. What these students typically do not understand, however, is that differences in grades result from the application of special performance skills in issue spotting and argument-making that are a *sine qua non* of the excellent student, the effective exam taker, and the competent lawyer.

INTEGRATED AND SYSTEMATIC APPROACH

I present then a systematic and holistic approach to empower you to identify, learn, practice, and master the skills-centered learning and performance skills that you need for law exams (and practice). In Chapter One, I specify the nature of the "beast": the different challenge posed by law-school exams, the six tasks you must perform in issue-spotting and exam arguing, and the six criteria by which your professor will grade you. I also specify an overall approach designed to equip you to perform these six tasks to fulfill the six criteria. In Chapter Two, I detail strategies, methods, and techniques to aid you to learn how to learn law most efficiently and effectively, both for exams and for practice.

In Chapter Three, a variety of methods and techniques for outlining your courses for exams are specified. In Chapter Four, the art and craft of issue spotting is decoded. In Chapter Five, a series of formats for outlining, organizing, and writing out your exam arguments is detailed. In Chapter Six, an array of typical and diverse essay-exam problems is set forth, and strong and poor student responses to the problems are detailed with some brief explanations of both strengths and weaknesses. In Chapter Seven, I specify common pitfalls that undermine student preparation and performance.

LAW AS ADVOCACY ARGUMENT

The law is a problem-solving procedure. So are engineering, social work, medicine, psychiatry, teaching, etc. In each area, a skills-centered panoply of concepts, categories, distinctive vocabulary, rules, and logic is applied to deal with different types of problems. As a law student, you immerse yourself in the legal panoply, just as you would if you studied medicine, psychology, engineering, etc. The marked difference from these other areas, though, is that legal problem solving generally requires advocacy arguments. Lawyers are not neutral or objective: they are one-sided advocates for their clients.[1]

Clients present legal problems rooted in torts, contracts, criminal law, etc. The appellate cases you study in class are a wellspring of a more rarefied version of such problem-solving and lawyerly argument. At the pre-trial and trial levels, however, lawyers engage in a different version. There, they apply a fact-driven set of skills that enable them to extricate the key legal facts, spot the issues, apply legal rules and principles to those facts to resolve the issues, utilize relevant legal policy to support their rule application, and do all of the above in concise advocacy arguments. More simply stated, lawyers fit facts into legal categories provided by the rules by spotting issues and resolving them with advocacy arguments in order to advance a client's interests. But lawyers mostly solve client problems outside of the trial framework using their expert knowledge, resourcefulness, negotiating skill, and insight into human needs, hopes and foibles.

It is, therefore, sound legal theory, sound legal practice, and sound exam practicality to adopt a skills-centered learning and performance approach aimed at issue spotting and argument making to the study of law, the taking of exams, and the practice of law. The common beginner's view of law—as a set of black-letter rules to be memorized and almost mechanically applied—is false and entirely misconceives the practice of law and the nature of law-school education and exam taking.

Often, the study of law is presented as unique and unrelated to other human endeavors, as if the experience and accomplishments students bring to law school are unimportant, and as if no student had engaged in analytical reasoning before law school. The opening speech of Professor Kingsfield in the film *The Paper Chase* is a classic example. But the truth is that all of us bring much to the study of law. We spotted issues and resolved them in our prior education, work experience, and everyday lives. All of this experience is relevant, since issue spotting and argument-making demand practical judgment that is a product of our experience.

---

[1] There are many exceptions to this advocacy role of course. Advising clients in the role of "counselor" and probating wills are ordinarily not adversarial, divorces are sometimes not adversarial, and business lawyers are often engaged in a continuing advisory role about a wide range of legal/business matters. Mediation is also gaining ground as a remedy, instead of litigation, in a variety of areas. Prosecutors also have an ethical obligation to ensure justice.

What you must do, though, is to adjust your present formulating and analyzing to accommodate legal vocabulary, concepts, categories, logic, knowledge, and experience. You must put on a "legal lens" for spotting the issues and then framing, analyzing, and resolving them with advocacy argument. In putting on this legal lens you do not disregard other methods of framing and understanding. You put on and take off different lenses, as you need them. To illustrate, my standing advice is to take off your legal lens at the end of the day of law school or law practice and keep it off until the next morning. An "advocacy lens" is definitely not for relating to loved ones, friends, and the pursuit of personal happiness. Be careful.

HOW TO USE THIS BOOK

If you have not yet started law school

Depending on your learning habits, you may read the book straight through or scan the book quickly for an overview. If overviews are important for you, and even if they are not, examine the Summary Table of Contents and the Analytical Table of Contents, which present a general and then a detailed road map for you. Such quick reading or scanning may lead you to focus on a particular chapter or two or three: perhaps learning for exams (Chapter Two) or issue spotting (Chapter Four) or exam writing formats (Chapter Five). You may need only a few chapters in this book, depending on what you bring to the challenge. Only you know what you bring—but you may be mistaken.

If your inclinations are to read in a more meticulous way, do so after you have gone through both Tables of Contents. Meticulous readers need direction, too. Give special attention to the brief Introduction and to Chapter One, which map the terrain through which you will be traveling.

Whether you proceed quickly or meticulously, embrace each section you select and do not be discouraged. Since you have not yet started law school, you do not bring legal understanding to your reading. Expect to encounter concepts, categories, and terms that are not altogether clear to you. But the clarification you seek may emerge from the next section or a chapter down the road. Since *How To Do Your Best On Law School Exams* was conceived, designed, and written with holistic themes permeating each chapter, a concept, category, or term presented in one chapter may be presented again in a different context in a later chapter. All the more reason to proceed, not bog down.

Be encouraged, too, by the maxim, "The more you know, the more you will see." Be confident, therefore, that as law school unfolds for you in the initial weeks, you will see more in these chapters because you will bring increasing understanding to them, including, I trust, important initial insights into your strengths and weaknesses. Hence, you may return, in reference fashion, to this book for particular needs: to Chapter Four on the critical skill of issue spotting, to Chapter Three on outlining your courses, or to Chapters Six detailing exam problems and concise, cogent argument-making in response.

Be kind to yourself. In various sections of Chapters Two through Six, there are many straightforward presentations that then progress to layers of complexities and challenge, the most difficult of which I suggest might be deferred until later. The complexities may then become understandable because you understand more. Many beginning students need a step-by-step learning approach. Others, however, need a preview of the entire terrain before concentrating on any part of it. A useful guide: if you feel overwhelmed or discouraged by the complexity of any presentation in the Book, come back to it later when your decoding skills are sharpened. Don't bog down.

If you are already in law school

If you are in the opening months of law school before taking your first-term exams, you should proceed in one of the ways indicated above.

But if you have received initial grades, even on a practice exam or possibly a mid-term, and you did not do as well as you expected and commensurate with your effort, it is vital that you identify both your strengths and weaknesses. Improvement, indeed even the direction your corrective efforts take, presupposes such diagnosis, as well as the courage and persistence to ferret out your weaknesses and identify your strengths. Many students summon this courage; they persist and improve, sometimes dramatically, even from a 'C' level to an 'A' level. But others do not summon it. They accept and are defined by their initial grades. They complain about the unfairness of life and fail to improve.

If you have not done well, I challenge you to forego wailing and other responsibility-evading schemes. I challenge you to confront that most elusive and resourceful opponent—the face in the mirror, your hiding-out self, your defense mechanisms, and any temptation not to persist and do your best.

An initial diagnosis, even if refined later, enables you to concentrate on the Chapter(s) in this book that address your weakness. To illustrate, if your weakness is in issue spotting, concentrate on Chapter Four and *practice* issue spotting. If you believe that your learning approach is not sufficiently efficient and effective, one consequence of which is to weaken your issue spotting, devote yourself also to Chapter Two to determine which of the suggestions might enable you to learn better—and *practice* them. If instead, your essays are unlawyerly (disorganized, wordy, meandering), concentrate on the writing formats detailed in Chapter Five—and *practice* writing lawyerly argument making.

Two brief stories illuminate how the above approach has worked for other students. Years back at the Bar Examiners in Albany, New York, I reviewed the bar essays with a former student. He had failed the bar twice and was discouraged. His essays were consistently ranked just below what was required. His issue spotting was consistently impressive, but his rule statements were habitually very rough, and hence his interweaving of element and fact was inevitably also poor. By correcting his single core weakness in stating rules, he also improved his interweaving and passed the bar exam on his next try. He is not unusual. Very often, there are one or two basic weaknesses that are related and ripple out, resulting in sub-par performance.

Second, also years ago, a first-year student who was performing poorly told me that she felt her undergraduate college program had been relatively weak and, as a result, her analytical and other school skills were comparably weak. She worked hard at her learning, and by third year was performing at an 'A' level. I remember congratulating her on her wonderful achievement while also feeling regret that she realized her potential so late in her law school career. 'A' grades in the first year get you on the law review and open up vistas of opportunity.

Finally, *How To Do Your Best On Law School Exams* exemplifies themes, perspectives and methods that are also embodied in my book, *Learning Legal Reasoning, Briefing, Analysis and Theory,* which is used by many first-year students and some first-year programs.[2] The themes, perspectives and methods from both books are also exemplified in my *Learning Criminal Law As Advocacy Argument.* The three books are designed for first year students and complement each other. I strongly recommend studying *Learning Legal Reasoning* before studying this book or *Learning Criminal Law As Advocacy Argument.*

---

[2] These commonalities are exemplified in the forty frequently asked questions of first-year law students in Chapter One; the sections on "Interpreting Federal Statutes" and "Principled Decision-Making" (pp. 35-37); "Narrow Versus Broad Statements of Holding and Precedent" (pp. 72-73); "Trial Judges' Discretion" (pp. 73-74); "Appellate Judges' Discretion" (p. 75); "Narrow and Broad Views of a Holding" (pp. 103-104); "The Principle of a Case" (p. 104); "The Interacting of Historical Context, Politics and Law" (pp. 104-106); and the jurisprudential insight detailed in the last chapter.

In Chapter One, I specify the objectives of this book: the concrete differences between law school and other exams, the six exam tasks your professors expect you to perform, the six criteria by which your performance will be evaluated, and an outline of how you can proceed to develop the necessary skills.

Have a good journey.

ON LOOKING BACK

As I read this Introduction again years later, it is still valid for most exams. However, the correct emphasis on "rules" needs to be augmented with an additional emphasis on "principles." Especially in courses such as constitutional law, civil procedure, family law, criminal law, torts and other areas, you also encounter broad, malleable principles that contrast with the concrete rules divisible into specific elements. Examples include due process, equal protection of the laws, and separation of powers in first-year constitutional law; minimum contacts and fairness for acquiring personal jurisdiction in civil procedure; equitable distribution of marital property and the best interests of the child in family law. Since principles do not have elements and are broader in scope, they resonate on different frequencies from the more concrete rules, as will be explained and illustrated throughout the book, and they offer almost endless interpretive possibilities.

Six Exam Tasks, Six Grading Criteria

THE OBJECTIVES OF THIS BOOK

- To show the differences between what you mostly do in class — analyze and decode appellate cases and what you must do on essay exams — spot and resolve issues raised by the fact pattern.

- To help you prepare for exams using skills-centered learning and performing aimed at practicing and refining the methods and techniques that are most efficient and effective for you.

- To help you develop skills in spotting issues and writing lawyerly arguments, and to avoid unlawyerly issue spotting and arguments by explaining and illustrating the characteristics of each.

- To help you avoid common mistakes and outright blunders by pinpointing what they are and how to avoid them.

- To build confidence in your demonstrated capacity to do well on exams.

To enable you to pursue these objectives, I will use numerous illustrations, mostly from first-year subjects such as torts, criminal law, contracts, constitutional law, and civil procedure. Remember, however, to keep your eye on the ball: our focus is on learning the skills that are a *sine qua non* for doing well on all exams — and that are not systematically taught in law schools. We are not engaged in any doctrinal review (rules, principles, policies) of these first-year subjects.

Assumption

I assume that you are attending each class and studying diligently on a day-to-day basis. This book is no substitute for attendance and meticulous, intense study and practice. An indifferent, episodic approach, or studying a couple of hours a day, will not do.

Caveat

If there is any conflict between anything I write in this book and what your professor says, always follow your professor's guidance on that item for that course. Later, I will specify how you make necessary changes in what I am presenting to dial into your professor's doctrinal, analytical and exam frequencies in each course.

WHAT IS THE CHALLENGE IN ANSWERING LAW SCHOOL EXAM PROBLEMS?

Prior schooling often emphasizes memorization of materials from a textbook and the teacher's lectures, and requires at most a sophisticated regurgitation on the exam. Clearly, this level of teaching and learning is prevalent in elementary and high schools and, unhappily, intrudes into college and beyond.

In law school, by contrast, the exam priority is on skills in issue spotting and then application of rules and principles to each given set of facts to resolve the issues spotted with advocacy arguments.

In addition, law-school exams differ radically in format from what you have been doing in the classroom since August. So far, you have mostly been studying and briefing appellate cases: facts, procedural history, issue, holding, reasoning, and judgment.

You are acquiring skills in after-the-fact dissection of appellate cases. In these "legal autopsies," you analyze how a judge marshals the relevant facts, articulates the issue, applies a rule or principle of law, and articulates reasons from the relevant repertoire of legal reasoning for her application of the rule or principle to the facts. Based on the logic of all your schooling experience, you might expect that a law-school exam would be akin to an analysis of a collection of appellate cases. Though logic and experience are decisively in your favor, your expectation is completely contradicted by the reality of law exams. Generally, there is only modest connection between your dissection of appellate cases in class and what you must do on exams. Even worse, the elaborated, often discursive, reasoning typical of many appellate cases misdirects you from the concise, cogent and time-pressured writing essential for law exams.

Generations of first-year law students have been confounded and disappointed by the realization, after their initial first-year exams, of this stark contradiction between the required class performance and the radically different exam performance that produces 'A' grades.

SIX EXAM TASKS

In typical exam problems, you are given a detailed fact pattern, often extending for a page or more, single-spaced, with your professor's question at the end. For most professors, you must:

1. Extricate the key facts from the non-key facts embodied in the often dense fact pattern (also called relevant and non-relevant facts).

2. Spot and specify the issue(s) raised by the key facts in light of your professor's interrogatory at the end of the essay problem.

3. Select the correct legal rules (or principles) to be applied to resolve the identified issues.

4. Apply the rules by interweaving the key facts with the elements of the applicable rules or with the principles-derived tests or standards

5. Indicate (sometimes) the policy purpose(s) served by the application of the relevant rules.

6. Do the above with mostly concise, time-pressured, lawyerly writing, and sometimes argue two or three ways as required by the facts, the rules/principles, and your professor's expectations.

THE CENTRALITY OF SPOTTING THE ISSUES

Students sometimes ask me a question that may be on your mind: which of these six tasks is the most critical? Most professors, I believe, agree that skill in spotting and specifying legal issues in a problem is the most important.

A moment's reflection on the above sequence of six skills verifies this view. Since steps three through six presuppose you have spotted the issue, it is obvious that these latter steps cannot be performed competently without the issue having been identified. To stress this conclusion is only to reflect the old maxim that if you miss the question, you miss the answer.

This logic would seem to pinpoint the first sequence, extricating the key facts, as most important since it is a presupposition of issue spotting. While there is a sense in which that is true, it is also true that the objective of extricating the key facts is to spot the issue. Extricating key facts leads, often intuitively and immediately, to issue spotting.

Thus, while extricating key facts can be analytically separated from issue spotting, the two usually go hand in hand in the actual decoding of exam problems. Indeed, while all six sequences can be analytically separated, they are best viewed holistically as parts of an integrated process.

To appreciate fully the centrality of issue spotting, it may help to see legal issue spotting as simply a reflection of the general truth, as underlined by the American philosopher, Suzanne Langer, in *Philosophy In A New Key*, that a question establishes a field, a framework, for analysis and for drawing conclusions. Scientists might agree, too, since scientific research and verification usually takes place within a framework established by a theory expressed in a more specific question in the form of a hypothesis.

Thus, the lawyerly emphasis on the quality of issue spotting conforms to philosophical and scientific tradition as well as jurisprudential requirements. If you articulate and frame with the right legal issue, you are on the right path leading you to the right rule and to apt interweaving. But if you have misstated the issue, you are on the wrong path leading you to the wrong rule and to incorrect interweaving. Indeed, as you gradually sharpen your issue-spotting skill, you can approach each new course, and its topics and subtopics, with an illuminating perspective: what are the core issues in each topic and subtopic? The answer to this question establishes the scope of issues you must be prepared to identify at exam time.

Even if you make mistakes in applying the right rule and in interweaving on an exam, you will likely receive substantial credit if you have framed the issue well and applied the rule implicit in the issue. The reason, in short, is that a sharply focused statement of the issue cuts to the heart of what the facts are really about, and that is what law professors, legal supervisors, and judges demand.

Clearly, too, issue spotting is an everyday lawyerly skill. Lawyers in extremely varied practices devote a great deal of time to serial and relentless fact investigation to uncover the key facts in cases and determine their legal significance, i.e., spotting and specifying the issues. You should emulate them as a law student by devoting substantial time to uncovering the key facts in exam essays and determining their legal significance — spotting and specifying the exam issues.

There are no good answers without good questions — not on exams, not in practice, and not in life. This skill of issue spotting pervades latter chapters but is systematically decoded in Chapter Four.

SIX CRITERIA FOR GRADING EXAMS[1]

You are graded on how well you perform your six exam tasks by six criteria

You should not be surprised that the six criteria by which most professors grade you are simply a reframing of the six exam tasks you must perform.

Six Grading Criteria

1. Your lawyerly skill in extricating the key facts from the non-key facts detailed in the exam problem.

2. Your lawyerly skill in spotting and specifying the issues raised by these key (red hot) facts.

3. Your lawyerly skill in learning, recalling, and applying the applicable legal rules or principles to resolve the specified issues.

4. Your lawyerly skill in interweaving (meshing together) the key facts with the elements of the applicable rules or with the principles (or their tests or standards).

5. Your lawyerly skill in sometimes applying the appropriate policy purpose(s) to support your rule application.

6. Your performance of all these skills with concise, cogent arguments within the allocated time, sometimes arguing two or three ways as required by the facts, the rules or principles, and each professor's expectations.

Notice that the six criteria are formulated as skills. This formulation is, of course, intentional. It captures the holistic, skills-centered approach that is central to dialing into the exam wavelength.

Grade differences result mostly from differences in skills

Many students are unaware of what professors know: the decisive difference between a mediocre, good and excellent exam paper is typically in the quality of the skills displayed. The reason is that knowledge tends to be broadly shared among many first-year students, since most study intensely. In contrast, however, the core exam skills specified above are distributed widely across the spectrum, from poor to outstanding. To be sure, arguments sometimes reveal differences in knowledge, and these differences can be important too, especially at the extremes.

Nevertheless, after grading thousands of exam papers over three decades, what leaps out are the radical differences displayed in legal skills. Briefly, some answers are lawyerly. They are directly responsive to the interrogatory at the end of the essay. They are lucid, logical, well organized and fact- and issue-centered. They display cogent legal reasoning. Issue spotting of all major issues is followed by apt rule application and interweaving of key facts with the relevant rules. Policy is briefly but appropriately applied when required. The writing is concise without meandering or regurgitating irrelevant knowledge. In essence, these arguments embody or approach the writing formats detailed in Chapter Five, and approximate the model and excellent student responses detailed in Chapter Six. These exam papers make professors smile.

In contrast, many other exam responses, in varying degrees of weakness, display unlawyerly qualities. They are often not directly responsive to the interrogatory. They are confused, not well organized, not systematically developed, and not sufficiently fact- and issue-centered. Major issues are missed altogether,

---

[1] Some professors have additional expectations for a standout 'A' exam argument that will be illustrated in Chapter Five.

rule application is often faulty, and interweaving with key facts is weak, or even missing. At worst, the paper is an unappetizing stew of relevant and irrelevant rules, principles, facts, and conclusions, mixed well with confusion, rambling, and often ending abruptly, sometimes with the words, "no more time." Illustrations of poor responses are also set forth in Chapter Six.

Improvement possibilities — So what do I do?

If you are graded by your professor's six criteria on how well you perform your six exam tasks, then the principle directing what you must do is clear. Your studying, reviewing, outlining, study group focus — and especially your practice with hypotheticals and argument making with old exam problems — must be approached with these six criteria in mind. The details for implementing this direction comprise the rest of the book.

To reduce your learning merely to an exam focus is unnecessary and foolish. But to overlook it, or in classic college fashion, to reserve it to the last week or two before the exam, may be folly for which you could suffer. For my fellow liberal-arts devotees, the time-pressured surface character of law-school exams is a lamentable reduction of the rich history, economics, culture, religion, and political struggle from which law has emerged over the centuries, and from which arise vibrant perspectives for critical appraisal. Yes, of course, I strongly agree. But keep in mind that you need not sacrifice any of your liberal-arts perspectives and critical reading and writing skills. You just need to add a new frequency for exam decoding, for singing this particular song, for dancing this dance. That's all.

Chapter Two concentrates on aiding you to get on the right frequency for learning law for exams (and practice). From my long experience in law teaching, it is clear to me that weak exam performances are often rooted in failing to dial into the exam frequency. Thus, the priority on strengthening legal learning skills that is embodied in Chapter Two is justified by an analysis born of much experience.

ON LOOKING BACK

1. In beginning to think about and practice the core skills of issue spotting and argument making, you should be aware that both vary greatly depending on the type of exam problem you confront. They are defined and illustrated especially on pages 48-50 and in Chapters Six.

2. The substantive revision in this chapter is the addition of principles to the specifications of rules for the reason detailed previously (p. xx).

Understanding, especially deep understanding, is the engine that drives exam and other skills. That is a theme animating the focus on specifics throughout the book, and stressed here in Chapter One. There are no skills without such understanding, and no performance of understanding without skills.

Don't be misled by the separate listing of the above skills; atomism doesn't work. The skills all flow together in a configuration and depend on each other. Holism does work and is emphasized throughout the book.

In a useful shorthand, the six exam tasks and related grading criteria can be summarized as two: (1) spotting the issues and (2) resolving them in a series of concise, well-crafted, advocacy arguments. Both skills are repeatedly illustrated in the many strong exam arguments detailed throughout the book, especially in Chapters Five and Six.

3. It might be instructive to know why I try to avoid the word "answer" (or "discussion") in describing responses to exam problems. I fear those words will be understood as inviting a collegiate answer that tends to regurgitate all relevant knowledge. That is definitely not what you must do. The word "argument"

better captures what you must do: write a series of legal arguments to resolve the spotted issues. I suggest therefore that you abandon use of the word "answer" as in "What is the right answer?" for the far more helpful word "argument" as in "What is the best argument?" Notice the added emphasis on "best" argument and always seek it and be able to demonstrate why it is superior. Of course, an argument always contains analysis but I recommend that you frame and write best arguments.

4. Lastly, if you are beginning your legal journey — and even if you have already started — my hope is that this book may help you to be clear about what you are doing and not doing. If you can achieve such clarity, you can work smart and avoid the prevalent anxiety, even freneticism, of many first-year law students. Thus, your time and energy will be channeled to meet your professors' priorities as detailed in their course outlines, classroom presentations, and old exams. You will not waste time, for example, in studying law review articles (with the exception of your professor's article). You will study hornbooks and primers in a highly disciplined way, concentrating only on those sections that correspond to and aid you in decoding and mastering your professors' course coverage in scope and depth. And you will avoid study groups that are off-base.

Indeed, it's more than possible that you might even enjoy parts of law school by seeking the deeper understanding and potential for insight and service embedded in your courses. To illustrate, in studying the First Amendment, you absorb part of the infrastructure of freedom that we all enjoy and tend to take for granted — freedom of speech, press, assembly, association, petition, and religion — and the implicit right to pursue happiness as we define it and not as government and advertisers urge. What would our lives — and America — be without these freedoms that we exercise every day? As you prepare to practice and participate in legal culture, you develop a special understanding about how this infrastructure of freedom and opportunity is rooted not simply in Constitutional law, but in all realms of law.

To illustrate, imagine the meaning later for you, your client and his family, in securing the freedom of an innocent person on death row or serving a long prison term because of DNA evidence you uncovered (as has happened many times in the nation). Or imagine the meaning for you and the families of victims in prosecuting and convicting an elusive serial killer because of DNA evidence, which has occurred in New York and elsewhere. Imagine the meaning for you and young clients in aiding them in the purchase of their first home or business. Of course, learning law also offers a negative potential, too. At heart, law and law practice are a moral quest, and you choose your path.

If, as the philosopher Ernst Cassirer said, culture is the main channel for human liberation, the principles and black-letter rules you study exemplify a fascinating and poignant evolution of history, politics, economics and culture, as well as opportunities for liberation. If you learn to work smart, you can excel on the exams, deepen yourself as a person, prepare to serve others, and continue to enjoy your life. Freneticism is not destiny in law school or in life. It is a *choice*.

CHAPTER TWO

Mastery Learning of Law for Exams And Practice

Know thyself.
Good learners are made, not born.
What you do is what you learn.

INTRODUCTION

As detailed in Chapter One, how well you perform on law exam essay problems is mostly determined by how well you spot the issues triggered by the fact pattern in each professor's exam, and how well you resolve each one with cogent lawyerly arguments. To prepare you to perform these critical exam tasks, I specify concrete direction in this Chapter for acquiring the skills-centered mastery learning and understanding that you need. Please see such learning and understanding as well as issue spotting, outlining, and practicing such cogent arguments as steps in a holistic process rather then as separate tasks. That view will best empower you.

Mastery learning and understanding is not easy. There is a tremendous amount to learn. And the college and LSAT skills that got you into law school are clearly insufficient for you to thrive in this new, very challenging setting. Understanding is a *sine qua non* and must inform each rule you learn in law school. You must also meticulously memorize the elements of each rule stressed by your professor so that you can carry out the two critical tasks posed by the typical closed-book essay exam requiring factual proof of each element of the applicable rule. There are numerous such rules in each subject, and memorizing and understanding each element of each rule stressed by your professor is an indispensable and formidable task. But don't be intimidated. Remember that generations of law students have successfully coped with this challenge. You can do it too. You just have to learn how to do it efficiently and effectively, and practice doing it throughout the semester to empower your exam performance of the two core tasks.

Don't worry. You cannot apply all of the learning suggestions specified in this Chapter. Indeed, if you gain a bit of insight into how you might study more effectively and a few new techniques for doing so in law school, that result alone can make an important difference in your exam results and justifies the time spent studying, reflecting on, and practicing with at least some of this material.

EXAM LEARNING METHODS AND TECHNIQUES

Skills-centered understanding and performing

First, while there are many paths through the legal thicket, the common aim is a skills-centered understanding of your professor's materials so that you can perform the two core tasks. That is the crucial output of all your preparation. It is crackpot realism to see doctrine (rules, principles, policies) as mere atomistic data to be fed into one's memory so that it can be regurgitated on cue, as if the ideal were a parrot mimicking back what it has been taught.

Even seeing the doctrine as a web of knowledge is also deficient, unless doctrine-as-data transformed into doctrine-as-knowledge leads to doctrine-as-understanding: its meanings, its purposes, its implicit interests, and its output in issue spotting and cogent argument. Put differently, you should strive to cultivate a personal relationship with the doctrine. Embrace it, so that you don't just know it but have cultivated the mental flexibility to quickly apply it to spot issues and resolve them. As you study the attitudes, methods, and performances specified in this book, please remember that a skills-centered understanding is the engine empowering all of them.

Legal mind-set: Problem-centered and fact-centered

A problem- and fact-centered approach to doing your best on law school (and bar exams) provides, both theoretically and practically, the preferred general path to such a skills-centered understanding and performance. This approach is at the same time a perspective, a method and an attitude. It is not merely speculative; it is born of experience. In my decades in law school teaching, many of the best students have used this approach or variants of it.

The animating idea is very simple: since the nature of lawyerly practice includes adversarial problem-solving, and since you are asked to spot issues and resolve them with cogent lawyerly arguments on the exams and in practice, your studying, practicing, and reviewing should be directed to increasing your skills in such problem-solving, issue spotting and argument-making.

Applying a problem-centered and fact-centered approach

Don't abandon the study and review habits and methods that have served you well in college or graduate school. Many of these habits and methods should serve you well in law school, too. Instead look on them as a solid foundation upon which to begin to cope with the new phenomenon of law-school essay problems with their different formats and expectations.

As you now know, the two overall performances (issue spotting and writing cogent arguments) can be deconstructed into six exam tasks. Thus, you study and review with an objective in mind: to increase your doctrinal understanding and skills necessary for carrying out the six tasks you must perform on the essay problems, and the six tasks by which you will be graded (p. 4). It's a blunder, then, simply to focus on increasing your knowledge of rules (and relevant principles and policies) independent of the skills that empower you to apply it.

I therefore recommend that you unlearn the prevalent dualistic approach to preparation for exams. Don't separate study aimed at acquisition of the required doctrinal understanding from practice aimed at developing and refining the skills needed to perform the six exam tasks. Rather, from the start of each course, you should integrate acquisition of such understanding with concurrent practice to deepen it while also sharpening your exam skills. The main method for doing so is relentless daily practice with hypotheticals, and at least weekly practice writing only those parts of old exams whose doctrine you have already covered in class. Contrast this holistic approach using hypotheticals and old exams with those students who have told me over the decades that they are going to begin practicing with hypotheticals and with their professors' old exams as soon as they "know the materials." Instead, you must begin such practice from the start of each course. The fallacy in waiting until you "know the materials" is that you never really know them completely, and the false pursuit of "knowledge" can devour all your time and energy. Such pursuit is both bottomless and wrongheaded since you only need to know the scope and depth of materials as telegraphed to you by each professor — her priorities become your priorities.

The integrated approach is exemplified when students study daily with a problem- and fact-centered approach, stressing hypotheticals for exam-focused understanding of each of your professor's rules and principles in order to spot issues and then to resolve each issue with mostly concise lawyerly arguments. This approach can be achieved both by disciplined self-study and in a well-focused study group. You also practice writing to resolve the issues spotted in the old exams as you recognize them, one by one, during the entire semester.

My next major recommendation is that in studying, reviewing, and practicing, you must dial into your professor's frequency. There are two parts to it: (1) a substantive frequency and (2) an analytical frequency. It might help you to see these two frequencies as the master *conceptual maps* that detail the limited substantive terrain to be covered in each subject and the analytical perspectives for traversing this formidable territory. But first, a short excursus on understanding your teacher's strategy.

Identifying your professor's teaching strategy

If you study intensely and still encounter difficulty in a particular class, one hypothesis to consider is that your professor is teaching, either altogether or in part, in a mode that is perplexing to you. To illustrate, many law professors do not teach basic doctrine and skills in a systematic manner. They regard that as "spoon feeding," a pedagogic vice of great magnitude to be shunned. Rather, they teach at a more rarified level, perhaps in a top-down or on a theoretical or policy frequency, which is rewarding for them as well as for students who resonate on those learning frequencies. But many students who resonate on other frequencies find such teaching confusing. In addition, some professors stress rules with less emphasis on policy and even less on theory, which can be confusing to top-down or theoretical learners. Yet other teachers forge a varying blend of theory, policy, and rules, a blend to emulate in that course and exam.

Since you are responsible for your learning and teachers are just guides to suggest paths through the legal thicket, you should not be surprised that some guides are better for you than others. If you spot your professor's mode of teaching as antithetical to your mode of learning, look elsewhere for help promptly. Consider the recommendations detailed on page 30. In contrast, identifying your professor's mode of teaching as harmonious with your own learning wavelength raises what can be very exciting possibilities for both scope and depth of learning, etc.

Dialing into your professor's substantive frequency

Contrary to what many students believe, you are definitely not studying torts, criminal law, contracts, civil procedure, real property, etc. in any comprehensive sense. Instead, you are studying an important introduction to torts as taught by your professor, an introduction to civil procedure as taught by your professor, an introduction to contracts as taught by your professor.

It is important for beginning students to appreciate that each subject incorporates a vast doctrinal terrain that can be taught in many different ways. Thus, there are numerous choices for a professor. In the limited class hours available (about forty-three in a three-credit, one semester course) what should I cover from the doctrinal terrain? What should I omit? What should I emphasize and what should I cover quickly? Which casebook and other collections of materials should I select and which mix of rule, principle, policy and theory should I present? Not surprisingly, answers to these questions vary widely. For example, a student from Columbia Law School told me that his criminal-law professor devoted three weeks to felony murder (only one of the forms of murder within a larger category of criminal homicide).

One of the criminal-law casebooks has over one hundred pages on conspiracy, another only a few. I do not mean to imply any criticism at all of the Columbia professor or of the casebook editors. They have a right, as each professor does, to mold their presentations in light of their choices, priorities and methods. This right is an exercise of academic freedom and pedagogic choice.

The point for students, however, is to *stop* trying to learn the subject in some "objective" and comprehensive sense. That is a classic first-year blunder. Start concentrating on your professor's substantive road map, her conceptual map for presenting her course, as revealed by her syllabus, her classes, and especially her old exams. Most professors are not shy about their course coverage. As you now know if you have started school, they detail it in their syllabi or course outlines. If they are not clear, you can still uncover it: which topics have been assigned from the table of contents of the assigned casebook? Which omitted? In addition, consider the weight or priority assigned to different topics by whether substantial or modest class time is allocated. If your professor, for example, spends four or five weeks on criminal homicide (murders and manslaughters), expect to see it on the exam. If your professor has spent some weeks covering remedies in contract, expect to see it on the exam. And so on.

Don't study, review, and practice what your professor has not covered in class and has not assigned. That's a lot you *don't* have to do. In addition, follow your professor's example in class and in assigned materials in calibrating your depth of preparation in each topic. Though not all students are aware of it, there is an implicit social contract between each responsible professor and her students: only those matters covered in class or assigned will be on the exam, and only in the depth presented in class and assigned materials. Only culpably aberrant professors (outliers) violate this social contract. If you go beyond the prescribed scope and depth, you risk entangling yourself in endless academic complexities that transcend the course and exam and that will likely distract and confound you.

Exam problems sometimes involve issues only quickly covered in class, or issues not covered at all in class but assigned. To protect yourself, you must be careful also to cover *all* that is assigned. Give some special attention to issues quickly covered in the last week or so of each course. The reason: many professors, especially new teachers, plan to cover more than what they can actually accomplish in the course. Typically, when they realize they cannot cover it all, near the end of the term, they quickly highlight what they consider most important. Exam issues sometimes emerge from this highlighting.

Avoid the common beginner's blunder — the anxiety-driven, frantic quest to learn all about torts, civil procedure, real property, contracts, etc. It's impossible: a thousand pages in your hornbook in torts, eight or nine hundred pages or more in your tort casebook, nine hundred pages or more in your contract casebook. Remember, you cannot and need not learn it all; the 'A' grades go to those who can best spot the issues and resolve them with cogent and mostly concise arguments. They definitely do not go to those who simply know the most or even understand the best. That's what I call the "scholarly fallacy," and it will mislead and confuse you.

Have you noticed that many of the second and third-year students study less than first-year students and are also far less anxious about exams? They know that knowledge acquisition is only one component of exam taking. They make their knowledge and understanding serve their exam skills. They realize that irrelevant knowledge can actually work against you. It may clutter your mind with obscurities and minor issues, distracting you from a mastery-type appreciation of central themes, problems and issues in each professor's course, the heart of most exams. This knowledge clutter often leads to missing basic issues in the exam problems in a frantic preoccupation with secondary, tangential, and irrelevant issues. Thus, it is not studying in itself that will help you. Rather, it is well-focused, skills-centered studying and practice aimed at issue spotting and cogent argument making that sheds light. Unfocused studying is like being on a high wire as crosswinds blow. The harder you try, the more dangerous it is.

Dialing into your professor's analytical frequency

"Our brains are pattern-recognition machines."
Benedict Carey

In addition to your professor's substantive frequency (the conceptual road map of her relevant course doctrine), you must also dial into your professor's analytical frequency for viewing the conceptual terrain. Sometimes, these analytical frequencies are explicitly stated in class; sometimes, they are implicit. If the latter, you must make explicit what is implicit. Use these analytical frequencies to organize and make sense of the mass of cases and other materials, and to direct your approach to the facts, issues and rules. These frequencies, with their set of relevant patterned categories, can prevent you from being overwhelmed. How do you cope with the amazing mass of cases and rules in the form of causes-of-action and defenses? Cope as your professor copes: use her patterned categories, particularly as exemplified in her lecturing, questioning and comments in class. She values them and believes them to be illuminating. She will therefore value your apt use of them on exams. Indeed, she has no choice but to do so.

Her analytical perspectives are not simply personal. Each course, like each area of law, has underlying patterns that specify rules with their required elements for a cause-of-action or defense. Even better, these patterned categories provide a lawyerly means to begin to frame and analyze any relevant exam (or practice) problem and to uncover the important issues. Even if you make mistakes in uncovering all the major issues and in arguing to resolve them, the apt use of these pattern-provided categories will get you credit because your argument is analytical, and thus lawyerly. The patterns also aid you in avoiding unlawyerly blunders that alienate and suggest to your professor that you do not know what you are doing.

To illustrate, for many students who are somewhat confused by discursive appellate cases that meander over sometimes esoteric terrain, it is clarifying and even exhilarating to realize that each rule spelling out a cause-of-action (e.g., trespass, breach of contract, tort negligence, extreme-recklessness murder) is comprised of a specific number of essential elements.[1] For example, each negligent tort cause-of-action has five core elements that can be briefly stated: (1) duty, (2) standard of care, (3) behavior breaching standard of care, (4) causation, both factual (but-for) and legal (proximate), and (5) actual harm. This skeletal pattern can then be amplified in six sequential questions.

TORT NEGLIGENCE PATTERN

1. Did the defendant owe the plaintiff a *legal duty*?

2. If yes, what was the *standard of care* owed by the defendant for the protection of the plaintiff (usually the standard of reasonable care)?

3. Did the defendant's conduct *breach* the required standard of care? (If duty and breach are established, there is negligence in an initial sense.)

4. If yes, was there *factual (but-for) causation*? Is defendant's behavior a cause in fact of harm to plaintiff? If yes, was there *legal (proximate) cause*, meaning a reasonably "close causal connection between the conduct and resulting injury"? And was the defendant therefore also the proximate cause of harm to plaintiff?

5. If yes, was there *actual harm* to the plaintiff?

---

[1] In sharp contrast to rules, principles do *not* have elements. Rather, they trail standards and tests or factors that help to apply such principles as due process, equal protection, and many others. In Chapter Five, this important and different type of argument making is explained and illustrated.

> 6. Two additional questions should be added:
>
>   a) Was plaintiff contributorily negligent (in some jurisdictions), or was the plaintiff comparatively negligent (in most jurisdictions)?
>
>   b) Did plaintiff assume the risk?

Of course, this skeletal pattern of core elements for analyzing negligent tort issues must be detailed. Each of these elements gives rise to the complexities that are illustrated in the cases. But this *pattern* of elements in the right sequence, and each other pattern in the right sequence, gives you a foundation for building, organizing and applying your doctrinal knowledge and understanding. It gives you a place to begin to extricate key facts, spot issues, and write cogent arguments. I trust your tort professor uses this analytical pattern, either explicitly or implicitly. Be sure to use it, too. If she varies the language somewhat and adds a lot to it, you follow, as always, your professor's language and direction, not mine.

INTENTIONAL TORT PATTERN

In intentional torts (e.g., assault and battery, trespass, conversion), the following six sequential questions lead to beginning lawyerly analysis of relevant exam fact patterns, including spotting and specifying issues. If your professor uses this approach, explicitly or implicitly, be sure to use it on the exam. Again, if she varies the language or adds greatly to it, use her language. The outlining of your professor's course will then detail these categories to embody her doctrinal choices, omissions, and voice.

> 1. What is the *intent* requirement and is it met on these facts?
>
> 2. If yes, what is the *act* requirement and is it met on these facts?
>
> 3. If yes, what is the *causation* requirement, if any, and is it met here?
>
> 4. If yes, what is the *harm* requirement, if any, and is it met?
>
> 5. If yes, is there *consent* to this intentional tort?
>
> 6. Do any privileges (defenses) apply?

CORE CRIME PATTERN

In teaching criminal law for decades, I emphasized, as most criminal-law professors do, a common sequential pattern for beginning to analyze common-law (core) crimes, which leads to issue spotting and argument making. Does your professor use it, explicitly or implicitly, or a variation of it? This pattern can be outlined in six basic questions. Since it emerges from embedded case law and statutes, it is hard for me to imagine a professor not using it. Like all these introductory patterns, the outlining of the course will add details, in this instance for each crime and defense.

> 1. What is the *mens rea* (mental) requirement and is it met here?
>
> 2. If yes, what is the *voluntary act* requirement (the *actus reus*) and is it met?
>
> 3. If yes, what is the *concurrence* requirement and is it met?
>
> 4. If yes, what is the *causation* requirement (factual and proximate), if any, and is it met?

5. If yes, what is the *harm* requirement (if any) and is it met?

6. Do any affirmative defenses apply?

CONSTITUTIONAL CRIMINAL PROCEDURE — FOURTH AMENDMENT
SEARCH AND SEIZURE PATTERN

Each search and seizure fact pattern may be decoded by systematic application of the following introductory step-by-step pattern. It's complex and you might want to defer learning it until you study it.

1. Did the defendant have any Fourth-Amendment right at all?
   a) Is there governmental action, and
   b) Did the citizen have a reasonable expectation of privacy?
2. If the answer is yes to both, did the police have a valid search warrant?
3. If the police did not have a valid search warrant, did the police nevertheless make a valid warrantless search and seizure; i.e., did one of the six exceptions to the search-warrant requirement apply?
   a) Search incident to a lawful arrest;
   b) Automobile;
   c) Plain view;
   d) Consent;
   e) Stop and frisk;
   f) Hot pursuit of a fleeing felon; evanescent evidence.

This very brief introductory pattern is detailed in the next chapter (pp. 35-37) and it models how such patterns should be detailed in your outlining of any course. Just look at it now.

CONTRACT PATTERN

An initial skeleton-like pattern for beginning to analyze contract issues is embodied in the mnemonic, **COCOA** plus **TBR.**

C	Capacity: do the parties to the purported contract have the capacity to contract (minor or mental capacity)?
O	If yes, is there a valid Offer and acceptance?
C	If yes, is there Consideration to support the offer and acceptance (or a substitute)?
O	If yes, is the Objective of the agreement not in violation of any public policy?
A	If yes, does the agreement embody the mutual Assent of the parties?
plus **TBR**	
T	If yes, what are the Terms of the contract at issue in the problem?
B	Is there any Breach of agreement? If yes, what is the nature of the breach?
R	What are Remedies for breach, including for seller and buyer?

Depending on how these topics are taught, the common law, the Restatement (Second), and the relevant UCC (Uniform Commercial Code) provisions should very often be considered. This introductory pattern of sequential elements will explode in detail in your outlining of the course to reflect your professor's choices, omissions, and voice.

CIVIL PROCEDURE PATTERN — ACQUIRING IN PERSONAM JURISDICTION

The United States Supreme Court has established dual, multi-step, sequential patterns of requirements for acquiring personal jurisdiction in one state over a civil defendant from another state or country. After all, such a defendant has to then defend in what may be a distant jurisdiction at substantial added cost and inconvenience. The procedural issue presented is: in which circumstances is this defense interest overcome by the competing interests of the plaintiff and the forum state that are seeking to compel such participation? In *Asahi* and related cases, the Supreme Court has detailed these dual patterns for ascertaining whether such personal jurisdiction has been established. In fact, this procedural doctrine may be the most challenging doctrine that you will encounter in your first-year studies. For that reason, I suggest deferring your study of this pattern until you begin to study personal jurisdiction in your Civil Procedure course, given in the fall or spring of first year (or for some perhaps after you have studied Glannon's well-regarded primer, *Civil Procedure*). Then, it should come to life, but not now.

ASAHI METAL INDUSTRY CO. v. SUPERIOR COURT
480 U.S. 102 (1987)

The two patterns of requirements/arguments in *Asahi* for establishing personal jurisdiction over a foreign defendant (either individual or corporate) are set forth below.

First Argument
(An influential but non-binding plurality opinion of the Supreme Court)

FUNDAMENTAL CONSTITUTIONAL PRINCIPLE: FOURTEENTH AMENDMENT DUE PROCESS CLAUSE

   Derived standards (or principles) from the Due Process Clause
   1. Limitation of state power in imposing personal jurisdiction over foreign defendant.
   2. Plaintiff must therefore purposely establish defendant's "minimum contacts" in forum state by:
   3. Act "purposely availing" itself of the market in the forum state so as to have
   4. "substantial connection" with it.

   Four factors for applying standards 3 and 4
       a) designing product for the forum state's market,
       b) advertising in it,
       c) establishing channels for providing regular advice to its customers, or
       d) "marketing the product through a distributor in it."

   Interweaving of key facts with these factors

Conclusion

Facts do not establish in *Asahi* the third and fourth factors and thus no "minimum contacts" exist; Cal. Ct. therefore cannot exercise personal jurisdiction over the foreign defendant. But even if the facts establish such minimum contacts, there is a second requirement that must also be met.

These dual patterns for sequentially analyzing such problems in civil procedure can also, of course, be matched with other complex patterns in basic constitutional law, real property, and indeed in many law-school subjects.

Do you appreciate how internalizing all these patterned categories, particularly when fleshed out in your course outline, guide you in learning, remembering and applying doctrine in a systematic exam-focused order for cogent issue spotting and argument making. Though professors often articulate and flesh them out quite differently, patterns are inherent in each subject. Learn and apply them. It is a key.

LEARNING RULES WITH LEGAL AND FACTUAL DIAGRAMMING

Legal diagramming

A core recommendation — and one of the most important — is always to learn rules with legal and factual diagramming. In legal diagramming, you see a rule as a *formula* composed of a sequence of essential elements, and you isolate each element in its correct sequence. Like a scientific formula, each element in the rule is essential.

For example, the rule sanctioning intentional murder has five elements: (1) intent to kill *(mens rea)* (2) actualized in a (3) voluntary criminal-law act *(actus reus)* that (4) causes, factually and legally, the (5) death of another person. It is this combination of elements in this logical sequence that comprises the rule. These constituent elements exemplify the shared requirements imposed by the explicated underlying pattern (pp. 12-13) that applies to common law crimes. Using this analytical pattern, you can diagram all core common-law crimes. To illustrate, intent to kill *(mens rea)*/ actualized (concurrence)/ in a voluntary criminal-law act *(actus reus)*/ causing (factual and legal cause)/ the death of another person (harm)/ equals intentional murder.

Another example: tort negligence requires, as you know, that there exist a duty owed to the plaintiff/ a standard of care that defines the nature of this duty/ followed by behavior that breaches the standard of care/ and that causes, both factually and legally/ actual harm to the plaintiff. This specification of these foundational elements of basic negligence applies common elements from the sequential structure for tort negligence (pp. 11-12). While tort negligence becomes increasingly complex with numerous additional rules, each such cause-of-action must nevertheless embody these common foundational elements.

Why bother? Why is legal diagramming useful for exams? Isolating the elements of each rule, especially causes-of-action and defenses, helps you to remember the exact rule by imprinting it in your mind. Inaccurately stating a basic rule (such as negligence or trespass) on an exam turns off graders. Isolating each element of a rule in its logical sequence directs your application of the rule on exams and in practice. A rule applies only if each element comprising the rule is concurrently established by facts. If so, the facts are sufficient to trigger application of the rule. If there are no facts to establish any element of a rule, the facts are not sufficient on that element, and thus the rule does not apply.

In addition, legal diagramming is an essential prelude to interweaving, a critical performance skill in making arguments on exams and in practice. Legal diagramming, using a pattern of sequential elements, is also useful for remembering the particular elements of those rules that deviate from the analytical pattern (e.g., strict liability crimes have no *mens rea* requirement; attempt, perjury and possession crimes have no causation and harm requirements; some contracts have substitutes for consideration). Lastly, legal diagramming is based on the comforting reality that there are *common patterns* in crimes, torts, contracts, and civil procedure (in each law-school subject), which offer a means to learn, analyze and apply an immense number of specific rules that exemplify such patterns.

You can't — and shouldn't even try to — memorize many hundreds, even thousands, of rules in crimes, torts, contracts, etc. You can — and should — *internalize* the patterns that enable you to recognize and analyze the common requirements in each subject, to see each rule as an embodiment of the relevant analytical pattern. You fit what you learn from the cases and other materials into the patterns, not the patterns into the cases and materials. The doctrine (rules, principles, and policies) learned from the cases, class and other materials, illustrates and details the patterns. With these patterns and legal diagramming, you don't necessarily have the complete response to exam problems. But you are on the right path to the best arguments. And you will discover that the right path is a large part of what you need to spot the issues and resolve each one with a concise, cogent argument.

Factual diagramming

In addition to legal diagramming, it is equally important to do factual diagramming of each rule. You match each element of a rule in proper sequence with the corresponding facts that establish that element. This meshing together of key facts with the elements of the applicable rule leads to the core exam and practice skill of interweaving, which is detailed and illustrated later. In my extensive experience, students who encounter difficulty with the interweaving performance skill in writing out exam arguments often need practice in legal and factual diagramming.

To illustrate practice in this meshing together of elements and the facts that establish them, consider carefully the following very simple examples that specify the elements with the key facts. Intentional murder: intent to kill (A shoots and kills B while saying, "You deserve to die"); concurrence (A's intent inspired her shooting); voluntary criminal-law act (shooting); causation, both factual and legal, (shooting produces B's immediate demise); harm of death (B dies).

Tort negligence: the defendant owed the plaintiff a legal duty (e.g., A, a motorist, owed B, a nearby motorist, a legal duty); the standard of reasonable care defines this duty (A, as a motorist, owed B a duty of reasonable care in driving); behavior that breached this standard of care (A looked to the back seat as she carried out an animated conversation with a friend); causing, both factually (but-for) and legally (proximately) (A's carelessness caused her to drive into B's car); and actual harm (B is injured).

Do not be troubled at all by the reality that the identical key fact(s) may be applied to establish *more* than one element, e.g., the fact of A shooting B obviously establishes the voluntary criminal-law act element, but it also underpins a strong inference that A intended to kill B. The underlying legal maxim is that the law permits an inference to be drawn that ordinarily we intend to do what we actually do. Naturally, if there are other facts that point toward another interpretation, say, of an accident, that is a different matter and the inference cannot be drawn.

It is important to verify early whether you have difficulty in legal and factual diagramming. Please do so by working with simple hypotheticals from class and your casebook or other source. If your performance with these simple hypotheticals reveals weakness, it is imperative that you practice to develop and perfect this foundational skill with rules stressed in your professor's classes, assigned materials, primers and, especially, arising from her old exams. The reason is that without such skill you will be unable to apply the formats for writing cogent arguments responding to the types of exam problems illustrated in Chapter Five. Even more fundamentally, such weakness may well alert the grader that you are not yet on the legal frequency in a basic sense. You are then unlikely, for example, to be effective in figuring out that a cluster of facts in an exam problem lacks facts on an element of an apparently applicable rule, and hence that the rule does not apply, and, of course, such omission must be stressed in your argument. Learning rules with iconic fact examples, as explained below, may also aid you in developing the skill in legal and factual diagramming that you need for exams and for practice.

LEARNING RULES WITH ICONIC EXAMPLES (PICTURES)

Iconic and related examples trigger issues and make rules come alive. You should therefore study, review, and outline rules with iconic fact examples (mental pictures) that together illustrate the coverage of each rule. Don't learn rules abstractly. Rules have no meaning without facts. Why? Rules are meant to apply only to a limited range of fact situations. Rules are *fact specific*. Your iconic fact examples should very roughly attempt to illustrate the accepted range of fact situations to which the rule applies, the scope of coverage created by the rule. It is also useful to learn each rule with at least a few counterexamples (also pictures) that illustrate fact situations that are beyond the accepted coverage of the rule, and an in-between example or two[2] that trigger two issues. Since all rules serve and particularize policy interests, remembering the specific interest that is served by the rule promotes the understanding that drives recall and performance skills. Unless you understand each rule as a servant of a policy purpose(s), you are likely to encounter difficulty in applying rules. Indeed, it is illuminating to see rules as policies writ specific.

Why is this method of learning and remembering rules so important for the exam? For almost a thousand years, common-law reasoning has been reasoning by iconic fact examples and, not surprisingly, law exams mirror this reasoning and require it. Hence, learning rules by such examples exactly matches the essence of both our common law and exam reasoning.

Thus, if you remember rules with iconic fact examples, there is a modest chance that you will see some of these examples in the exam problems, but there is an excellent chance that you will see *similar* fact examples in the exam problems. It is an exciting feeling of recognition. These facts are key facts. They trigger issues and the application of legal rules to resolve the issues.

Since you see such fact examples on exams, this method of studying and remembering rules matches the form of the exam: from facts to issues to rule application embodied in an argument. Remember always

---

[2] As detailed below, exam facts, of course, do not routinely fall neatly inside or outside of the usual scope of coverage.

that you are *not* asked to define rules and their elements on exams (e.g., define bilateral and unilateral contracts, define torts of trespass to chattel and false imprisonment, and define personal jurisdiction).

Instead, you are given a dense fact problem and you must identify (spot) the legal issues and determine which form of tort, contracts, etc., applies, if any, and you must apply the correct rule(s) by interweaving each element with the key facts. There are other advantages to this method, but first, two examples from torts and two from criminal law, each of which could be detailed on both sides of an index card.

In your practice during the semester, you should emulate these examples. If you do so, you will gradually empower yourself to spot issues and resolve them.

Intentional Tort Examples

RULE: BATTERY

Elements of Rule: Intentional infliction/ of a harmful or offensive contact/ on a person/ without his or her consent

(Remember this rule with the examples that roughly illustrate the coverage of the rule)

Iconic Examples

A slaps B

A makes a sandwich for B's lunch—with a little arsenic in it

A punches a book, bag, pocketbook or umbrella held in your hand

A spits in B's face (perhaps not harmful but certainly offensive)

A has his hand in your pocket or pocketbook

Policy

Rule protects against invasion of personal bodily integrity

(Remember the rule and illustrative examples in light of the policy interest that is protected)

Counter-Examples

Casual jostling on a crowded train, subway, elevator, bus, street or in a concert
    (Consent to such jostling is assumed or implied in all examples.)

A reaches for a supermarket item on a shelf and inadvertently strikes B (no intent)

RULE: ASSAULT

Elements of Rule: Intentional infliction/ of apprehension of imminent harmful or offensive contact/ on a person/ without his or her consent.

Iconic Examples

A shakes fist in B's face

A threatens B with gun, knife, club, piece of glass, can, etc.

A rushes at B yelling, "I'll get you."

Policy

Protection of personal integrity from a "purely mental disturbance," i.e., an apprehension of harmful or offensive contact embodied in an imminent battery.

Counter-Examples

A points weapon at you, but you are not aware (no apprehension).

A stares at you (test is whether a reasonable person would be apprehensive).

"If I had my sword, I would smite thee" (no present ability)

In-between Example

A, an old enemy of B, jokes and smiles, as he twirls a stick in his hand and points it near B (Is A joking or serious — or both?)

Criminal Law Examples

RULE: INTENTIONAL MURDER

Elements of Rule: Intent to kill/ actualized/ in act/ that causes (factual and legal)/ death of a person.

Iconic Examples

A, meaning to dispatch B to a meeting with his ancestors (intent to kill), shoots, stabs, strangles, beats, poisons B who dies from shooting, etc.

Policy

Interest protected: safeguards life from intentional violation (too obvious, don't mention on exam ordinarily)

Counter-Examples

A, drunk, speeding, talking to passenger in rear seat, kills B, a pedestrian (no intent to kill, but creation of risk of death: easily criminal-negligence manslaughter)

In-between example

A fires into a crowd and kills B, a stranger (facts are ambiguous as to whether intentional murder or extreme reckless murder applies)

RULE: DEPRAVED HEART MURDER (also called extreme-recklessness murder or willful and wanton murder)

Elements of Rule: Act committed with extreme recklessness/ under circumstances evincing depraved indifference to value of human life/ and which causes/ death of a human.

Iconic Examples

A shoots into an occupied car, bus, train, or house, or drops boulders off a roof on a crowded street. B dies. A was trying to just miss in shooting, etc.

A plays Russian roulette with B. B dies.

A sets a zoo lion free to scare the public on a crowded Sunday. B dies.

A sets a bomb in a public place. B dies.

A places heavy lumber on train tracks just before a scheduled train arrives. B dies.

Policy

Interest protected: safeguard life from extremely reckless conduct threatening death.

Counter-Examples

A shoots and kills B with intent to kill (it's then intentional murder).

A, a doctor, installs artificial heart in B knowing that B is virtually certain to die within a week or two. B has acute heart disorder and is close to death (risk is justifiable). B later dies.

In-between Examples

A, who has sometimes threatened to kill B, kills B while demonstrating how his new pistol works (facts are ambiguous: did A intend to kill B or was B's death accidental, negligent or reckless).

A plays "Russian roulette" with B who dies during the game (depending on factual context, may be argued as depraved heart murder or reckless manslaughter).

Advantages and risks of learning rules with iconic and other examples

These simple examples demonstrate how the fact-centered approach to distinguishing key and non-key facts leads to issue spotting and specification. Key facts trigger issues; non-key facts do not, and some facts are in-between the two categories.

A few examples previously used illustrate this process. In the tort of assault, the iconic example of A shaking his fist in B's face equals key facts because an issue is raised (is such threatening behavior assault?). Such facts also then trigger rule application. In contrast, the counterexample of A staring at B represents a non-key fact: no legal issue is raised as no legal rule is triggered. Such behavior may violate a rule of etiquette, but that is a different realm.

Suppose in any of the examples previously applied, A is described as a seven foot dropout from your law school, a computer wizard, a leader in "Big Brothers," and as especially devoted to his mother. Legally, such facts in all prior instances of A are non-key facts; no legal issue is triggered by such facts, as no rule application is authorized. With the example-centered approach, you can avoid a common beginner's blunder of the first magnitude: a broad conceptual approach to learning rules leads to applying rules where they do not apply. Since rules are fact-specific, any tendency to apply rules beyond the intended fact coverage is an error. You must restrain such concept-driven habits and attitudes. The example-centered approach restrains you. Do you see how all these fact examples are not just conceptual; they also present pictures (images) that do not simply mirror the conceptual reality. Rather, they are an integral part of the reality, and our mind remembers pictures in strikingly more efficient and effective ways than just concepts. Such images are also a core part of the common law tradition. With this method, you imprint the rule, its elements, and its examples into your conscious and beyond conscious mind so that you can pluck them out on exam day.

But two risks are posed by the example-centered approach. The first is example reduction: that the rule will be swallowed up by the iconic examples. Recalling that such examples illustrate the rule, but do not exhaust the rule, can contain this risk. Rules apply to similar fact situations. But rules also remain open to new examples and thus are not altogether fixed in meaning by the iconic examples drawn from prior decisions. This risk, however, has an advantage: it works against the common beginner's blunder of applying rules too broadly.

The second risk is that a simple "either/or" categorical structure — either within or without the scope of coverage of the rule — could blind you to the in-between examples that require you to argue for the application of two or more rules. Many professors love to present such in-between examples in class. If the old exams also stress such in-between examples, it is especially important to add such a category to the appropriate index cards with a few illustrations, and to practice issue spotting and arguing with such examples as detailed later. With practice, two-way arguments with in-between examples could become as familiar as one-way arguments with "in" or "out" iconic examples. As always, follow your professor's guidance in decoding and stressing these in-between examples and, indeed, all examples. Remember here, as always, basics first, then in-between complexities. Clarity comes from first understanding the "in" and "out" examples that then enable you to spot the issues that arise from the in-between examples. On exams, you may see issues from both categories; check all the old exams to see where your professors place in this spectrum of choice. Illustrations of "in" or "out" and "in-between" examples proliferate throughout this book. In jurisprudential language, iconic examples correspond to "core" fact examples of the coverage of a rule, while the in-between examples are called "hard" cases at a rule's "edge" or just beyond — its "penumbra."

ANTICIPATING EXAM ISSUES: MASTERY LEARNING OF SIGNATURE PATTERNS

Another helpful example of mastery learning applied by outstanding students is systematically and confidently mastering the signature pattern of issues from the pinpointed testable doctrine in each topic and subtopic of each course as spot-lighted in your professor's class, course outline and/or assigned sections in the casebook. Then they practice writing cogent arguments to resolve such issues. While passive, less confident, and less effective learners believe that exam questions are endlessly varying and thus the particular questions asked are purely arbitrary and hence unpredictable, the most effective learners know that such an impression is false. There is an identifiable signature pattern for each professor

Worse, this impression misleads you as you prepare, and limits your expectations as to your potential level of achievement. To be sure, the impression is not sheer illusion. The facts presented in exam problems do vary; resourceful and imaginative professors can endlessly vary the factual face of exam problems. Nevertheless, discerning students pierce this vivid factual variation, spotting the pattern of underlying core issues that tend to be raised again and again with different factual faces. If you identify the pattern and then practice with the issues, you are on the path to mastery understanding.

Why are these core issues raised again and again? The reason may be helpful: each topic and subtopic intrinsically contain a pattern of iconic core issues that arise from the core doctrine. Most professors present, or attempt to present, such issues when they purport to teach that area. How could they not aim to teach this pattern of core issues, or at least some of these issues, arising from the core doctrine? To illustrate, the requirement of factual cause for tort negligence raises a modest number of issues, while the related requirement of proximate cause raises an identifiable, but much larger range of issues. But the task for you is not at the macro level. It is very concrete.

In each topic and subtopic in each course, what is the likely testable doctrine? Which doctrine (rules, principles and policies) has been emphasized by your professor in class, in her assignments, and especially in her old exams often on file in the library? What is her angle of vision into the doctrine, her substantive and analytical frequencies (pp. 9-15)? Students with agile school skills know that each professor telegraphs her preferred responses to the question about what is most important, what is secondary, etc., and thus, what is the most likely testable doctrine out of the mass of cases and doctrine taught and assigned. An effective study group with many "eyes" should more thoroughly identify her telegraphing.

Thus, each professorial signature pattern of likely issues in each area can be identified, practiced and mastered. The exam questions from each topic and subtopic will very likely come from one or more of the issues in her pattern for that topic or subtopic. If you have practiced with hypotheticals and old exams and then resolved each issue with a concise and cogent argument, the issues and arguments should flow out of you on the exam as you recognize many issues you have practiced during the semester, alone and in your study group. Since you have practiced quick cogent writing of such arguments, you also cope more effectively with the severe exam time pressure that bedevils many students. You can be aided here by an illuminating article, "A Meta-Framework for Mastery Learning of Law," on our website (www.JohnDelaneyPub.com). I recommend it. It is also included as Appendix A in my companion book, *Learning Legal Reasoning, Briefing, Analysis and Theory*.

VERIFYING VIA OLD EXAMS

By gradually decoding your professor's old exams, you should be able to verify that the signature pattern of iconic issues and related doctrine stressed by your professor in the course also reappears on her old exams, at least in good measure. Indeed, from the first week or two of class, make copies of these old exams and, as each professor gradually raises these exam issues and teaches the relevant doctrine in class, identify and later practice responding to each such issue from the problems in the old exams. See each issue as a hypothetical to be specified, understood and argued. Thus, by the end of the semester, you've decoded all the issues in the problems detailed in her old exams. You spot all of them and, even without the often absent model or strong arguments, you write your own cogent arguments to resolve these issues and then discuss them in your study group. Gradually, too, you see the repetition of certain iconic issues from one old exam to the other. You have pierced to the underlying structure of signature issues emphasized by each professor. Indeed, this verification procedure also enables you to see any degree of deviation between what she stresses in class and syllabus, and highlights in her exams. By decoding her old exams, you have also added another illuminating dimension, an exam focus, to the unremitting "legal autopsies" of appellate cases in class.

PRACTICE BY WRITING: TEST YOURSELF

From early in the semester, you should practice writing concise arguments, devoting more and more of your time to working with hypotheticals and entire problems as the semester proceeds. Work with hypotheticals and problems from old exams, from your casebook, from primers, this Book, and those of your own making or from your study group. Remember the advantage of practicing and testing by writing. On the exam, you write out your arguments; you don't talk them out. Talking them out can be worthwhile but can also be misleading. You can inadvertently convince yourself that you know a pattern of issues and doctrine because you can talk about them, though you cannot competently spot issues, apply rules, and interweave in a cogent written argument.

Writing will reveal what you really know. It will also show what you really don't know — what you can't use in issue spotting and argument making. You will write your exam arguments with a much higher degree of skill, confidence, and speed if you have practiced throughout the semester with gradually increasing time pressure, even with a timer, to create exam-like conditions. How counter-productive it is to write your first exam argument in torts, contracts, civil procedure and the rest on the day of your exam! Without relentless practice, you are at risk of regressing to powerful old habits and writing what you know; regurgitating college exam answers, the very opposite of law exam arguments. Practice these skills yourself and then, at least weekly, discuss your written arguments in your study group. Seek constructive criticism and reciprocate with the arguments of your study-group members. Outlining and writing out any model arguments from old exams pinpoint and imprint your professor's patterns and 'A' argument-making at both conscious and beyond conscious levels.

This self-and-study-group testing with hypotheticals and old exams finds support in accumulating research that testing aids learning, and works better than some other learning methods. One researcher said, "…learning is all about retrieving, all about reconstructing our knowledge." Another commented, "…when we use our memories by retrieving things, we change our access" to that information…" what we recall becomes more recallable in the future…you are practicing what you…need to do later."

SEE RED-HOT FACTS AS LIGHTNING RODS FOR ISSUE SPOTTING

Initially, you might be wondering, what are red-hot facts and how are they different from the conventional category of "key facts"? After all, the conventional legal language and classification for legally relevant facts that raise one or more legal issues is "key facts;" you may already have frequently seen and heard this classification in class and assigned materials. Within this broad, somewhat fuzzy category that sometimes includes some context, however, certain facts are unmistakable lightning rods for issue spotting. They rivet your immediate focus on certain topics and rules in your professor's course, and resulting issue spotting as detailed in Chapter Four.

To illustrate, all of the mostly obvious prior fact examples of tort assault, battery, intentional murder and extreme recklessness murder are, as you know, key facts, but they all additionally qualify as red-hot facts. And, in marked contrast, the counterexamples are, of course, *not* key facts for the rule and certainly *not* red-hot facts. If unsure about red-hot facts, look again at these glaring and iconic examples (pp. 18-20). On exams, however, use only the conventional language of "key facts" (or "relevant facts," whatever is your professor's usage). In following chapters, we'll see the utility of embracing red-hot facts in each course for outlining, spotting issues and writing concise and cogent arguments. Note that I sometimes also refer to them as "iconic facts" and "iconic fact patterns."

MISCELLANEOUS POINTS ABOUT PREPARATION

Memorization

Memorization that is not accompanied by understanding leads to a mechanistic reduction that will bewilder and confound you. All the memorized legal knowledge in the world, all the mnemonics, will not empower you unless it is informed by understanding, is skills-centered, and you are able to apply it to extricate red-hot facts, spot issues, and select and specify the proper rule(s) or principle(s), which are essential for a cogent argument.

To the often-asked question, "How much should I memorize?" there is no single answer, but there are some guides. All professors insist that you be precise in defining the elements of the core rules (and principles) that you apply in your arguments, especially the basic causes-of-action and defenses. There should be no fuzziness, no omissions, no additions, and no paraphrasing. There is much more to law, law school, and the exams than black-letter law, but your statements of rules stressed by your professors must be precise, with all elements specified. An inaccurate statement of a basic legal rule creates a very poor impression, raising the suspicion that the student doesn't know what she is talking about.

Some professors want you to memorize a lot; some much less. You must follow your professor's guidance. To illustrate the range of possibilities, at New York University Law School, where I taught for many years, one criminal law professor required students to memorize the elements of a very large number of crimes. Other criminal-law professors, including me, had no such requirement.

In addition, do not spend any time memorizing citations. They are unnecessary. Do not spend time memorizing the names of cases. I suggest, however, an exception, especially in constitutional law and civil procedure. The accurate use of the case names of a modest number of landmark cases in applying a correct rule or principle, or in apt borrowing of legal reasoning, is a plus. Be careful, though, to avoid the use of case names if you are unsure about the applicability of the rule, principle, or reasoning contained therein. Memorize and use majority and minority rules (and Restatement rules) where your professor does so or recommends that you do so. Do not do more than she expects.

Legal language

On exams, you demonstrate to your professor that you know what you are writing about by using legal language correctly. More precisely, you demonstrate skills in legal argument by correctly applying the relevant rhetoric of the law, i.e., the *rhetoric* of contracts, civil procedure, real property, etc. In your studying, reviewing and practice writing, you should seek to sharpen your precise understanding of relevant legal language. Your knowledge of issues, rules, policies, principles, and legal argument is made manifest by your precise use of legal language. There is a specialized legal language just as there are specialized vocabularies in statistics (multiple regression analysis), in Freudian psychiatry (the id, ego, and superego), in medicine (crescendo angina), and elsewhere.

More specifically, there is a specialized legal vocabulary in each subject. In intentional torts and crimes, for example, you demonstrate your knowledge by using such words as assault, battery, consent, assumption of risk, privileges, murder, manslaughter, robbery, and larceny in their correct legal meanings. In contracts, your use of such words as capacity, offer, acceptance, consideration and remedies must be precise.

Seeing each such specialized vocabulary as a distinct language may be useful, e.g., contracts is German, torts is French, civil procedure is English. There are similarities as well as differences among these subject vocabularies, just as there are in the actual languages with common roots. Nevertheless, making a separate glossary of certain of these words in each subject's notes may aid you to absorb their definitions. Incidentally, don't hesitate to use your own non-legal language, perhaps in brackets, that enables you to make sense of the legal language that you will actually write later on the exam.

A typical beginner's mistake on exams is to use common English words, which have particular legal definitions, in the non-legal sense. Examples from torts, crimes, and contracts include "provocation," "intent," "entrapment," "negligence," "necessity," "offer," "acceptance," and "consideration." With few if any exceptions, these words and others should be used on exams only in their technical legal sense. If on an exceptional occasion you should happen to use such words in the non-legal sense, make that clear in your argument.

In addition, legal language includes words not ordinarily used outside the legal world. Examples include *mens rea, actus reus, sua sponte,* and *res ipsa loquitur.* Make sure that you understand and use such words correctly. As you read cases, check the meaning of legal language you do not understand in *Black's* Laws Dictionary, and include these words in your glossary in your notebook for each subject. If you are not sure about the meaning of any legal term or its application on an exam problem, don't use it.

Sometimes, beginning law students mistakenly believe that the use of legal language requires that artificial or pretentious words be employed. To the contrary, such language is unwarranted and unlawyerly.

Study groups

As with studying in general, study groups or partnerships can be illuminating or confusing. Some are wasteful, even debilitating, squabble-filled and ego-dominated. They engage in excessive socializing and nitpicking, have egomaniacs and situational psychotics, are preoccupied with secondary or tangential issues, and are relentlessly preparing for a college exam. But other groups are very useful in sharpening focus and providing mutual support and encouragement. Clearly, you also have to be able to get along together. I don't mean *like* each other, just not hammer each other (I recommend running, swimming, etc., for release of aggression and tension). You must keep your eye on the ball: your objective is to sharpen your skills-centered doctrinal understanding and performance required for the exam. Use your study group time to your best advantage. You can study by yourself, work on outlines by yourself. But studying only by yourself may lead to premature physical and emotional exhaustion, and sometimes even discouragement and worse as you fall prey to your fears. In your study group, you can reenergize yourself and provide mutual aid, both analytical and emotional. You accomplish this initially by talking out what you have studied individually, and by clarifying what is uncertain.

This group process in talking like a lawyer is a measurable step better than only studying by yourself. If you can state, explain, and illustrate a rule in a hypothetical and argument, you know it at another level beyond mere passive recognition-type knowledge. Such talking is more than unembellished articulation of what is in your mind. It can sharpen and deepen your performance. As you talk and listen to others talk, you gain clarity and insight, a rationale that can also apply to class participation.

Study groups can be especially useful in refining core skills: in extricating red-hot facts, in spotting and specifying issues using hypotheticals and old exams, and in critically assessing argument-making from different angles. It is a mistake, however, to devote disproportionate study-group time only to knowledge acquisition without stressing the core skills or to defer a concentration on such skills until you "know the subject," a classic beginner's cop-out.

Warming up

If actors, singers, comedians, and lawyers warm up before a performance, law students can warm up before an exam (or class) to enable more effective use of below-surface awareness, including long-term memory. Do you have trouble getting started on an exam? Do you tend to do better — recall, spot issues, and write better arguments — later in the exam? If so, you may have a need to warm up for each exam by practicing a bit of writing of an essay-type argument immediately before the exam begins. If the exam involves multiple-choice questions, practice answering such questions immediately before the exam begins. Experiment with this technique before your next exam. It can't hurt, and it may lubricate your capacity for extricating all that is encoded below the surface, all that you have studied and absorbed. It may also aid in reducing the beginning-exam nervousness that afflicts many.

Multiple-choice questions

Increasingly, law professors appear to be using multiple-choice problems on law school exams. They may constitute only a small part of the exam, or all of it. Some professors may choose multiple-choice problems because they are temptingly easy to grade in contrast to essay exams (at least for conscientious professors). I could only grade perhaps eight exams in a day, for fear that exhaustion might lead me to approach additional papers with a jaundiced eye before I even began. Other professors use multiple-choice problems because they are teaching a class based on a specific code, e.g., the Uniform Commercial Code or Federal Income Tax; they believe that multiple-choice problems effectively test that type of material. Others may use multiple-choice problems to help students prepare for the bar exam. Regardless of the professor's motivation, it is critical to find out early in each course whether (and to what extent) you will confront such problems, so that you can prepare accordingly.

Unlike essay exams, the good news about law-school multiple-choice problems is that all your prior experience in taking such exams in college, on the SAT, and the LSAT is relevant, at least to some degree. Of course, the content and complexity of the problems will be different and the fact patterns will typically be longer, but the form will be familiar (e.g., what is the best or worst of the following choices?). But, despite your familiarity with this format, your preparation for them will be different from that for prior multiple-choice tests, and certainly different from your preparation for essay exams.

Multiple-choice problems require sharp focus on a variety of subtle distinctions between one cause of action or another, one defense or another (including exceptions to exceptions), one statutory section versus a similar or different statutory section, etc. While issue spotting may still be relevant in multiple-choice problems, it is generally far more important to grasp the subtle distinctions emphasized by your professor in class dialectics and assigned materials. Of course, you'll also see such distinctions raised by essay problems, but for multiple-choice problems they are routine.

Preparing for multiple-choice exam problems (as you'll find when you prepare to take the bar exam) is best achieved through relentless practice over many weeks. Some professors indicate the type of multiple-choice problems that will appear on the exam. Others do not. To the extent that they are available, scour the old problems your professor has used in prior semesters. If unavailable, the best alternative is to use Bar-prep multiple-choice problems from PMBR or Bar-Bri (first year subjects are all typically tested on the bar exam), concentrating on the topics your professor emphasized. The Bar-prep problems should aid you since they, as well as your professor, often focus on similar distinctions — though in different ways. When you make a mistake in answering, pinpoint the reason why you got it wrong. Was it simply a lack of knowledge? Did you understand the relevant doctrinal distinctions but selected the wrong choice out of confusion? Whatever the reason, study that narrow doctrine to make it clear or correct any confusion. Mark your wrong answers and return to them at a later date. By the end of the semester, you'll likely have figured out all problems, answers and explanations, especially those that your professor has stressed.

One suggested technique for any particular multiple-choice problem follows. First, look at the question at the end of the fact pattern; then read the fact pattern with that question in mind. Before looking at the listed choices, hypothesize the correct response, and then examine the actual exam choices in light of your hypothesis.

SUMMARY OF RECOMMENDATIONS

- Stress skills-centered understanding (p. 8)
- Adopt and apply a problem-centered and fact-centered approach (pp. 8-9)
- Identify each professor's teaching strategy (p. 9)
- Dial into your professor's substantive and analytical frequency (pp. 9-15)
- Learn rules with legal and factual diagramming (pp. 15-17)
- Learn rules with iconic examples (pp. 17-21)
- Anticipate and verify exam issues (pp. 21-22)
- Practice by writing (p. 22)
- See red-hot facts as lightning rods for issue spotting (pp. 22-23)
- Miscellaneous points (pp. 23-26)

CONCLUSION

Before proceeding to the next chapter "Outlining Your Courses for Exams," ponder and then answer these questions to your own satisfaction and that of a study group friend. Which learning methods and techniques do you currently apply? Which additional methods and techniques, if any, will you try? Can you identify each professor's strategy and dial into their substantive and analytical frequencies — their signature patterns? Are you refining your skill in learning rules with iconic and other examples? Are you practicing daily with hypotheticals and at least weekly with old exams?

ON LOOKING BACK

First, on reflection, the materials detailing "Mastering Learning Rules with Legal and Factual Diagramming" and "Learning Rules with Iconic Examples" (pp. 15-20) are clearly even more important for exam performance and practice than I previously believed. I trust you now see that the iconic examples, the counterexamples and the in-between examples (each remembered with a vivid image) should all be transformed into questions, into hypotheticals for practice.

Second, a deeper understanding of policy and its layering begins with an appreciation of what rules and policies are. As you already know, a straightforward and useful definition of rules is that they are policies (and principles) writ specific. A policy then is simply the purpose of the rule. To illustrate, intent-to-kill murder is a specification of the underlying deep policy that, given our history, culture and religions, using the mind — the highest, most God-like human faculty — to crystallize the decision to kill another human being, and translating that decision (deploying mind and will) into an actual killing, is deeply culpable and should be very severely punished. Do you see how the essential elements for this form of murder (intent to kill/concurrence/voluntary act/causation/harm) exemplify and specify the underlying deep policy? Do you also appreciate how policy can be articulated somewhat more concretely at yet another level in emphasizing deterrence or retribution as decisive policy ends for intentional murder? Of course, rules can serve more than one policy purpose. Avoid the fallacy of "one rule equals one policy at only one level." It is often plural and multi-level as demonstrated in this example.

Do you see, too, how remedies for breach of contract, criminal and tort negligence, trespass in real property and the Bill of Rights all have sharply varying policy purposes? No rule—no principle—is an island. Legislatures and appellate courts do not create and change rules without policy purposes. No wonder an experienced colleague, Professor Cheryl Meyer, calls policy "the level of understanding." No wonder, too, that absence of policy understanding leads to mistakes in issue spotting and selecting and applying rules for lawyerly argument. Avoid them. Do not reduce law and its learning simply to the level of rules, a reduction that will weaken your exam performance.

Third, Professor Howard Gardner, the noted educational theorist, suggests four levels in learning that may be useful for you in learning all professor-emphasized rules, principles, and policies: (1) knowledge, (2) understanding, (3) performance of your understanding, and (4) feedback on your performance. Take, for example, the elements of the foundational tort-negligence rule: existence of a duty to act or not to act, the relevant standard of care, breach of the standard, causation (factual and proximate), and actual harm. While knowing these elements in a surface way is an essential beginning, understanding them requires knowing them in depth, including their complexities and interconnections; performance requires using this understanding for issue spotting and argument-making. Since law schools do not typically provide feedback on your performance in core first-year courses, you provide that for each other in your study group. This multi-level pedagogic framing suggested by Professor Gardner matches well the law school learning challenge. I would add a vital fifth level: legal judgment and imagination that can gradually emerge, especially from understanding, performance, and feedback. Legal judgment informs all of your technical decisions as a student and lawyer. Legal imagination is a quality of great lawyers and judges.

Fourth, Tracy Kidder's *Mountains Beyond Mountains, The Quest of Dr. Paul Farmer, A Man Who Would Cure The World* (Random House 2004) illustrates the utility of "flash cards." While enrolled at the Harvard Medical School and concurrently studying for his doctorate in anthropology there, Farmer also performed extensive medical work in Haiti and did not attend most of his classes. Yet he ranked as one of the top students. He compiled "thousands of flash cards," with a medical question on one side of an index card and the detailed response on the other. The question side of the card [sometimes] had "symbols for musical notes" directing the singing of the response. The answer side of the card often also had drawings to assist in understanding. Though preoccupied with his extensive Haitian medical work, Farmer squeezed in study of the cards whenever he could do so. While Farmer is brilliant and extraordinary in so many ways, his amazing use of flash cards may be a lesson for at least some law students. But I do not suggest skipping law-school classes.

Lastly, for those so inclined, the use of mnemonics and "memory palaces" to imprint and recall on cue is illuminated in *Moonwalking with Einstein, The Art and Science of Remembering Everything* by Joshua Foer (Penguin 2011).

CHAPTER THREE

Mastery Outlining Of Your Courses For Exams

*"A big [exam] mistake people make is just basically copying their
outline. This matches up with that. So I'll write it down."*

Harvard Law School Professor

INTRODUCTION

In preparing to do course outlines, keep in mind that you not outlining a course for a college exam. College exams are not given in law school. It's not about "memorize and regurgitate." Nor are you outlining a law review article, casebook, hornbook, or the "subject" in any comprehensive sense. All these paths risk ensnaring you in a trap of misconceptions and misbegotten results. Instead, your purpose is clear: Your outlines should provide exam road maps for you. They should re-organize and re-present your professor's assigned materials and class priorities — her signature pattern of issues and related doctrine — to enable you to perform the two core exam skills: (1) spotting the issues and then (2) writing a cogent argument to resolve each issue. They should impose an exam-based order on the proliferating course data for these twin tasks. This ordering accords with the powerful patterning character of our minds and thus aids you to make the course your own, especially for performance of the twin tasks. Mastery learning requires mastery outlining.

In preparing to do course outlines, build upon your semester-long studying, reviewing, issue-spotting and argument-making practice with hypotheticals and old exams. Don't conceptualize a course outline as something apart from such preparation and practice. Your course outlining should flow naturally out of this exam-focused studying and reviewing, and your growing skill in issue spotting and argument making. Holism, as always, is the theme. If you found it useful in studying and reviewing to use your own non-legal language (perhaps in brackets) to make sense of the legal language, continue this practice in outlining, but always use the apt legal language on the exam.

Remember that there is no one-way to outline. There is relativity of method — but not of aim. Whatever method you use should aim first to sharpen your performance of the twin exam skills by deepening your understanding of each professor's course: her signature issues and related doctrine (rules, principles, and policies), especially as spotlighted in her old exams. It is the exam-centered process of thinking through her course by outlining that helps you to embrace it, to make it part of yourself. This process should occur throughout the semester as you complete each unit and later refine it, rather than a task you tackle near the end of the term. The more you understand, the better your outlining becomes, and the sharper your outline, the better you understand.

Selecting materials to help you outline

In preparing to outline, it is important to recall the unpleasant but compelling fact that casebooks typically do not clearly and systematically present the related problems, issues, doctrine, and relevant argument. Usually, as you now know, the presentation is not from basics to complexities. Confusion often abounds, whether inherent in the cases, or due to the editor's selection and comments, or failure to comment. The cases stress idiosyncratic facts and bizarre exceptions as well as landmark cases and the cutting edge of law as it evolves, but not basics to complexities. In practice, where you presumably know the basics, you do not ordinarily rely on such casebooks for assistance; for students, the casebook presentation you concentrate on in class can be very confusing for learning the foundational doctrine and the issue-spotting and argument-making skills you need for exams. Even worse, some professors and casebooks unwittingly spread confusion.

I regret to say that many casebooks often seem to be prepared not for students but rather to impress other professors who may assign the casebooks for use in classes. Professors gain credit toward tenure and enhance their prestige and status by editing casebooks that other professors assign to their students. The professors, not students, are mainly served by this arrangement. What's more, frequent new editions of increasingly expensive casebooks, often with the most dubious changes, enrich publishers and professorial authors.[1] If you're thinking that this is a heck of a way to run a railroad, I agree.

Recall, too, that appellate cases are best seen as examples of the law in application: as a problem-solving procedure with *de facto*, often contrasting advocacy-type presentations by various appellate judges arguing their positions. While a typical casebook is not like a college textbook presenting basics and then complexities, be assured that other legal texts are systematic, clear and actually aid you to learn the materials. With luck, your professors — or at least some of them — will present their course materials clearly and systematically. In the end, however, the challenge is upon you to outline your professor's course for the exam, even if her assigned casebook and teaching reflects some pedagogic mystification and obfuscation.

In outlining, too, I strongly recommend that you again *personalize* your search for the right supplementary materials. Your guiding principle: which materials will best aid you to absorb each professor's course and exam priorities as detailed by her old exams. The best guide in your search is Atticus Falcon, the author of *Planet Law School II*. I find his book a presentation of a great amount of useful and vital information about preparing for law school, surviving the experience, doing your best, and pursuing diverse career paths. All those planning to become law students and those in law school will benefit from its careful study. After painstakingly assessing a remarkable number of legal texts, outlines and primers, he recommends those he believes will be most helpful to you. His recommendations include: Dobbs' *The Law of Torts*; my own *Learning Criminal Law As Advocacy Argument, How To Do Your Best On Law School Exams* and *Learning Legal Reasoning*; Glannon's *The Law of Torts* and *Civil Procedure*; Burke and Snow's *Property*; and Blum's *Contracts*. He also has valuable specific schedules to direct your preparation before law school, depending on how much time you can devote to it.

With all the assigned and other materials you use, always concentrate first on basics and then work your way to complexities. Exercise self-discipline. Again, do not attempt to learn the subject in a

---

[1] There is yet another form of corruption at work. Ever more expensive casebooks now are often a thousand pages or more in length. But the static three-hour, fifteen-week course for many subjects utilizes only a few hundred pages or so from these increasingly massive tomes. You pay big bucks for more than a thousand pages and use only a fraction of it. With digital printing and publishing, it is easily feasible, of course, to produce casebooks tailored for individualized professorial coverage with only the few hundred pages that are actually covered, and a much lower price, but the rip-off system and greed prevail.

comprehensive way; concentrate only on those topics in the materials that your professor has covered in class and in assignments. Ordinarily, don't go beyond her scope and depth. Otherwise, you risk drowning in materials. Use the cases she has emphasized as important illustrations of the rules, principles, policy and reasoning explicated in her class, not as an organizing structure. Why? You are definitely not outlining her appellate cases for a compelling reason: these cases are typically not the direct focus of her exam.

As you scrutinize the three outlining methods set out below, keep in mind that the outlining process in one course may result in different outlines. To illustrate, if your torts professor spends three or four weeks covering intentional torts, eight weeks covering negligence and related topics, and two weeks or more covering product liability and perhaps one other topic, your outlining process for this course should have four parts corresponding to the three or four largely separate parts of her course. Your time allocation in outlining her course should also roughly parallel her allocation of class time.

Outline in the right margin as the semester progresses, making checkmarks in the left margin to specify which parts you understand well and which require additional work as measured by your increasing skill in performing the twin tasks. Gradually, your weekly reviews enable you to eliminate such checkmarks.

FIRST APPROACH: OUTLINING WITH RULES AND EXAMPLES

From learning to outlining

Learning rules and their elements, with iconic and other examples (pp. 17-20) leads naturally to outlining the entire course with each rule and related policy and examples on a separate index card. Such outlining is just this learning method writ large, so review the details for implementing it as well as its rationale, advantages, and limitations. I suggest creating an actual or virtual index-card compilation of all the course rules organized systematically into categories and sub-categories. As stressed in the previous Chapter, learning the rules with iconic examples, relevant policies, a few counter-examples, and at least one or two in-between examples, should empower your issue spotting and enable you to resolve each exam issue with cogent arguments (detailed in Chapters Four and Five). Remember that all iconic examples are also red-hot facts.

As noted, while you may not see your iconic examples on the exam, you are likely to see comparable illustrations that express the same underlying pattern of issues. More importantly, if you set forth the iconic examples on one side of an index card, and the rule by elements with the policy on the other, you can train your mind throughout the semester in the required exam thinking sequence: (1) from the red-hot facts in the essay (2) to the issues raised by them and then (3) the relevant rules necessary to resolve them. Once habituated to this sequence (by your daily practice throughout the semester), you should be able to apply it almost automatically on the exam. You have trained your mind in this distinctive way of thinking. Each iconic example is also, in effect, a hypothetical, so that you can practice them alone and in your study group. After you know them well, vary the facts as professors do in class to develop the mental flexibility required for the exam problems, which are often just an aggregation of such hypotheticals into an overall story (as detailed in Chapter Five). Remember the words of one law professor: "There are only so many issues in torts, contracts, etc. If you take enough exams you'll see the same issues, just with different fact patterns and be able to spot them." So true and so focusing.

Thus, outlining each course — including all covered examples, rules, principles, and policies — prepares you with the doctrinal knowledge and understanding you need, and at the same time, with practice in most of the required exam skills: extricating red-hot facts, issue spotting, selecting the relevant rule, and the use of policy as appropriate. This form of preparation omits only practice in interweaving, which you perform by writing responses to hypotheticals and old exam problems (as detailed in Chapter Five).

In compiling these index cards, I reiterate what you now know: the utility of learning each element-centered rule in light of the policy purpose(s) to be served by said rule. Rules are best viewed as policies (and principles) writ specific, and this policy level is the level of understanding. It is the engine that drives your skills in issue spotting, rule applying, etc. Without such understanding, you are in a storm without a compass. Hence, to use another metaphor, outlining by rules and their elements, without understanding the relevant policy served, is like learning specific moves in chess without knowing the purpose of such moves. While virtually all professors emphasize policy as well as rules and principles, the range is from a modest level to an unremitting focus. Where are each of your teachers on this continuum? But sometimes the teacher most policy-preoccupied in class gives an exam that is surprisingly rule focused. Old exams provide answers in locating each of your professor's placement in the policy spectrum. In outlining, too, see principles as akin to policies because of the similarity in their abstract and flexible language (e.g., principles of federalism, separation of powers, justification, reasonableness in many subjects, freedom of speech, press, assembly, and religion).

Sequencing of your index cards — building from basics to complexity

As you study each topic, systematically extract each relevant rule, element by element, from your professor's presentation and from other materials that specify the rules she emphasizes. Keep in mind that casebooks are only sometimes helpful in presenting the basic rules, and you may have to obtain them from other materials. Begin with the basic rule in each topic; then add the additional elaborating rules, each one on a separate index card. You are thereby learning from basics to complexities. This method fits naturally for basement-up learners. But this method should also aid top-down learners if they first acquire an overview of the topic from a *Nutshell* or other materials. Rule formulations vary, especially case-based rules, but always use the formulation that your professor prefers. There is nothing objective about it. Always follow her choices for her course.

To illustrate, in applying this outlining method to learning tort negligence, your first index card might specify on one side the basic tort negligence rule, element by element as your professor taught it.

> Tort negligence requires as elements: (a) the existence of a legal *duty* owed by the defendant to the plaintiff; (b) the specification of this duty in a *standard of care*, usually reasonable care; (c) behavior by the defendant in *breach* of this standard which; (d) *causes*, both *factually* (but-for) and *legally* (*proximately*); (e) actual *harm* to the plaintiff[2]

On the same side of the index card, briefly specify the policy purposes served by this rule. For example:

> - compensate victims for unreasonable and harmful behavior of others
> - fairness to such victims
> - deterrence of such future behavior

On the other side of the same index card, set forth some iconic examples of facts to which the rule clearly applies, as well as a few counter-examples to which the rule does not apply because they embody intentional harms.

---

[2] Use of your own abbreviations should greatly shorten this detailing of rules, policies, and examples.

> **Iconic examples**
>
> A, driver, takes her eyes off the road while talking with a passenger in the car's rear seat, and hits and injures B, a pedestrian.
>
> C, a camp counselor, directs the children to shelter under a lone tree during a lightning storm; lightning strikes the tree and injures three campers.
>
> F, a construction foreman, fails to adequately inspect a construction elevator that malfunctions and injures a visitor.
>
> S, a coal mining company, fails to provide basic emergency equipment to protect miners from methane gas, resulting in death and injuries to miners.
>
> **Counter examples**
>
> A drives his car and intentionally hits B.
>
> B, a camp counselor, intentionally and falsely tells a camper's mother that her son died in an accident, thereby causing the mother severe emotional distress.
>
> **In-between example**
>
> A, a lifeguard, is distracted from a drowning swimmer by his reading, listening to music, and his flirting with an-off duty lifeguard. Negligence or gross negligence?

After this initial card, envision *each* element above, (a) through (e) as a subtopic for card making. Then, systematically extract the rules as laid out above for each subtopic. You will have few cards covering the subtopic of factual (but-for) causation, but numerous cards covering the subtopic of legal (proximate) causation. The reason may be apparent: factual (but-for) causation has only a modest number of issues while legal (proximate) causation is very complicated and challenging with a stunning number of issues, so your professor will probably spend modest class time and assignments on factual causation while devoting a great deal of energy and time to the complexities of proximate causation. It is just common sense to make her priorities your own in card making as in all other outlining, learning methods and techniques.

Two final points on the first recommended approach to outlining your courses: first, while commercially produced index cards are available, I recommend that you make your own cards stressing each rule by elements, relevant policy purposes, iconic and other examples. The physical act of producing your own written or computer-produced cards may help to imprint each rule, policy and related examples in your long-term memory, from which you can *extract* them at exam time. Merely studying commercially produced cards is less effective than learning from your own card making and reviewing. Second, in contrast to the commercial cards, your own cards are tailor-made for your professor's course and exam, and thus for your own needs.

Again, always keep in mind who gives the exam (it's not Gilbert or Emmanuel) and whose rules and priorities you embrace, e.g., contrasting (as your professor typically does in class) common-law rules with modern statutory rules, Restatement rules with statutory rules, common-law rules with Model Penal Code rules, etc. In addition, if, as is typical, she emphasizes in-between examples in class and in her old exams (requiring that students argue for the application of two or more rules) be sure to stress such an in-between category with examples on the appropriate index cards in your outlining (pp. 18-20). Though you always begin with basic examples, be sure also to stress these in-between examples in your practice of hypotheticals during the semester. You are training your mind to spot such issues and argue two ways.

A disadvantage and a remedy

Finally, this first and preferred outlining method — where rules, policies, and relevant examples are detailed on index cards — has a disadvantage. It does not contain a visual portrayal of the entire course, its various topics, subtopics, and the possible complex connections between and among these parts. This limitation can be remedied by a chart that highlights how these parts (say, offer, acceptance, consideration, breaches, remedies in contract) fit together and show connections between and among such topics and their sub-topics. For visually oriented learners and top-down learners, such charts can materially sharpen and deepen understanding. For bottom-up learners, they may provide the overall connections and principles that may be obscured by devotion to important details. For others, charting may shed light, and the risk of harm seems slight or nonexistent. In addition, there is another technique that provides a conceptual overview: add the "summaries of your outlines" (pp. 39-43).

SECOND APPROACH: A MORE TRADITIONAL OUTLINING

As an alternative to outlining with systematic use of index cards, consider the following approach.

Topics and subtopics

As you learn a topic/subtopic in each course, begin the outlining process as soon as possible (after completing the segment), while the material is still fresh in you mind. How do you do this? How does such outlining differ from briefing cases? With each topic/subtopic (take your cue from your professor's syllabus or course outline, her class coverage, and her casebook's table of contents as to what a topic/subtopic is), say to yourself: "I've studied the cases and other materials that elucidate her course. I've been awake in class and taken notes. I've a good or fair idea of what this is about so far including my professor's substantive and analytical wavelengths (pp. 9-15) and priorities. I've practiced daily with hypotheticals and weekly with relevant parts of the old exams. What I have done so far, though essential, is insufficient. I must now outline this segment for the exam."

Key questions

Your outlining emerges here from a systematic response to the following questions.

- What are her signature issues in each topic and subtopic in her course?

- What set of issue-related, red-hot facts trigger these signature issues?

- What are the basic rules (and principles) required to resolve each of these issues?

- Which are the important exceptions to the rules that she emphasized?

- Which statutes (if any) are relevant?

- Which policies (from the cases, statutes and other materials) provide the rationale for these rules (and principles) and drive their application?

- Which rules (if any) has she taught by contrasting common-law rules with modern rules embodied in statutes or the relevant Restatement or Model Code?

- Which in-between issues has she stressed in class and on her old exams?

The advantage of prompt outlining of each topic in response to these questions is that you are translating your knowledge of cases and other materials into the skills-centered understanding that will empower you to spot the exam issues and resolve them. You do not wait until the end of the course to focus on this understanding, these skills and signature issues. You do so all through the course. You are not simply putting on an exam "lens" near the end of the course: you are practicing your twin exam skills in each course as you proceed, step by step during the semester, with each topic and subtopic. From knowledge to skills-centered understanding and performing is the path to 'A' grades.

Sample outline of topic in Constitutional Criminal Procedure

Please review the student illustration below of this second recommended approach below. Note the numerous iconic examples that illustrate the meaning and scope of a professor's coverage of the relevant rules. Emulate this example-laden outlining of a challenging multi-step doctrinal topic. When you study Criminal Procedure, not now, you should be able to extract the multi-step pattern that is spelled out in the cases and applies to every fact pattern that may raise a Fourth-Amendment search-and-seizure issue.

Fourth Amendment Search & Seizure Outline

Purpose: the Fourth Amendment is designed to promote fundamental privacy interests of individuals against federal (and now also state) governmental intrusion.

Thus, it bans unreasonable searches and seizures of "persons, houses, papers, and effects." What follows is a brief outline of certain core constitutional cases detailing this interest: what "unreasonable" means, the requirements of a valid search warrant, and important exceptions to the general rule that a search warrant is essential.

On the given exam facts, is there a Fourth Amendment right?

I. First Requirement — Government Action (threshold requirement) — the Bill of Rights protects us against Government intrusion but not against private intrusion

Who is the government for this purpose?
Publicly paid police, government agents, public school officials, etc. — also private persons acting as agents of government (e.g., deputized citizen). Note — private security guards are not agents of government unless deputized to arrest.

II. Second Requirement — Subjective Expectation of Privacy that is objectively reasonable ("totality of circumstances" test should be applied — *Rawlings*)

a. Expectation of privacy presupposes standing.

b. No standing = No Fourth Amendment Right

Standing requires:

1. ownership of the property, or a right to possess the property subject to the search (e.g. renter of apartment)
2. legitimacy of presence on premises at time of search (e.g. permission, occupancy, etc.)
No standing examples:
- passenger in car to object to search of car
- prisoner to object to search of cell or personal property found therein
- automatic standing to object to introduction of evidence against defendant in a possession (i.e. narcotics) case on basis of illegal search and seizure rejected — *Salvucci*

No reasonable expectation of privacy in property if publicly held out; examples:
- dog search for odors
- observation (e.g. property on car seat)
- aerial surveillance — *Ciraolo, Dow Chemical*
- open fields beyond curtilage of house (outer border of house & outbuildings) — *Oliver*

- voice — *Dionisio*
- handwriting — *Mara*
- bank account records — *Miller*
- magazines offered for sale — *Macon*
- listening devices — eavesdropping is okay if second party to the conversation consents. This is not wiretapping
- homing devices

III. If there is both government action and a subjective expectation of an objectively reasonable privacy interest — was there a search warrant?

If yes, check the validity of the warrant against the necessary tests:

PROBABLE CAUSE — an officer must allege in an affidavit sufficiently *specific* facts that would enable a magistrate to determine probable cause independent of the officer's conclusions. Restated: if an officer alleges sufficient facts, even if hearsay, to meet probable cause standard, the warrant is valid; if only conclusions alleged, not valid.

INFORMANTS — under the "totality" standard of *Gates,* the requirement means the whole affidavit of the officer, its "totality," enables the magistrate to be able to reach independent conclusions.

NEUTRAL and detached judicial officer (magistrate) issuing warrant must be role neutral — attorney general or law enforcement personnel are not neutral. Also not valid if magistrate gets paid per warrant, or if magistrate accompanies search (abandonment of judicial role).

SCOPE of search limited — warrant must "particularly describe" names and places; police must have probable cause upon arrival to go beyond those names and places, although unnamed persons can be detained. Police may seize contraband or fruits or instrumentalities of a crime that they discover in executing a valid warrant.

PRECISION of warrant — must describe with reasonable precision the place to be searched and the things to be seized. Vague descriptions will not suffice (e.g. apartment building without specific apartment #). In some areas, precision is more stringent than others (e.g., First Amendment & seizure of books) *Stanford.*

EXECUTION of the warrant — police must execute warrant without unreasonable delay. They must knock and announce their purpose except in cases of true emergency.

IV. If no search warrant, the search is unconstitutional.

V. But there are SIX IMPORTANT EXCEPTIONS[3] to this general rule prohibiting searches without warrants:

SEARCH INCIDENT TO LAWFUL ARREST — The arrest must be authorized by statute and the search contemporaneous in time and place with the arrest. The scope of the search is restricted to the person and her "wingspan"— her "grabable area". The policy purpose is to protect an arresting officer from any weapon that might be hidden and to preserve any evidence that might be destroyed, whether felt by the officer or uncovered by the search.

AUTOMOBILE — only after a car is stopped for probable cause, otherwise the police must have a warrant. If the police have probable cause to stop the car (e.g., fits description of informant)

---

[3] In addition, in a small number of cases, the Supreme Court has also applied a limited "special needs" doctrine to validate drug testing, on the basis of health and safety justifications, of student athletes, customs agents, and railroad workers involved in train accidents.

or have probable cause to search after stopping a car (e.g., plain view), then they may search the car because of mobility and later unavailability for search plus the lesser expectation of privacy. Search may include packages, containers, etc., even in trunk.

PLAIN VIEW — if the officer is (1) legitimately on the premises and (2) the instrument or evidence of crime is in plain view, the officer may seize it (e.g., inventory of stolen cars).

CONSENT — must be voluntary and intelligent and can be given by anyone with equal right to use or occupy the premises.

STOP AND FRISK — reasonable suspicion standard. If there is *reasonable suspicion* to stop someone, a frisk (pat-down) is valid if the person apparently has a dangerous weapon. (If no weapon, how much like a weapon did it appear?)

HOT PURSUIT, EVANESCENT EVIDENCE AND EMERGENCIES — if not within fifteen minutes behind suspect, not hot. Police in hot pursuit can enter a house to apprehend defendant but no pretext.

This example of a student outline of a difficult course topic demonstrates the "Second Recommended Approach." Note the basics-to-complexities presentation, the numerous iconic examples (the red-hot facts) that trigger issue spotting, and how cases are fitted into the outline rather than the focus of it. Note also the pattern for any search-and-seizure issue. First, given the facts, is there a Fourth Amendment issue? Second, to answer this question, is there government action? Third, if yes, is there a subjective expectation of privacy that is objectively reasonable and violated? Fourth, if yes, is there a valid search warrant? Fifth, if not, does one of the exceptions to a valid search warrant apply that could justify the search and seizure?

Using the table of contents and hornbook

With each topic/subtopic, it's useful to begin in this second approach from any relevant outline of the topic in your professor's syllabus and from the table of contents in her assigned casebook, hornbook or other materials, provided that you focus only on her assigned topics and subtopics.

Systematically answer the above-specified questions (p. 34) as you review the cases and other materials covered in class or assigned by your professor. Use your casebook, your briefs, class notes and other materials that help illuminate her course priorities. I suggest that you should use any commercial outline or primer that you find useful. If it helps you, use it, but don't rely on it exclusively. A commercial outline provides the author's view of the subject; but what you are interested in is an outline of your professor's conception of it. Do not confuse the two. To illustrate the danger, I reacted quite negatively if students blundered by using a commercial-outline rule on my criminal-law exam, after I had directed them to apply only New York/Model Penal rules that I specifically gave them. In addition, such outlines may have mistakes, omissions, or divert you from your professor's approach. Again, remember who is giving the exam.

Using your assigned cases — from case specifics to rule application

As you now know, you do not outline the appellate cases you covered in class. Rather, you *fit* the cases into your topic-centered outline as illustrated above. You proceed to review the cases assigned in each course, case by case, to extract the issues and rules applied to resolve them. Outlining from your cases and other materials differs, however, from your case briefing in that you are now aiming to extract from the cases the set of issues, rules and policies essential for the exam. In determining what is essential, recall what your professor has emphasized. Which cases did she stress; within them, which facts, issues, rules, principles, policies, and arguments?

You extract them from the cases that birthed them because the rule applies more broadly to similar fact patterns as illustrated by examples from old exams, class, casebook, primer, etc. This liberating of the rule from the case context is crucial. It enables and trains you to apply the rule to similar fact patterns in exam problems, to cultivate the mental flexibility that is crucial.

At the end of your outline of each topic, ask yourself again the key questions (p. 34). Also ask:

- Do I understand the set of red-hot facts and related signature issues presented here?

- Do I understand which rules and principles apply, and which relevant policies apply to which iconic facts?

- Given my professor's doctrinal and analytical priorities, and especially her old exams, which issues are likely to appear on the exam?

- Have I verified whether I can apply my understanding of her doctrinal priorities to numerous hypotheticals and her old exams?

Refining your initial outlining efforts

Understandably, your initial efforts at outlining of your first year will inevitably be beginner's efforts. They will be like your first efforts at briefing cases or working with your professor's old exams: awkward, unsure, incomplete, or verbose. As you gradually study and outline, based on the materials, cases and exams, your sophistication in outlining will grow by leaps and bounds. After a couple of months, you may smile as you review your initial efforts of September. What you will see in the cases, exams and in your professor's comments is not simply a matter of what's written and what your hear. It is also a matter of what is in your head: as you learn more about doctrine and analysis of it, you will see more in all of these sources.

You will revise your earlier outlining efforts because you will better see their strengths and weaknesses. As you sharpen and deepen your analytical focus, you will perfect these topic outlines. And your entire effort in studying, reviewing, compiling of red-hot facts, issue spotting, argument making and outlining will be the engine of this process.

Check for interweaving threads

As you revise and perfect the outlines, be alert for connections among them. Assume that the topic in a course is not always an entity unto itself. See each topic and subtopic as an integral thread in a tapestry, interwoven often with other threads. Your professor likely signals such interweaving threads in her class comments and questions, explicitly and implicitly. Be alert for these signals. One example: in criminal law, the iconic examples of criminal negligence, reckless manslaughter and extreme reckless murder illustrate a threading of related but escalating culpability that is usually emphasized by professors who teach these homicides. Don't overlook such highlighted interconnections. Always use iconic and related examples to demonstrate similarities and differences in exam argument. Manufacture your own examples, too, your own hyotheticals to practice the different fact possibilities in applications of rules.

Doing these topic outlines with regular review and revisions gradually builds to a complete outline in each course. At the end of each overall outline, you should also write out — and memorize — a one-page Exam Checklist (see Appendix B, p. 165) that enables you to extract quickly on the exam what you need from your internalized overall outline.

THIRD APPROACH: SUMMARIES OF YOUR OUTLINES

In addition to the prior recommended approaches, many outstanding students do a prose summary of their detailed outlines, and many add a chart. You must discover if these methods aid you to spot and resolve issues and argue. The functions of these methods are clear enough:

- You see the overall structure of the professor's course, its signature issues and related facts.

- You acquire a more concrete grasp of the segments of the course and how they are related; how segments and related issues are tied together — or not.

- You specify how you will approach certain likely exam issues, the steps in your argument.

Examples of student prose summaries or outlines of an outline are set forth below. These summaries are intended only as illustrations of what you might do in each course. But they are not tailor-made for your professor's course. That takes individualizing, which you must do to reflect her issues and priorities, her choices and omissions, and her language.

Negligent Tort Pattern Summary

STEP I: DUTY

D [defendant] is potentially liable to P [plaintiff] in negligence only if there existed some basis of legally obligatory care towards P. Such duty may be based on a statute but many traditional duties arise instead from the case-based general obligation each person in society has to act so as not to create unreasonable risk of harm to others. (Indeed, the creation of such injury-causing and unreasonable risk of harm to others is the definition of negligence in tort.) If D had no duty towards P, D will not be legally liable to P for negligence in tort, even though D's conduct toward P was in fact negligent (in its everyday, popular sense of "careless").

STEP II: DETERMINING THE APPLICABLE STANDARD OF CARE

You must identify the yardstick against which D's conduct will be measured in order to determine if his conduct was a deviation from the norm expected of him, i.e., whether his conduct amounts to a breach of his duty of care towards P. The standard applicable to D might be found in a statute (e.g., a speeding ordinance), the accepted level of practice within a profession ("malpractice" is the name of negligence committed by professionals), or the common reasonable-person standard. All three formulations represent the societal imposition of an external, objective standard of conduct imposed on the individual, subjective behavior of D.

STEP III: BREACH OF DUTY

Breach of duty is the failure by D to conform to the particular standard of care owed to P. The breach consists of D's negligent conduct. It is no excuse that D was unaware of his careless risk-creation, because it is *precisely* that actual lack of awareness (subjective standard) which under circumstances where a reasonable person would have been aware (objective standard), that constitutes the culpable state of mind of negligence. Check to see if the facts of your problem give rise to the evidentiary presumption of *res ipsa loquitur.* Check for a violation of an express statutory duty, thus creating an instance of negligence *per se.*

STEP IV: CAUSE IN FACT (ACTUAL CAUSE)

Is there an empirical link between D's negligent conduct and P's harm? If there is one such cause, it is termed "but for"; if more than one, each could be a "substantial factor." A given causal factor must first be found to be a factual cause before it can be evaluated as a possible proximate (legal) cause.

STEP V: PROXIMATE (LEGAL) CAUSE

P must show a sufficiently close causal link between his suffered harm and D's negligent conduct. This legally relevant link, termed "proximate cause," is really a matter of policy determination by the courts, and depends for its determination on the reasonable foreseeability to D of harm to P. If two or more factual causes are found to have been severally necessary and jointly sufficient to create P's harm, these multiple proximate causes are labeled "concurrent causes." A cause that arises after the initial cause and contributes in some relevant way to the ultimate harmful outcome is factually described as an "intervening cause." An intervening cause which operates so directly, immediately, and completely as to become the new and effective cause of the ensuing harm is legally concluded to be a "superseding cause," and the liability of the original tortfeasor is ended.

STEP VI: DAMAGE OR HARM

P must in fact have suffered some legally recognized form of actual (compensable) damage or harm, as contrasted with the rule in intentional torts where nominal damage is sufficient and assumed. In addition to actual damage, ask whether there is some basis in especially shocking facts for punitive damages (e.g. a surgeon cutting off the wrong leg).

STEP VII: POSSIBLE DEFENSES

Contributory Negligence: any amount of fault by P in causing P's injuries (some jurisdictions), or more than 50 percent (in others), will totally cut off P's right of recovery against D

Comparative Negligence: recovery for P equals total amount of damages minus that amount attributable to P's percentage of fault in causing those injuries

Assumption of Risk: P's recovery cut off entirely if he voluntarily encountered a known risk

Statutory Immunity: e.g., Workmen's Compensation

Core Crimes Pattern Summary

STEP I: VOLUNTARY ACT (*ACTUS REUS*)

What is the voluntary criminal-law *act* (e.g., the shooting of another human in intentional murder, the "trespassory taking" of property in theft) that the definition of the crime prohibits? There must be such an act, or there can be no criminal liability; the criminal law doesn't punish mere bad thoughts. Further, in order to count as a criminal act, the act must be voluntary, not the product of automatism, sleepwalking, unconsciousness, hypnotism, bodily reflex, or convulsion. Mere status or condition (e.g., drug addiction) is not punishable in itself, but the knowing possession of material that is contraband (e.g., drugs) is a sufficient act for punishment. The willful or knowing failure to act when there is a legal duty to do so (based on certain relationships such as parent-child, lifeguard-swimmer, or statutory obligation) constitutes criminal omission, and is a sufficient criminal-law act. Finally, there are exceptional situations — based again on party relationships, such as employer-employee, principal-agent — where D may be held strictly liable (no *mens rea* needed) not for his own acts, but for those of another; this is known as vicarious liability and usually entails low-level liability.

STEP II: *MENS REA*

Mens rea is defined as the culpable state of mind that a defendant must have in concurrence with the act in order to commit the prohibited criminal conduct. In analyzing *mens rea*, focus on both D's actual state of mind, as given in the facts of the problem, and the kind or degree of *mens rea* that the definition of the crime requires; there must be a match for conviction. Be wary: at common law, *mens rea* is an especially complicated and confused segment of the law. Words in such statutes and cases requiring *mens rea* (also called *scienter* or criminal intent) do not have uniform meanings and are applied to convey different meanings.

At common law, these words include intentionally, willfully, knowingly, purposely, designedly, wantonly, feloniously, fraudulently, culpably, negligently, recklessly, and others. A practical approach for exams is to learn the specific *mens rea* requirement for the crimes you have studied and use the language used in the cases and statutes and articulated by your professor. For example, larceny: "intent to steal"; intentional murder: "intent to kill"; forgery: "with intent to defraud"; burglary: breaking and/or entering of a dwelling of another requires "general intent" to do so, and "a specific intent" to commit a crime therein.

The strong modern trend — e.g., the Model Penal Code and now many state laws—seeks to rationalize and clarify the common-law proliferation and confusion by defining just four major categories of *mens rea*, also known as *mental culpability*: (1) purposely; (2) knowingly; (3) recklessly; (4) and negligently. (See Model Penal Code, §202) If your professor has covered these Model Penal Code definitions, study them and their application carefully. A limited number of crimes are defined so as not to require any kind of *mens rea*. Known as strict liability crimes, they are mostly statutory offenses covering public morals, health, and safety. Distinguish strict liability, which totally eliminates *mens rea*, from criminal negligence and recklessness that are forms of *mens rea*. Strict liability makes irrelevant and inadmissible any defense claim by D of mistake of fact since such defense, if successful, is aimed at a *mens rea* element that does not exist.

STEP III: CONCURRENCE

There must be concurrence between the *mens rea* and the voluntary act; the act must manifest the relevant *mens rea*; concurrence may be with any act that suffices as a legal (proximate) cause of the harm. For those crimes defined in terms of a particular harm (e.g., death), the better view is that concurrence must also exist between the *mens rea* and such harmful result.

STEPS IV AND V: CAUSATION AND HARM

Required in "result" crimes (i.e., crimes that are not merely preparatory [inchoate] crimes which category includes solicitation, attempt, and conspiracy). Causation describes the link between D's act and the harmful result. State must prove that D's act was both a factual (generally "but for") cause and a legal (proximate) cause of the prohibited harmful result; a finding of factual cause is a necessary prerequisite to a finding of proximate cause. Murders and manslaughters are examples of such result crimes (death).

Factual Cause is subdivided into the following: (1) "but for," where the harmful result (e.g., death) would not have occurred in the absence of D's conduct, which is thus both a necessary and sufficient cause of V's injury; or (2) a "substantial factor," where D's act by itself may or may not be sufficient but in any event is not necessary to cause V's injury, because the conduct of a third party is sufficient for that. Even though it falls short of a conventional "but for" cause, D's conduct can still be deemed a factual cause of V's injury if it was a substantial factor in achieving that result.

Proximate cause is the legally relevant cause, determined by the court's analysis of the facts in light of policy considerations. Even though D's conduct qualifies as a factual cause of the harm, another question must be asked: is the connection between the factual cause and the harm so attenuated that it would be unfair to hold D criminally liable for the result? As there can be more than one factual cause of the result, so too there can be more than one proximate cause, each termed a "concurrent cause." For example, where D-1 and D-2 independently shoot V so that either wound would have been fatal, and V dies from the combined effect of both wounds, the acts of D-1 and D-2 will both be deemed to be the concurrent (legal or proximate) causes of V's death. Key factor to note in causal link for homicide: victim's death must occur within statutorily specified time period from date of D's infliction of injury (in many states, 365 days). Proximate cause is more strictly interpreted to D's advantage in crimes than in torts because liberty and even life itself is at stake, not just money as in torts. In both areas of law, a tighter link between D's act and Victim's death (or injury) must be shown when D's act is done with recklessness or criminal negligence than when it is done intentionally.

Whether or not acts that intervene (factual description term) between D's original act and V's ultimate injury will break — i.e., supersede (legal conclusion term) — the original causal link, thus relieving D of criminal liability, turns on how the intervening cause is classified: (1) if it is deemed independent of D's act, and unforeseeable by D, then the causal chain will probably be broken, and it will be deemed to be a *superseding* cause; (2) if it is deemed dependent (e.g., ordinary surgery following D's wounding of V), then in order to break the causal chain, the intervening cause must be abnormal (e.g., grossly negligent surgery that converts a routine operation into a fatal one).

STEP VI: DEFENSES

If your analysis of each STEP thus far supports a charge against the defendant, you still must consider — before reaching any final conclusions as to the ultimate question of D's liability — the applicability of one or more of the following defenses as presented in your professor's course.

Incapacity: If D is in any of the unusual states listed in STEP 1, D's acts will be held involuntary, because D performed them *without* volitional capacity, and hence, there is no criminal-law act. Similarly, if D can successfully show that when he did the criminal act, his cognitive and/or behavioral-control abilities were either totally (insanity) or partially (diminished capacity in some states) impaired, such that he could not form the required general criminal intent, or particular intent (e.g., specific intent), this should result in, respectively, an acquittal in some states, or likely conviction on a lesser included offense requiring some lesser level of *mens rea* than does the crime originally charged.

Justification: D acknowledges that he intentionally did the prohibited act, and achieved the harmful result, but asserts that it was, given the circumstances, the right and socially useful behavior to perform. If accepted, D's claim results in acquittal. The main justifications are as follows: necessity, "choice of lesser evils," where the threatened harm has a non-human source, (e.g., nature); duress, where the threatened harm does have a human source; self-defense; defense of another; defense of habitation; law enforcement defense; consent.

Excuse: D acknowledges that he did the act, but asserts that — for reasons centering on D's mental state — it was not his fault, that he is either completely or partially without blame. The main excuses are as follows: mistake of law (very limited) or of fact (relevant only when it can operate to negate a *mens rea* required by the crime's definition); duress (similar to the justifications of necessity, but here D's will is overborne by threats from human agent); entrapment (very narrowly defined).

DANGER IN THE LAST OUTLINING APPROACH

There is danger as well as benefit in the top-down approach. You could acquire good, even excellent, conceptual understanding from these summaries of your overall outline, but still be unable to apply that understanding well in performing the two core exam tasks. The very familiarity of this third approach to conventional collegiate outlining could mislead you into believing that such understanding automatically translates on law exams into success. It doesn't.

Many students then convert the professor's micro interrogatory about specific issues (and responding arguments) into a difficult-to-resist opportunity to show off their conceptual understanding, often just copying a relevant section of their outline ("This matches that so I'll write it down"), thereby exemplifying the vice of "legal lecturing." Your professors did not ask for, and do not appreciate, such mini-lectures. Instead, they require issue spotting and cogent arguments based on their classes and materials that resolve their exam issues. To be sure, such understanding can empower you but you also need a pervasive *micro* approach in all your preparation. The remedy for this danger: daily practice with hypotheticals for each rule you are learning, and at least weekly incremental practice with old exams, and make sure your detailed outline contains numerous examples.

TALK YOURSELF THROUGH THE COURSE

You may find it useful, alone and in study groups, to use your outline, whatever form it takes, to talk yourself through the course. Such talk is disciplined and systematic from beginning to end, unfolding the broad course categories into subcategories, and beginning with the basics. In each subcategory, articulate which issues can be raised and how you would resolve them with an argument. Ask yourself in each topic and sub-topic: which issues did each professor stress in class and in her old exams? By so doing, you are practicing an advanced technique of preparation, orally recapitulating the signature issues that drive your professor's course, and practicing how you will resolve them. You may want to chart issues and your responses and discuss them carefully in your study group. Such a chart can help spotlight these driving issues and their interconnection.

VERIFYING THE UTILITY OF YOUR OUTLINING

As you refine your outlining throughout the semester, I suggest asking yourself, "Does my approach to outlining actually aid me to spot issues and resolve them with cogent arguments as I work (and rework) with hypotheticals and my professor's old exams?" If so, you are on the right track. If not, you have to re-think and revise what you are doing in light of the twin skills. Such revision presupposes that you have some insight into the strengths and weaknesses of your outlining. Better to gain such insight and be alerted earlier than later. In this quest, please don't see these three approaches as sharply separate. You may well find a congenial blending that works best for you as you outline during the semester.

Again, keep in mind always that what is true and valid here is personal: what works best for you is your guide, and remember you not outlining a college course for a college exam.

ON LOOKING BACK

1. The main substantive change is adding an emphasis on principles and relentless practice with hypotheticals and old exams throughout the semester. Keep in mind that there is a real danger in excessive outlining: it risks detracting attention and time from this practice. Outlining is only a means to prepare you for this empowering practice. Resist the temptation to make it a *de facto* end by devoting grossly disproportionate time and energy to perfecting it. For many, it seems to become the centerpiece of their preparation as they diligently and tirelessly prepare for a college exam that law schools do not give. Since they have worked so hard to produce the outline, they are then driven, in a sad and misplaced logic, to quote mini-sections of this time consuming product in serial mini-lecture form in response to triggers in the exam fact pattern. Avoid this very common exam blunder which leads to C range grades. On reflection over the years, it's increasingly clear to me that outlining has an equal potential to help you — or harm you.

I recently heard of a student who prepared a three hundred-page outline for a first-year course. Imagine the internal pressure she must feel on an exam to incorporate "mini-lectures" from her massive outline. She may know more than any other student in the class, but she may have misconceived the nature of a law school exam and the results could be very disappointing.

2. The previously recommended article, "A Meta-Framework for Mastery Learning Of Law," could also direct your outlining focus to repeated iconic fact patterns and the resulting set of repeated signature issues in each course. I again recommend studying it before you begin outlining. You'll find it on our website — www.johndelaneypub.com — under "Professors Advice", and in my *Learning Legal Reasoning* (Appendix A).

Spotting Issues on Law Essay Exams

INTRODUCTION

Professors, second- and third-year students and lawyers all agree that spotting issues is the *sine qua non* in decoding multi-issue exam problems (only with extraterrestrial help can you resolve issues you have not spotted). But there is, nevertheless, little systematic instruction in the specific steps necessary to perform the skill and the corresponding techniques for practicing and mastering it. Mostly, professors simply advise students to spot the issues as if spotting issues were simply a matter of a pure and natural legal aptitude rather than a skill that can be practiced and mastered. This Chapter provides specific, step-by-step direction from the basics to the complex. I assure you from decades of teaching experience that while some students have a gift for spotting issues, virtually every law school student can learn to do it well.

This chapter is intended as comprehensive, to serve those with and without natural skill. There are at least a few insights that will help every student in mastering this skill. For the typical beginning law student, it is important first to carefully identify the different types of problems your professors present and then to practice issue spotting with those types throughout the semester with their old exams. Otherwise, all your efforts in law school may be undermined by a defective foundation. For those who are not yet in law school, this Chapter is especially challenging since issue spotting is quite different from what you must do for success on most college exams, and you cannot identify each professor's choice of exam problem types until school begins. Acquaint yourself now with the four major types (detailed below) before school begins and concentrate on the nationally predominant types of exam problems — the Type One, Type Two and Type Three problems. Then identify each teacher's *actual* choices during the first week or two of class. While learning all four types may be initially perplexing, once you identify which types your first-semester professors apply, your exam challenge may be narrowed since, e.g., they clearly deploy only two or three of the four types.

As you immerse yourself in your courses, issue spotting will gradually become clearer in your mind. Deepening doctrinal understanding provides fuel for sharpening this skill. Indeed, doctrinal insight and issue spotting are inseparable twins: each reinforces the other, and they therefore should be learned together, not separately. Daily hypothetical practice provides such blended learning.

The importance of identifying issues on law exams matches the centrality of spotting issues in everyday class and in practice: it is the nucleus, the catalyst, of legal argument across the spectrum from the most basic levels to the most advanced levels. It directs and even molds your argument. In fact, in practice it is common for friendly experienced lawyers to query one another informally about their cases by asking, "What is your theory of the case?" This means, "Have you figured out yet the crucial issue(s) on which you will seek to win the case?" Thus, spotting issues on exams is but a particular application of a far more broadly applied skill that you will use for the decades of your professional career. Moreover, in business, government, the non-profit sector, and politics, where many lawyers migrate, you will also apply issue-spotting skills in these equally challenging arenas.

The most-frequent challenge in spotting issues on exams is still the Type One, in-class, closed-book, multi-issue essay problem[1] — an often dense, intricate fact pattern sometimes extending for one or two single-spaced pages, at the end of which you are typically asked to "identify and resolve all relevant legal issues" or an equivalent question. As you know, there may be anywhere from four or five to eight or more issues packed in many of these multi-issue problems. Typically, each problem will have a suggested time allotted, often fifty or sixty minutes but sometimes longer or shorter[2] and each exam is usually three or four hours. To pass this law-school genre of exam, you must learn by meticulous reading to spot quickly the basic issues posed by the fact pattern, issues which are often straightforward and even manifest after the right preparation and practice. But to do well, you must also learn to quickly uncover the less obvious, major issues. Semester-long practice in gradual decoding of these exam problems is the key to excelling.

Skill in spotting issues presupposes a repertoire of related skills that enable effective and efficient learning for law school now, and for practice later. This foundational infrastructure of relevant learning and outlining skills, as detailed in Chapters Two and Three, leads naturally to the superstructure of skills embodied in spotting issues. Thus, do not see issue spotting as an autonomous category of skills separate from other learning and performance skills. Rather, visualize a holistic skills continuum: concurrently learning rules, outlining courses, and issue spotting, all of which lead to writing cogent arguments to resolve the exam issues.

Before immersing yourself in the detailed methods for practicing and finding out which of them works best for you, it is necessary first to define precisely what you are doing and why.

WHAT IS A LEGAL ISSUE?

Skill in identifying issues presupposes that you clearly understand what a legal issue is. A good legal issue "cuts to the heart" of the question posed and frames the argument. It is a question raised by key facts about a particular legal liability or a defense to liability. To elaborate, a legal issue poses a question about liability arising from a cause-of-action (or criminal charge) rooted in tort, contracts, civil procedure, constitutional law, etc., or a question about a defense to such a cause-of-action (or charge). In evidence or in civil or criminal procedure other issues also arise about, for example, the admissibility of evidence, the credibility of witnesses, the sufficiency of evidence, and the standard of proof to be applied. But these issues are best viewed as derivative, typically arising out of questions about liability for a cause-of-action (or a criminal charge) or a defense to such liability.

---

[1] While the art and craft of extracting issues from appellate cases is beyond the scope of this chapter, it is nevertheless important to contrast the extracting of issues for briefing appellate cases from the altogether different task of identifying the issues lurking in essay exam problems. In many appellate decisions, extracting the issue upon which the case pivots is straightforward, since the court explicitly defines the issue. Indeed, in the common law tradition, it is a requirement of good judicial form to so articulate the issue(s) from which the holding is a derivative and the judgment a consequence. In contrast, spotting essay exam issues is usually not straightforward but rather a central challenge in decoding the often dense fact pattern presented to you as a given.

[2] You surely can see essay problems that look different. For example, I helped to proctor a three-hour, in-class, family law exam in which the single essay was worth eighty-five percent of the exam, with multiple-choice questions comprising the rest. On closer scrutiny, however, the two-page-plus essay had at least three major parts, so the appearance of a "single" almost-three-hour-long essay was misleading. I have seen other essays that contain many issues, even twelve or more with intense time pressure. Indeed, law exams have many different faces (pp. 48-50, 110-111).

It is vital to appreciate that issues arise from facts rather than from abstract conceptualizing. You must therefore begin your search for issues by scrutinizing the facts in your professor's exam problem with often a sharp paragraph-by-paragraph focus. The problem and fact-centered approach to learning law (pp. 8-9) matches this issue-spotting sequence: from facts to issues and rules.

Consider this facts-to-issue sequence with a familiar simple example: is there a legal issue raised by the fact that A stared at B on the street? The first requirement is satisfied — there is a fact. But we have not satisfied the second requirement: this fact does *not* pose a question about legal liability. It is therefore not a key fact, meaning it is not a legally *relevant* fact. The reason is simple. No legal entitlement follows: no arguable claim of a cause-of-action (or crime) arises from such a fact, not in tort, criminal law, or in any other subject. Stated differently, no legal right of B is violated by such staring and A violates no legal duty owed to B by such staring. To be sure, there may well be an issue about an Emily Post violation of etiquette: A may well have been rude to B. Rudeness, however, is different from legal liability. Legal liability pivots on legal rights and corresponding duties spelled out in legal rules. Distinguish issues about legal liability, therefore, from questions about violations of etiquette, custom, or morality.

But if some of the facts in the essay problem specify instead that A stared at B and then rushed at B waving a menacing fist in B's face, these different facts pose a question about A's liability to B for the intentional tort of assault. These facts spell out an intentional affirmative act by A that creates an apprehension in B of an immediate battery, i.e., the tort of assault.[3] B has a right to be free from such threat, and A has violated his obligation to respect B's right. The issue arising from these limited facts might be formulated as follows:

> Is A liable to B for the intentional tort of assault when A rushes at B waving a menacing fist in B's face?

Note the three component parts of this issue statement: (a) a concise question that (b) incorporates red-hot (key) facts (or some of them) and (c) points to the applicable legal rule. Almost all issue statements should include these three parts. With a clear understanding of what a legal issue is, you can concentrate on the issue-spotting methods detailed below with the suggested techniques for practicing and developing your issue-spotting and issue-specifying skills. As you study and practice these decoding methods, please keep in mind that, as always, the truth of what works most efficiently and effectively for you is highly individualized. Two basic examples follow of valid and invalid issue statements.

Examples of lawyerly and unlawyerly spotting and specifying of issues

Note that the two lawyerly issue statements below are factually focused on the act, the parties, and the harm — the three parts that comprise each legal conflict. They incorporate only necessary key facts, and they all point to the applicable rule. Thus, they "cut to the heart" of the question posed and frame and direct the argument. The unlawyerly examples are shot through with weaknesses that I (and other professors) have heard and seen too many times over decades of teaching and grading. Practice to avoid them. Keep in mind that a good issue statement is the linchpin for outlining and writing of the cogent exam argument that resolves the issue (as illustrated below).

Lawyerly issue statements beget strong arguments; weak statements beget weak answers.

Lawyerly: Is A liable for extreme-recklessness murder for shooting near or into a crowded gondola and killing X and Y? [A did not intend to kill anyone.]

---

[3] Criminal liability is omitted.

Unlawyerly:	Is A liable for murder for shooting near or into a crowded gondola and killing X and Y? [The use of the word "murder" is vague and fails to identify the precise form of murder at issue here, extreme-recklessness murder.]
	Did A kill X? [Legal issues inquire about legal liability. They do not merely inquire about a factual matter such as, "Did A kill B?" a fact which here is a given and thus not a matter of inquiry.]

Lawyerly:	Is X liable to Y for breach of a unilateral contract when Y accepts X's offer by mowing the lawn as X requested and X then refuses to pay?[4]
Unlawyerly:	Does X owe Y the money promised? [Too vague, not focused on the key facts (and relevant element) that Y's mowing X's lawn per X's request is an acceptance of X's offer and forms a unilateral contract.]
	Is X liable to Y for breach of contract? [No key facts whatever, and "breach of contract" is not precise.]

TYPE OF ISSUE SPOTTING DEPENDS ON THE TYPE OF PROBLEM

Identifying the types of problems you confront on each exam clearly precedes the search for key facts and issues. Contrary to what is sometimes said, professors do present a variety of types of essay exam problems. It is essential then to quickly and accurately identify the types of problem actually presented in each exam since the nature and scope of issue spotting (and argument making) varies widely depending on which types are specified. These types are explained below and illustrated later. Each professor typically has a signature pattern that can be identified early and practiced during the semester.

Type One Exam Problem: Paragraph-based multi-issue problem

By far the Type One problem is still the most common type of exam problem. It is the classic multi-issue problem, detailed often in a dense fact pattern of one or two pages presenting a series of paragraph-based mini-problems (legal conflicts) that are sometimes only loosely tied together in an overall problem, an overall narrative. Each conflict contains at least one issue and sometimes two or more. Each conflict should be viewed as a separate hypothetical, usually a very short story. To illustrate this most popular exam type, see the "Mary Lee" tort problem (p. 114), and my own "Speluncean Explorers" problem for a criminal law exam at the New York University Law School (p. 123). The late Tip O'Neill, former Speaker of the House of Representatives, said, "All politics is local." Similarly, with this most common type of multi-issue problem, issue spotting is local, i.e., rooted in these mostly separate paragraph-based conflicts and *not* in the problem viewed overall. While most of these multi-issue problems raise four to eight issues, some teachers detail an extreme version with ten, twelve or even more issues.[5] At the other extreme, you may see a short version with only a few issues and less allotted time.

Type Two Exam Problem: An overall multi-issue problem

The Type Two problem is also a multi-issue problem, but is not paragraph based: you simply cannot mine the separate paragraphs for separate issues. Rather, and in pointed contrast to the Type One approach, you must consider the problem as an overall entity, and then decode it. Often, the overall issue

---

[4] Professors expect a well-focused, often narrow issue statement that frames and then directs a matching cogent argument — instead of the disorganized, jumping-around responses that they often see.

[5] While the issue-spotting process does not change with this extreme version of the multi-issue problem, the format for writing out the arguments to resolve the multitude of issues is even more concise than usual (pp. 85-86).

is an actual or virtual professorial gift, so that the issue-spotting challenge is instead to unfold it into its sub-issues. For a revealing contract example, see "Olivia Warbucks" and the detailed unpacking into numerous separate sub-issues in the strong professorial argument (p. 137). For another version, see the civil procedure problem, "Blowing In The Wind" (p. 150), and the strong responding argument (p. 151). For yet another example of clear, step-by-step unpacking of a single overall issue into the separate but closely related steps necessary to resolve it, see the criminal-law mini-problem and the "standout" responding student argument (p. 104). For an instructive constitutional-law example, see "Let Them Eat Cake" (p. 152), and the strong responding argument (p. 153). In addition, there is a popular and challenging type of contract problem, "Books, Books, Books (pp. 144-149), featuring back-and-forth efforts at offers and counteroffers set forth in a number of paragraphs and sometimes in two pages or more. To spot the issues raised by such a problem requires assessing the relevant group of typical shorter back-and-forth paragraphs, rather than simply one paragraph at a time. As these examples demonstrate, do not be misled by erroneous advice that all multi-issue essay problems can always be broken down into autonomous paragraphs and then separately mined for paragraph-based issues. They can't.

Type Three Exam Problem: Policy problem

The Type Three problem contrasts markedly with the above two most popular types of multi-issue problems. It is the policy problem that asks you whether an existing or proposed legislation, rule or principle should be continued, abolished, changed, or adopted, and requires you to specify the policy reasons for and against said proposal and your choice for or against it, with supporting reasons. You could also be asked to draft legislation relating to, for example, so-called tort "reform" or changing sentencing guidelines. The possibilities are endless. For a criminal law example of this contrasting genre of exam problem, see my "Policy Problem" for an NYULS exam (p. 133), and the responding strong and mediocre arguments (pp. 133-136). Policy questions can occasionally even be a substantial part of the exam. But they are also often omitted altogether. Check each of your professor's old exams to verify both the extent of her use of such problems in each course (if at all) and the kind of policy issues she presents. Since your task in such problems is specified, there is ordinarily no issue-spotting challenge, but you do have to embrace your assigned role in responding, including argument making from a distinctive perspective, usually as a lawyer, trial or appellate judge, or legislator. In my own Criminal Law and First Amendment exams, I always included one pure policy problem along with two other Type One or Type Two problems. While clearly not a standard, my exam practice was also not remarkable at all.

Type Four Exam Problem: Legal issues that spring from but transcend the facts

The far less common Type Four problem also contrasts markedly both with the Type One and Type Two multi-issue problems, as well as the Type Three policy problem. Although triggered by facts, of course, the issue posed is purely legal, rather than the fact-centered issues or the policy-centered issues posed by the first three types of problems. Consider the following example: when a person is arrested for using vulgar words to a police officer, the issue may be framed as whether a statute criminalizing "offensive words" violates the guarantee of freedom of speech? With this broad issue framing, though triggered by the particular facts, you respond with a more abstract level of argument than you would if the issue were only centered on the facts and harm posed by the specific case (pp. 105-107).

The example further illustrates that there are two framings — two standards — for arguing First Amendment free-expression issues. Using the initial "as applied" standard, the issue is whether a statute may be invalidated only "as applied" to the narrow, particular facts and claim of harm posed in the specific case. In sharp contrast, in applying the "facial analysis" standard (as in the example), the particular facts and harm fade in importance as the issue is transformed and generalized to address whether the statute itself should be invalidated and declared null and void on its face for all applications, present and future. Keep in mind, however, that legal issues can be posed on any exam.

49

In conclusion, you can clearly cultivate your skill in identifying all these four different types of exam problems by practice with the old exams of each of your professors during the semester. Forearmed with this identification skill, on exam day you then quickly summon the right wavelength for spotting the relevant issues and then resolving them with cogent arguments, as detailed below and in Chapters Five and Six. As with other exam skills, what initially may be daunting becomes routine and with practice even quickly performed.

Assume now that you will most likely encounter the most popular Type One (paragraph-based multi-issue) problem, and you'll know what to do and where to begin: you must mine each paragraph-based legal conflict for the issue(s) that it poses. The following issue-spotting methods show you how to do so.

THREE ISSUE-SPOTTING METHODS FOR THE TYPE ONE ESSAY EXAM

1. Light-bulb Issue Spotting:	Intuitive method aided by an Exam Checklist[6]
2. Systematic Issue Spotting:	A five-step process, also aided by an Exam Checklist
3. The HATRI Decoder:	An exam safety net — and systematic method for practicing

Students vary in their mastery of the initial intuitive method for issue spotting. Even for those who cultivate powerful intuitive skills during the semester, those skills, when applied on the exams, may not be uniformly effective on all exam problems in a single exam or in all exams. While the five-step systematic method is also detailed below, the two methods overlap and I suggest rejecting any either/or choice. Instead, practice all three approaches during the semester. For most students, a blend is probably the most effective way to proceed. But the reality here as always is personal: you have to determine the right blend through practice — and it may vary from course to course and even from problem to problem.

First issue-spotting method for the Type One Problem: Light-bulb issue spotting

Here you quickly and intuitively identify many, most, or even all of the issues raised by the serial key (red-hot) facts in the essay exam problem. It's harvest time. You've learned the rules (and policies and principles) daily in each course with iconic examples as well as counterexamples and in-between examples (pp.17-20). You've learned the iconic mini-fact patterns of each professor and her signature pattern of issues in your struggle for mastery learning of each topic (e.g., p. 21). You've also practiced weekly during the semester with the old exams of each professor (p. 22). Your confidence has grown. After an initial quick reading, study the exam fact patterns carefully twice, beginning with the question at the end of the problem — and issues begin to jump out at you right away. Sure, the facts are likely different but many are similar to what you practiced throughout the semester. There's far less systematic figuring out of the issues then in the second and third methods detailed below. Your issue spotting is mostly quick and intuitive — but it is a cultivated intuition that flows from all your daily and weekly practice. You feel you can ace this exam and you can!

For a vivid example of this intuitive issue-spotting method and how it leads to quick outlining of your exam arguments, examine the issue decoding of the Type One, paragraph-based tort essay problem on page 116. But please don't spend time now with the 'A' argument that results from this method, and the quick outlining on page 117. We'll return to it later in the next Chapter that details formats for writing exam arguments. Two caveats here. First, don't rely entirely on this intuitive method. It's possible to miss some or more of the important issues. You routinely verify whether there are any such missed issues by

---

[6] An Exam Checklist is simply a one-page list of the topics you have studied. In closed-book exams, you write it our from memory as soon as possible at the beginning of the exam or as the exams are being distributed (See, Appendix B, pp. 165-166).

applying your one-page Exam Checklist of all the major categories studied in each professor's course. We'll detail use of this Exam Checklist shortly. Second, as we later decode other types of exam problems, we'll revisit the varying ways to apply this intuitive method to these other types of problems that are not paragraph based.

Second issue-spotting method for the Type One Problem: Systematic five-step approach

Please note in applying this systematic five-step method that at any point in tackling any of the steps, especially three, four or five, the light bulb can ignite in your mind: you immediately and intuitively know that the key (red-hot) facts in a particular legal conflict trigger an issue that you may well have practiced with hypotheticals during the semester. Since you have the issue, you happily short-circuit the remaining steps. Sure it's five steps initially but after semester-long practice, those five steps should collapse; you spot many of the issues in seconds. So, it's daunting and dense only initially.

STEP ONE AND TWO: DECODE THE INTERROGATORY AND
IDENTIFY THE TYPE OF ESSAY PROBLEM

Often called the interrogatory (or "call of the question"), this question at the end of each problem typically falls into one of two main categories. The most frequent may be the classic open-ended question, what are the rights and liabilities of the parties? Decoded for torts this question means, is there liability on the instant facts for intentional torts, negligence, product liability, and whatever other categories you may have studied that are spelled out in the fact pattern and any relevant defenses? Decoded for contracts, it often means whether back-and-forth statements and forms establish the offer, acceptance and consideration (or a substitute) necessary for a valid contract, as well as breaches and remedies. And so on for each subject.

Other interrogatories you will see are more specific and helpful, as illustrated in the following examples and in the Sample Exam Problems in Chapter Six. In a tort problem: "What are Lee's remedies? What are Barr's remedies? In a criminal law problem: "As a local prosecutor, what charges, if any, would you bring against Happy, Hopeful, and Captain Kirk?" And in any subject: "As a legislator…" signals a policy problem.

Such interrogatories often signal the likely type of exam problem that the professor is presenting. To illustrate, the first interrogatory above in its focus on "remedies" of two parties implies a likely multi-issue, Type One problem (p. 48). The second interrogatory that assigns a role as a "prosecutor" and asks about "charges" against three potential defendants clearly signals another multi-issue, Type One problem.

Do you see how the more specific interrogatories, in signaling one or another type of problem, also often identify the parties at issue and your legal role in responding, e.g., as a plaintiff's or defense lawyer in a civil trial, or as a trial or appellate judge? Since these different legal roles will invoke quite different wavelengths, it is essential to identify your designated role in each problem before you begin to spot the issues and resolve each one with a cogent argument. Do you appreciate how misconceived your response will be if you spot an issue from the wrong perspective, and argue as a defense lawyer when you were asked to argue as a prosecutor or plaintiff's lawyer, or to rule as a judge? Be careful, then, about always identifying and accepting your professor's type of problem and your designated role. Don't ignore it and don't fight it. After semester-long practice, you'll likely perform this initial task in seconds.

Apart from mining the exam interrogatory, you should be able quickly to identify the likely type(s) of essay problems you confront in each exam, a skill you've practiced for each professor during the semester.

STEP THREE: IDENTIFY EACH LEGAL CONFLICT BY IDENTIFYING THE PARTIES

Next spotlight the series of legal conflicts within the overall problem by identifying each specification of parties in conflict. What does this mean? Common Type One essay problems signal the legal conflicts contained therein by serial detailing of the parties in conflict. There is no mystery at all to such detailing and identification. Indeed, it's easy to extract them. Beginning with the first paragraph, you simply look in each paragraph for party couplings: in criminal law, A who kills B while committing a felony; in tort, C who carelessly injures D; in contract, B, a buyer, who does not pay S, a seller, and so on. Just extract these transparent party couplings on scrap paper, three or four to a page: A and B, C and D, E and F, etc. Each such coupling signals a legal conflict. Once you have identified and specified all these party couplings in the paragraphs and detailed them on scrap paper, proceed to quickly complete each legal conflict by adding two obvious additions.

STEP FOUR: COMPLETE EACH LEGAL CONFLICT BY ADDING THE ACT AND THE LEGAL HARM

For the fourth step, to decode the legal conflict all you have to add to the specification of parties is the legal harm inflicted by one (or more) of the parties against the other party (or parties). Each legal conflict has not only parties, but also a legal harm and an act causing the harm. Each such legal conflict poses at least a single issue, and sometimes two or more.

You launch your search for this fourth step in the first paragraph of the problem. But sometimes the first paragraph has no such conflict; it is just an introduction, a stage-setter (e.g., see "Mary Lee" p. 114). Look for people who are harming other people with different behaviors, the "parties" and "harm producing acts." In criminal law, the harms and acts are vivid; A robs and assaults or kills B. In tort, the harms can be compelling too: you are looking for intentional, negligent or reckless acts by C that hurt D (and maybe others) or damage property. In contract, the harms are also compelling in a commercial sense: e.g., E has not paid F after promising to pay her if she delivered goods that F then actually delivered (to appreciate the harm, imagine yourself as the unpaid F facing a payroll deadline). In real property, the harm is yet different: a purported transfer, for example, by G to H of a property interest pursuant to an oral rather than the required written agreement.

Spotlighting the three parts of a legal conflict (the parties, act and harm) is essential, but you must also now capture the legal meaning of the conflict — the resulting issue, or issues, that are raised by it — the fifth and culminating step. Let's explain and illustrate this fifth step by applying the entire five-step process, aided by the intuitive method, with basic criminal law, tort and contract examples.

STEP FIVE: ARTICULATE THE ISSUE

Let's do it initially in a criminal law context. In a criminal-law essay problem you have identified in seconds as a Type One (paragraph-centered, multi-issue) problem, you are asked in part to specify the criminal charges you would initiate as a prosecutor against A (steps one and two). You read in the first paragraph of the essay problem that A aimed and shot his rifle very near a crowded gondola transporting skiers up the mountain. A's objective was to terrify, but to avoid actually hitting, any skier — but she nevertheless killed X and Y, two skiers in the gondola. You identify (steps three and four) the three parts of the legal conflict: (1) the *parties* (A — and X and Y[7]), (2) the *harm* (the death of X and Y), and (3) the harm producing *act* (A aiming and shooting his rifle to just miss the gondola). So far, identifying this legal conflict by applying the four steps is mostly mechanical; a good high school student could do it. But the legal challenge comes next, the crucial fifth step: you must capture the *legal meaning* of this pinpointed conflict, i.e., the issue raised by these red-hot facts. How do you do that?

---

[7] With public, not private, prosecution in the United States, the state or federal prosecutor is technically the official party, she acts on behalf of the public, including X and Y and their families. That fact, however, does not change the suggested steps here.

If you have studied criminal-law rules with iconic examples for each rule and have embodied them in persistent practice with hypotheticals (pp. 18-20), you might quickly recognize that these facts spelling out an extremely reckless shooting risking and then actually taking life are strikingly similar to iconic examples of extreme-recklessness murder you've practiced with during the semester (shooting into or near an apparently occupied apartment, house, car, bus or train without intending to kill a particular person). You could quickly underline these red-hot facts in the problem and immediately abbreviate the issue on scrap paper (or in the margin) as follows:

> Is A l. f/ E.R.M. f/ aim. near. but shoot.. into a cr. gon. & k. X and Y?
>
> Is A liable for extreme reckless murder for aiming nearby but shooting into a crowded gondola and killing X and Y?

Please note that this fifth issue-spotting step flows from all your practice. You learned this murder rule with all or many of the above iconic examples; you practiced hypotheticals with all of them. Your persistent practice cultivated your mental flexibility, so that you correctly intuited in seconds that no problem is presented by extending the iconic examples you practiced to include the similar example of shooting into or near a crowded gondola. You may not need the systematic five-step method for decoding these facts; these one-sided facts do not require you to ponder here for more than a few seconds any question about legal claims that can be brought by A against X and Y, who on these facts are pure victims. You know from your semester-long practice that the one-sided issue here is only about this extreme-reckless type of murder (also called "depraved heart" murder or "willful and wanton" murder).

But suppose you were still uncertain here as to which murder is applicable of those you studied. Glance quickly at your one-page Exam Checklist listings under "Murd." (p. 165) and see a listing for "Ex. R. M." [Extreme Reckless Murder], which should then jog the iconic examples you studied into your conscious mind, and you are now certain about your issue spotting. Even when you are clear about your intuitive issue spotting, it's a good habit to quickly visit your Exam Checklist to verify it.

ISSUE SPOTTING WITH A MORE CHALLENGING TORT EXAMPLE

Let's illustrate again the easy identification of a legal conflict, and another blend of the systematic and intuitive light-bulb processes with help from your one-page tort Exam Checklist for spotting the issue. Suppose you read in the second paragraph of a Type One paragraph-centered, multi-issue problem inquiring about liability of A (steps one and two), that A silently approached B from behind and punched B on the back of his head? The three parts of the legal conflict are clear (steps three and four): the parties (A and B), the harm (the violation of B's physical integrity, and the harm-producing act (A's punch against B's head). Fine so far, but what about the fifth step: what issue is raised by these red-hot facts that comprise this conflict?

Again, if you have prepared by learning rules with iconic examples and have practiced them with hypotheticals, the light bulb should switch on as you recognize another gift from your professor: an iconic example of the intentional tort of battery, i.e., an affirmative act (the punch), with the intent to touch another, that results in an unprivileged harmful or offensive contact with another. You might, without spending more than seconds on any claims A might have on these facts, underline these one-sided, red-hot facts and outline the issue on scrap paper as follows:

> Is A l. to B for int. t. of bat. f/ pun. B on back of head?
>
> Is A liable to B for the intentional tort of battery for punching B on back of head?

If you learned rules as specified above, you might then pause on the unusual fact of "A silently approaching B from behind" before punching B on the "back of his head." The identical red-hot facts spelling out the first legal conflict pose a second issue. You might intuit there's a issue lurking here without being exactly sure of what it is. A glance at your Exam Checklist entry of assault and battery under Inten. Torts (p. 168) could remind you that these facts illustrate a classic exception to the general rule that assault and battery in tort go together, as Prosser says, like "ham and eggs." Such classic exceptions to general rules often provide grist for issue spotting on both law-school and bar exams. You have seen this fact pattern before (or one like it) in studying assault. Indeed, it is a prime counterexample for assault liability. Assault, you recall, requires an apprehension by the victim of an imminent battery. On these facts, since B is unaware, there is no apprehension and hence no assault. The parties and the act are established (steps three and part of four), but not the legal harm of "apprehension" that step five mandates. You quickly underline again the red-hot facts of "A silently approaching B from behind" before punching B on the "back of his head." These facts pinpoint the pivotal missing element of apprehension, and this negative second issue[8] could be outlined in seconds on scrap paper as follows:

Is A l. to B f/ ass. f/ pun. B fr. beh. w/ no app. of att. by B? No!

Is A liable to B for assault for punching B from behind with *no apprehension* of attack by B? No!

ISSUE SPOTTING WITH A STRAIGHTFORWARD CONTRACT EXAMPLE

Suppose in the third paragraph of your Type One paragraph-centered, multi-issue contract exam inquiring about the liability of X (steps one and two), you see the following familiar facts: X said he would pay Y thirty-five dollars if Y mowed X's lawn, and Y said nothing in reply but mowed the lawn, and X then refused to pay Y. The three parts of this legal conflict (steps three and four) might be crystal-clear to you at this point: the parties (X and Y), the act (Y mowing the lawn in response to X's request), and the harm (X did not pay Y). You might quickly, even intuitively, recognize the next step from all your preparation during the semester: these straightforward and one-sided facts illustrate an iconic example of a unilateral contract, and therefore raise an issue as to whether Y can accept X's offer by actual performance of the requested act rather than by a promise to perform. You might quickly underline these red-hot contract facts and outline the issue focused on the pivotal element as follows:

Is X l. to Y f/ br. of unil. K wh. Y acc. X's off. by perf. the req. mow. & X no pay? [9]

Is X liable to Y for breach of a unilateral contract when Y accepts X's offer by performing the requested mowing and X refused to pay?

But even if intuition left you uncertain, a quick perusal of your contract Exam Checklist should jog your memory when you see its listing of "Unil. K." These facts represent a simple, clear example of an acceptance by performance that results in a unilateral contract (the parties, act and harm are manifest). Again, the light-bulb process or a blend of intuition triggered by your Checklist could serve you well. These first two methods for issue spotting really work together hand in glove. As we proceed, you'll see many examples of this blending applied. While all these illustrations so far are plain, more formidable ones follow, illustrations of the pedagogic principle: basics first, then complexities.

---

[8] It is labeled as a "negative issue" in the sense that the correct argument spells out the absence of liability.

[9] Note the precise framing of the pivotal element at issue. This issue framing illustrates more advanced issue spotting and specifying. Also, your abbreviations might be shorter than mine: viz., X l. Y f/ b u k wh. Y acc. X's O by perf. mow. & X no pay.

The Third Issue Spotting Method for Type One Problem: HATRI, a safety net

Let's suppose you are not feeling well on exam day. As you mine the separate paragraph-based legal conflicts for issues, your intuitive issue-spotting skills are not flowing well. The five-step method, including scrutinizing your Checklist, is not jogging your conscious or below conscious mind. Or perhaps you are merely drawing a blank on a few sentences or paragraphs. You are not without recourse. During the semester, you also practiced issue spotting for the Type One fact pattern by applying a different systematic decoding method: HATRI, an acronym for (1) Harm, (2) Acts and Parties, (3) Topics, (4) Rules, and (5) Issues. It could restart you.

HATRI decoding skill unfolds into five questions. First, ask "who has harmed whom" (H). For the familiar facts that "A silently approached B from behind and punched B on the back of his head," the parties and initial legal harm are clear: A harmed B by violating his legal duty to respect B's physical integrity. Second, you pinpoint the specific act (A) that caused the harm, by asking yourself "How did this legal harm occur?" Here, the back-of-the-head punch obviously caused the legal harm. Third, consult your tort Checklist for the relevant topic (T) that applies. It isn't negligence (nothing negligent about a deliberate punch), product liability (no product), or defamation (no vicious verbal or written attack). If only by systematically excluding other course-covered topics, you should spotlight the broad topic of "Intent. Tort" in your Checklist that is relevant. Of course, you might also go to this topic directly without much or any figuring out at all, and after practice you will do so.

Fourth, ask "which of the intentional torts (R) listed in your Checklist under this broad topic, reflecting class coverage and assigned materials, is most applicable to the specified harm and harm-causing behavior?" The listing of "Batt" (battery) should jump out at you. Why? The relevant intentional tort certainly isn't conversion, trespass, trespass to chattel, etc. (no facts at all for any of these torts). In the final step, you formulate the issue in abbreviated form: "Is A, in punch. B, liab. f/ batt?" Voilà! You have quickly applied HATRI to decode these clear facts into the relevant issue as outlined below.

THE HATRI PROCESS

HATRI	Harm & Parties	Act	Topic	Rule	Issue
	A harms B	Back of head punch	Intent. Tort	Batt.	Is A, in punching B, liable f/ battery?

Decoding by applying the five HATRI steps could also be joyfully short-circuited by your jogged intuitive realization that these facts are an iconic example of the intentional tort of battery. The two prior issue-spotting methods and systematic HATRI decoding complement each other. With practice, you'll have many more of these "Eureka!" moments, not only with straightforward facts but also with increasingly complex legal conflicts.

Remember the previously specified exam facts that "A aimed and shot his rifle to just miss a crowded gondola transporting skiers up the mountain but killed X and Y, two skiers in the gondola,'" and that "A's objective was to terrify but to avoid hitting any skier." Applying the first HATRI question, you identify who has harmed whom (H). For these facts, the parties and legal harm are again clear: A harmed X and Y by violating his duty to respect their right to life by very risky shooting. Applying the second question, you pinpoint the specific act (A) that caused the harm-producing behavior by asking yourself, "how did this harm of loss of life occur?" Here, A's shooting of X and Y in the gondola obviously caused the harm. Third, you consult your Checklist for the relevant broad topic (T) that applies. It obviously isn't rape, robbery, larceny, arson, conspiracy, fraud, etc. (no facts at all for any of these crimes). Again, if only by systematically excluding other clearly irrelevant topics, you should promptly spotlight the broad topic of "Crim, Hom." as applicable.

Fourth, ask yourself: "which of the murders and manslaughters rules (R) listed in your Checklist topic under "Crim. Hom." (Appendix B, p. 165) is most applicable to the specified harm and harm-causing behavior?" The listing of extreme reckless murder should jump out at you. Why? The relevant homicide plainly isn't felony murder (no underlying felony), it isn't any form of intentional murder (no conscious objective to kill a specific person on these facts), and it isn't reckless manslaughter (these facts don't match the iconic examples). Instead, the facts are similar (the magic legal word) to shooting into or near an apparently occupied train, plane, bus, car, trolley, the relevant iconic examples for extreme reckless murder. In the final step, formulate the issue (I) in abbreviated form: "is A, in fir. into a crowd. gond, l. (liable] f/ ex. reck. mur?" Again voilà! You have quickly applied HATRI once more to systematically decode the facts into the relevant issue.

HATRI	Harm & Parties	Act	Topic	Rule	Issue
	A kills X & Y	A sh. X & Y in gond.	Crim. Hom.	Ex. R. M.	Is A, in sh. X & Y in gond. l [liable] f/ Reck. Mur?
Is A, in shooting X & Y in gondola, liable for reckless murder?					

Of course, systematic decoding by applying HATRI could again be short-circuited at any point by your belated intuitive realization that, of course, these red-hot facts are strikingly similar to the iconic examples of this type of murder. You are restarted, re-sparked! Intuition and systematic decoding again complement each other. (For additional practice with HATRI as applied to straightforward and much more challenging hypotheticals, see Appendix A, p. 159). As may be obvious now, you determine from practice during the semester the particular blend of issue-spotting methods that best work for you in each course.

ISSUE SPOTTING WITH A MULTI-ISSUE TYPE ONE EXAM PROBLEM

All of the above short examples of red-hot facts raising issues are straightforward and even transparent. But on the exams, the problems are far more challenging. At first glance, they often seem perplexingly intricate and intimidating. As you begin to practice with them during the semester, however, you can be pleasantly surprised when you recognize that these common Type One, essay-exam problems are, as noted, just a collection of separate paragraph-based legal conflicts tied together in an overall entity, a series of mini-stories woven into an overall narrative. The intimidating becomes manageable with practice, one legal conflict and issue after the other.

You'll probably be pleased to see that some of the legal conflicts in these exam-level multi-issue problems are also straightforward. However, other conflicts burst with legal issues, some obvious while others will only be uncovered with practice. With persistent practice during the semester, these initially intimidating fact patterns, now to be unpacked into individual legal conflicts, can also be decoded with one or with a blend of the methods you have just learned.

Let's begin with the application of these methods to a classic and challenging tort-exam problem including typical fact and issue patterns. Some of the issues should be familiar.

Old Friends At Work and Play

D and F are old friends who often take rides together for both fun and business purposes. They have taken many such rides in both the city and the country. All such trips have been conducted without any accident. D and F pride themselves on being careful drivers, and they generally do drive in a careful manner. Though the car belongs to D, sometimes F does the driving. During these excursions, they often engage in intense discussions about politics, friends and business.

One day as D drives the car, the two friends engage in such an animated discussion. During this discussion, D, while turning his head to the rear and talking in animated fashion with F in the back seat, hits and injures P, a pedestrian. Both D and F are distraught, immediately stop the car and call for an ambulance, which struggles through clogged traffic and arrives ten minutes later.

A, the ambulance driver who works for the Acme Ambulance Company, carefully loads P into the ambulance, but is drunk as usual and distracted and therefore collides with another vehicle while driving P to the St. Good Luck Hospital; P is further injured from this collision. Happily, A succeeds in carefully unloading P from the ambulance and transporting him into the Hospital.

I, who just graduated from medical school and who is a new and unsupervised Intern in the Hospital's emergency room, is called and promptly leaves the cafeteria, where she is eating and discussing new medical developments with other doctors, and returns to the emergency room. I does the best she can, and is supportive of P, but she fails to administer routine tests on P and that results in additional injury to P. When she later realizes what she has failed to do, I is deeply remorseful and apologies to P.

S, the Hospital's experienced surgeon for decades, is a nationally known surgeon with outstanding credentials and experience. She is operating on another patient when she is summoned to come to the emergency room, but she quickly finishes her operation and goes directly to the emergency room to treat P.

She decides that P needs immediate surgery and has P brought to the operating room. Unfortunately, though experienced and highly credentialed, she mistakenly amputates P's right leg instead of his badly injured left leg. When she realizes what she has done, she is also deeply remorseful and apologizes to P.

Identify the rights and liabilities of the parties.

(55 minutes)

THE FIRST AND SECOND ISSUE SPOTTING STEPS: DECODE THE INTERROGATORY AND IDENTIFY THE TYPE OF PROBLEM

Let's begin by applying the five-step process. As with any exam problem, begin decoding by focusing on the interrogatory at the end of the fact pattern. Here, it's the classic, "Identify the rights and liabilities of the parties," suggesting a multi-issue problem. Applied to this tort problem, that formulation means: which issues of intentional torts and negligence (and related issues) should be raised and resolved? Why only these two tort topics? Because those are the only topics covered in your one-semester tort class; your professor chose not to cover product liability, defamation, etc. You then verify the type of exam problem you confront. The interrogatory implies the answer and if you have practiced such identification during the semester, you could in seconds confirm that you clearly have an example of the most popular Type One problem, a multi-issue paragraph-based problem, here with a bunch of parties.

THE THIRD ISSUE-SPOTTING STEP: IDENTIFY THE PARTIES IN CONFLICT

In the easy third step, you spotlight the serial, paragraph-based legal conflicts within the overall problem by identifying and then extracting each specification of parties in conflict. Remember that all Type One issue-spotting problems signal the legal conflicts contained therein by sequential detailing of the parties in conflict. Beginning with the first paragraph, simply look in each paragraph for party couplings. Here, since the first paragraph is clearly just an introductory stage setter, you identify in the second paragraph two parties in conflict: D, the driver, and P, the pedestrian. In the third paragraph, you identify A, the ambulance driver, and P again. In the fourth paragraph, you identify I, the Intern, and again P. In the fifth and sixth paragraphs together, you identify S, the surgeon, and again P. You have finished the third step, and written these four transparent party couplings signaling four legal conflicts as follows:

1) P v. D	3) P v. I
2) P v. A	4) P v. S

THE FOURTH ISSUE-SPOTTING STEP: ADD THE ACT AND THE LEGAL HARM

In the fourth step, you complete each legal conflict you have identified by asking another easy question: who inflicted the legal harms against P and with what act? Recall that all legal conflicts have one party causing a legal harm against another party with an external act. In this tort exam, you are looking for one party causing harm by intentional or negligent acts, the topics you studied in your course. In the first legal conflict, D, the driver, while turning his head to the rear and talking in animated fashion with F in the back seat, hits and injures P, a pedestrian. In the second legal conflict, P is further injured when a distracted and drunken (as usual) ambulance driver, A, who works for the Acme Ambulance Company, collides with another vehicle and further injures P while driving to the Hospital. In the third legal conflict, I, a new and unsupervised Intern in the Hospital's emergency room, fails to administer routine tests on P that causes additional injury to P. In the fourth legal conflict, the Hospital's experienced surgeon, S, mistakenly amputates P's right leg instead of his badly injured left leg.

THE CULMINATING FIFTH ISSUE-SPOTTING STEP: ARTICULATE THE ISSUE

Before proceeding to the fifth step, please consider what you have accomplished already by application of these first four steps. The five-paragraph, almost page-long, multi-issue problem is now reduced to mostly four sentences spelling out four core conflicts with their parties, and the harms caused by various acts. Not bad at all, especially when with practice you sense that you'll be able to rapidly perform these four steps on actual exams. What about all the other facts in this twenty-sentence problem? Well, these four sentences capture the red-hot facts in the problem that raise issues. The other sentences set the stage. They detail and contextualize the conflicts, and help to build a coherent story. But they are definitely not red-hot (key) facts, and therefore raise no legal issues at all. From twenty to four sentences! You could feel good about this decoding. Excellent progress, so far.

But the legal challenge comes next, the crucial fifth step. And you cannot perform this step unless you have studied negligent torts. If you have, the challenge is to capture the legal meaning, the issue(s) raised in each of these four pinpointed legal conflicts. How do you do that? Again, if you have studied tort rules with iconic examples of each rule and have embodied them in persistent practice with hypotheticals from the beginning of the semester (pp. 17-20), you might immediately recognize (the light-bulb ignites in your mind) that the red-hot facts contained in the first conflict are strikingly similar to iconic examples of tort negligence. Remember: D, the driver, who while turning his head to the rear and talking in animated fashion with F in the back seat, hits and injures P, a pedestrian. D is obviously breaching his duty owed to P of driving in a reasonable manner; this breach causes, factually and proximately, harm to P. You could immediately abbreviate the issue as follows:

> 1. Is D, w. hits & inj. P , wh. talk. to pass. in back seat, l. to P. f/ neg? [P v. D]
>
> Is D, a driver, who hits and injures P, a pedestrian, while talking to a passenger in the back seat, liable to P for negligence?

In the actual exam, you would then briefly outline your argument with this issue as its linchpin, and later in Chapter Five I'll show you how to do that quickly. At this point, however, you are concentrating only on issue spotting, so proceed to the second conflict: A, the drunken and distracted ambulance driver, who further injures P by colliding with another vehicle while driving P to the Hospital. These striking red-hot facts are just a variation from the initial facts, another gift from your professor, and the light-bulb should ignite again for the compelling reason that you have practiced similar hypotheticals during the semester. You also abbreviate the issue.

> 2. Is A, drun. & dist. am. dr. f/ Acme Co., wh. coll. w/ an. veh. & fur. injures P, l. f/ neg?
>
> [P v. A] Is A, the drunken and distracted ambulance driver for the Acme Ambulance Company, who collides with another vehicle and further injures P, liable for negligence?

Proceed to the third conflict that presents yet another gift from your professor. Concentrate first on the red-hot fact that I "fails to administer routine tests on P that results in additional injury to P." You have practiced relevant hypotheticals during the semester and thus you know immediately (the light-bulb ignites) that there are no excuses for new doctors: all are held to the relevant professional standard of care that imposes a duty to administer "routine tests" without harm, another variation on basic tort negligence. If you apply what I call a "mother's rule," you might say: the Intern is new and unsupervised, cut her some slack. But you know that's ridiculous; think from P's perspective, even P's mother, and you then make no excuse for the Intern. The issue could be abbreviated as follows:

> 3. Is I, wh. fails admin. rout. tests & addit. injur P, l. f/ med. malp? [P v. I]
>
> Is Intern, who fails to administer routine tests and additionally injures P liable for medical malpractice?

The fourth conflict presents an outrageous illustration of medical malpractice that actually does occur: "the Hospital's experienced surgeon, S, mistakenly amputates P's right leg instead of his badly injured left leg." No need to ponder this red-hot and appalling example of medical practice. You could almost instantly abbreviate the issue:

> 4. Is S, the H. exp. Surg., who amput. P's wr. leg, l. to P f/ med. malp? [P v. S]
>
> Is S, the Hospital's experienced surgeon, who amputates P's wrong leg, liable to P for medical malpractice?

Perhaps you're wondering why I initially labeled this tort problem as "challenging," but then characterize these four conflicts and their resulting issues as "easy." As you'll shortly see, these four issues are just the beginning. Some of the remaining issues are not so transparent, and the overall problem with time pressure is definitely not easy. I hope you've learned something important: a demanding problem at the macro level can contain some easy issues at the micro level. The presence of these easy issues in a demanding overall problem is intentional. Professors often insert them as a gate-keeping test. If you spot (and resolve) these foundational issues, you are in the ballpark, and you are on track to spot at least some of the remaining ones. You are on the road for at least a 'C' and perhaps a much better grade. But if you miss these issues, or most of them, professors know from experience in grading that you are very likely to miss, miscast or mangle the remaining issues. You are in trouble. The lesson for all tests: look for the easy issues, too, and make sure you spot, specify and resolve each one with a concise and cogent argument. Reject the false idea that they are too obvious and, "my professor did not intend them as part of the challenge." She did.

Always confirm with your Checklist

To repeat, you never rely completely on either the intuitive lightbulb, issue-spotting method, the systematic five-step method or HATRI for issue spotting. Always verify each issue spotting by checking your Exam Checklist. As you do so here, remind yourself of the definition of a legal conflict: it raises at least one issue, but sometimes two or more. Thus, you are not only verifying the four issues that emerged from the four conflicts. You are also asking yourself whether or not these easy surface conflicts trigger additional issues, as they often do. Indeed, I suggest you routinely hypothesize that there may well be a second (or even a third) issue raised by each conflict on any test.

As you scan the "Intent. Torts" part of your one-page Tort Checklist, you could conclude in seconds that none of these listings apply to this fact pattern: no iconic or other examples of assault, battery, conversion, trespass, etc. are spelled out. This negative knowledge is useful and leads to the positive focus: you need, of course to concentrate only on the "Negl." (and related issues) listings. As you scan these listings, you might wonder, and certainly should, why the facts pointedly specify that A, the usually drunken ambulance driver, "works for the Acme Ambulance Company." As you routinely traverse your Checklist, you should see a listing for "Respondeat Superior" (Appendix B, p. 166). If you learned this doctrine with iconic and other examples and practiced with hypotheticals, the listing should easily jog your memory that the Ambulance Company is plainly an employer of A and, of course, all employers are vicariously and strictly liable for the negligence of their employees committed in the course of their employment. Acme is plainly liable as such an employer. Your Checklist has helped you to uncover the issue-spotting significance of this red-hot fact that you may have initially missed. The issue could be quickly abbreviated as follows:

> 5. Is Acm. Am. Co vicar & strict, l. to P in *resp. super.* f/ neg. of its ambul. driver wh. work?
>
> [P v. Acme] Is the Acme Ambulance Co. vicariously and strictly liable to P in *respondeat superior* for the negligence of its ambulance driver while performing his job?

Once you've recognized the red-hot fact that the usually drunken ambulance driver is an employee, which raises an issue that should also lead you to uncover two other red-hot facts that initially may have escaped your focus: the new Intern in the emergency room (I) and the "hospital's experienced surgeon" (S) are also employees of the Hospital.[10] This additional issue could be quickly abbreviated as follows:

> 6. Is St. G. L. Hos. vic. & str. l. to P in *respondeat superior* f/ I's and S's negligence? [P v. Hos.]
>
> Is the St. Good Luck Hospital vicariously and strictly liable to P for I's and S's negligence?

To repeat, you should never be content with the easily spotted surface conflicts and related issues. When you see a collection of such issues, you should always presume that there are additional issues to be uncovered, and emphatically so when there are *untapped* facts in the legal conflicts that you should postulate almost certainly are pregnant with issues. Indeed, here that postulate blossoms: these four

---

[10] Though not explicitly cited as employees, the description of I, the "new Intern in the Hospital's emergency room" and S, the "Hospital's experienced surgeon for decades," should lead you to infer that they are employees. Indeed, this inference illustrates the kind of limited and reasonable inferences that you can certainly draw from exam facts, the difference between drawing such inferences and the grossly inappropriate practice (unless specifically authorized) of changing or adding facts, thus transforming your professor's problem into a student version. Professors do not appreciate such transformations, and neither would you.

surface conflicts and issues raise others. In abbreviated form, you have spotted and specified six issues at this point:

> 1. Is D, w. h. & inj. P, wh. talk. to pas. in back seat l. to P. f/ neg?
>
> 2. Is A, drun. & dist. am. dr. f/ Acme Co., wh. coll. w/ an. veh. & fur. injures P l. f/ neg?
>
> 3. Is I, wh. fails admin. rout. tests & addit. injur P, l. f/ med. malp?
>
> 4. Is S, the H. exp. Surg., who amputates P's wr. leg, l to P f/ med. malp?
>
> 5. Is Acme Am. Co vicar & strict, l. to P in *resp. super.* f/ neg. of its ambul. driver?
>
> 6. Is St. G. L. Hos. vicar. & strict. l. to P in *respondeat superior* f/ I's and S's negligence?

Remaining issues in "Old Friends at Work and Play"

With quick detailing of these additional issues in lawyerly argument, you are now sailing toward a B or better. Why? Well, most students will spot the four surface legal conflicts, the gifts from your professor. But you have gone beyond the gifts: you have spotted the issues arising from the Ambulance Company's strict liability for A's negligent driving and the Hospital's strict liability for the medical malpractice of I and S. To be assured of sailing into the B+ and A realm for issue spotting, however, there are some remaining issues to be identified.

If you prepared in the recommended ways, two of these issues could/should be uncovered by light-bulb issue spotting ignited by your scrutiny of the still untapped red-hot facts in the conflicts. Why? Both are iconic examples of the relevant rules. First, the facts of S amputating P's wrong leg should rivet your attention. Yes, of course, it's an iconic example of gross medical malpractice. Such a shocking blunder should ring a bell in your mind, even if you did not study negligence with this specific example. It's comparable to operating on the wrong patient, or leaving an astonishingly large medical instrument in a patient after an operation (an x-ray picture of such a horror appeared in a Philadelphia newspaper). This type of blunder is therefore not simply the frequent failure to exercise a duty of reasonable medical care that harms someone. Rather, it catapults such routine failure into the different category of gross negligence. And it definitely should. If light-bulb issue spotting with its search for red-hot facts failed you, a quick scanning of your Checklist might well have a bare listing of "Gross Negl." that should jog your mind to trigger the issue spotting you need (p. 166). The fourth issue above would now be reformulated as follows:

> 4. Is S l. to P f/ gross med. malpractice f/ amputat. wrong leg of P? [P v. S]
> Is Surgeon liable to P for *gross* medical malpractice for amputating the wrong leg of P?

As soon as you spot this riveting issue, you have to extend the existing issue about the Hospital's vicarious liability for the Intern's negligence to also include the Hospital's vicarious liability for the surgeon's gross medical malpractice. That reformulated issue (from number six above) would now read:

> 6. Is St. G. L. Hosp. vicar. & strict. L to P in *respondeat superior* f/ I's neg. & S's gross med.malp.?
> [P v. Hos.] Is St. Good Luck Hosp. vicariously and strictly liable to P in *respondeat superior* for Intern's negligence and Surgeon's *gross* medical malpractice.

In addition, if you studied the doctrine of *respondeat superior* with illustrative red-hot facts, and embodied at least some of them in hypotheticals from exams and elsewhere, then you are primed to look also for additional untapped facts also spelling out negligence in supervision or failure to supervise. Why? You know that negligence is doctrinally separate from respondeat superior and its strict liability. From much practice with old exams, you also know that these two issues are frequently linked together in a pattern. Your professor is testing you: can you see that there are three issues to be raised when "the new and unsupervised Intern…fails to administer routine tests on P and that results in additional harm to P?"

To recapitulate, the initial issue arises from the Intern's clear medical negligence (malpractice), the next issue arises from the vicarious liability of the Hospital for the Intern's negligence, and the latter issue arises from the red-hot facts that the Hospital failed to supervise a brand-new Intern in its emergency room. It's a classic instance of "Failure to Supervise," which might be a listing in your Checklist, especially if your professor stressed it in class, in materials, or old exams. Here, these red-hot facts explode with issues. The third of these issues could be abbreviated as follows:

> 7. Is St. G. L. Hos. l. to P f/neg. f/fail. to super. new Intern in its emerg. room? [P v. H again]
>
> Is the St. Good Luck Hospital liable to P for negligence for failure to supervise the new Intern in its emergency room?

Spotting the issue about the Hospital's failure to supervise the brand new Intern in its emergency room could also trigger a reassessment of the facts about A, the drunken ambulance driver, who further injures P. Yes, you already have, of course, an initial issue about A's negligence, and another issue about the strict liability of his employer, the Acme Ambulance Company. But there is yet another untapped red-hot fact here: A is drunk "as usual," raising another issue about the failure of the Company to supervise A, one of its drivers. Since the ambulance driver, whose negligence harmed P is drunk "as usual," the failure of the Company to supervise A arguably rises to gross, not ordinary, negligence. Do you see the pattern again that can be learned and practiced? A negligent employee may raise three issues as illustrated here and above. The third issue follows: .

> 8. Is Acme Am. Co. l. to P in gross neg. f/ its fail. to super. A, its usually dr. emp.?
>
> [P v. Acme again] Is the Acme Ambulance Co. liable to P in gross negligence for its failure to supervise A, its "usually drunk" employee?

If the Acme Ambulance Company is liable for gross negligence for failing to supervise D, the driver, it might also occur to you at this point that D, too, is also liable for gross negligence for driving "while drunk as usual." Yes, indeed, so the second issue (p. 59) is reformulated as follows. What's illustrated here is how your issue spotting in any exam can be refined as you outline and write it out.

> 2. Is A, drun. as usual driv. f/ Acme Co., who coll. w/an. veh. & fur. injures P, l. f/ *gross* neg?
>
> [P v. A] Is A, the drunken as usual ambulance driver for the Acme Ambulance Company, who collides with another vehicle and further injures P, liable for *gross* negligence?

The remaining issue is hidden, unless you have practiced finding it during the semester. As you see, the notion of what is hidden is very fluid and hostage to your preparation. This issue isn't on the surface and it is not accessible simply by the systematic, paragraph-based decoding that has uncovered all the other issues. It requires a look at D in a new legal light, a new casting. Sure, he's plainly the first tortfeasor, and liable for his negligence. But recognizing him as the first tortfeasor in this cast of tortfeasors also brands him with a new legal classification: he is also an "original tortfeasor," meaning that he is additionally liable for all ensuing ordinary, but not gross, negligence that flows from his initial negligence. If you learned during the semester always to be on the alert for such a pattern triggered by "original tortfeasors," you might have spotted this issue by light-bulb issue spotting, perhaps assisted by your brief Checklist listing of "Orig. Tortfeas." You might also have learned during your semester-long practicing always to hypothesize that the first tortfeasor in negligence exam problems is a likely candidate for this additional legal branding. The issue follows:

> 9. Is D also l. to P as an orig. tortf f/ all ensu. ordin. neg, aris. from D's init. neg.?
>
> [P v. D again] Is D also liable to P as an original tortfeasor for all ensuing *ordinary* negligence arising from D's initial negligence?

Since D's liability, as the original tortfeasor, is not restricted to the facts in the first episode, it also ripples out to other episodes, illustrating vividly that some episodes are definitely not completely discrete and autonomous. Even in this first type of multi-issue problem, issue spotting is not always exclusively paragraph based. Look for such rippling-out facts and issues.

The fact pattern detailed above is a familiar one that can be formidable when first seen but is a joy the second or third time you have seen this matrix of issues (or something comparable), especially after you have practiced resolving each issue with a cogent argument. You have prepared for this pattern; thus you know you can ace this essay with an 'A' grade.[11]

With all the issues identified, you are ready for quick outlining and cogent writing of your arguments to resolve each issue as detailed later in Chapter Five. There is another bonus from this quick and well-focused issue framing on scrap paper or in the margins: it directs and flows easily into such outlining and writing. Incidentally, you did not apply HATRI to these facts for a simple reason. You did not need it.

ISSUE SPOTTING WITH ANOTHER TYPE ONE PROBLEM: THE SHORTER MULTI-ISSUE PROBLEM

There is a shorter version of the popular multi-issue problem that you will also likely encounter that can nevertheless explode in issues.

> ### The Rampage of the Hothead
>
> X, a hothead, sees Y, an old enemy, on the sidewalk, and immediately chases Y with knife in hand while shouting at Y, "I'll kill you." Y, who is ordinarily a slow runner, is inspired and outruns X who is then furious that Y escaped. A group of passersby had witnessed the drama and crowd around X. A minute or two pass, and then X, still in a fury, suddenly flails out with his knife and stabs Z, a member of the crowd who said and did nothing to X and who is a complete stranger to X and Y. Z dies from the stabbing. The local prosecutor, who is also your criminal law professor, asks you, an Intern in her office: Which criminal charges should be *considered* against X (no weapons charges at this time)? She also wants to know the reasons for your recommendations.
>
> (40 minutes)

---

[11] Please note that this challenging problem poses issues that result mostly in one-way arguments, in sharp contrast to the "Olivia Warbucks" problem, "Blowing in the Wind" and other examples in Chapter Six that require two or even three way argument. With practice, you gradually develop judgment and skill in deciding whether one-way or two-way argument is triggered by the facts, relevant rules, and each professor's old exams and expectations. While two-way argument is certainly possible in these multi-issue problems, the predominant tendency appears to stress one-sided facts that result in mostly one-sided argument as here. The stand-out response here spots most of the issues and resolves them with concise, cogent arguments under intense time pressure.

To decode this seven-sentence, one-paragraph, multi-issue problem, you need to have studied both murder, manslaughter, and attempt. But again, even if you have not studied these core criminal-law topics yet, you can perform the first four steps in the five-step protocol and learn much about the process of decoding for issue spotting with this different version of a Type One problem. Applying both intuitive and systematic issue spotting and checking your Checklist with its course categories should quickly begin to illuminate these red-hot facts. Incidentally, a juror related the facts in the actual homicide case to me after the trial.

EXTRACTING THE SURFACE LEGAL CONFLICTS

The five-step protocol directs you again. First, read the interrogatory at the end of the problem that makes you an intern in the prosecutor's office recommending which charges to consider. Second, scan the problem, clearly a short Type One. Third, identify the two surface legal conflicts posed by extracting the two party couplings: first X and Y, and then X and Z. Fourth, to detail and complete these conflicts, underline the harm inflicted by X in each conflict: i.e., X chased Y with knife in hand with a shouted, though thwarted, intention to kill Y, and X actually killed Z by suddenly flailing out with his knife into the crowd. You have spelled out the two conflicts and thus you have also spotlighted the red-hot facts that constitute these conflicts. The fifth step is to determine the legal meaning posed for you, as an intern in the prosecutor's office, by these facts: which charges should be considered?

Having studied the substantive criminal law, two issues (charges) should jump out at you even as you underline the red-hot facts as you read them. Again, this jumping out is intuitive, light-bulb issue spotting. As soon as you see the riveting facts that X chases Y [an old enemy] with knife in hand while shouting at Y, "I'll kill you," you could instantly react that X is obviously trying to intentionally kill Y and plainly only falls short because Y outruns X. Yes, your learning of rules with iconic examples and hypotheticals almost instantly opens your eyes wide here. These facts are glaring iconic facts for attempted intentional murder: an intention to kill is dramatically displayed here in the act of chasing and shouting with "knife in hand" as X tries to kill Y. To be sure, there are moderate challenges down the road in decoding this problem, but this first issue is a gift from your professor that must not be missed. It's emphatically clear, one-sided facts cannot be argued to the contrary.

Second, the additional red-hot facts that a "minute or two pass," and then "X...suddenly flails out with his knife and stabs [and kills] Z," who he did not even know, should lead you almost instantly to hypothesize a bizarre killing and, therefore, probably an issue about extreme reckless murder. Indeed, as soon as you see a bizarre killing, such as X's act of stabbing a complete stranger, you should react: probably extreme reckless murder. Why? You've learned this murder rule with, as you know, the bizarre iconic examples that illustrate it, including someone shooting into (or near) an apparently occupied apartment, house, car, train, or bus, or someone shooting just above or into a crowd, all without intending to kill a specific person. X's flailing-out killing is roughly similar in the risk posed[12] to an utterly reckless, life-threatening act — flailing out into a crowd with a knife thereby killing a stranger.

ALWAYS CONFIRM WITH YOUR CHECKLIST

The five-step protocol and the light-bulb issue hypothesizing lead to the initial framings, but as you know you always confirm with your Checklist. A quick rolodex-type perusal of your listings under "Crim. Hom." and its sub-category "Murd." (p. 165) should lead you quickly to exclude felony murder (no underlying independent felony (such as robbery, arson, kidnapping, etc.); exclude premeditated and deliberated murder (no facts at all); and exclude intentional murder (no conscious objective to kill the stranger Z). Confirming this first issue should flow from your listing of "Attemp," and "Inten. Murd."

---

[12] The legal standard — similar — does *not* mean factually comparable in a surface sense. The iconic examples here obviously vary widely on the surface but all pose this extreme reckless risk to life. This insight should be writ large for all your courses. Look for the interest that is at stake in deciding whether certain exam facts are arguably similar to iconic examples of a rule.

with its *mens rea* requirement of intent to kill that is crystal clear on these initial facts; and the often troublesome question as to whether the voluntary act comes close enough to completion for attempt is no trouble at all on these glaring facts. Y saved himself, as noted, only by his inspired speed in escaping the murderous X chasing behind him with knife in hand. X's voluntary act (*actus reus*) for attempt could not be clearer on these searing facts.

Maybe you didn't need, or hardly needed, to check your Checklist for its listings under "Crim. Hom.," "Murd." and "Attemp." All these list-based categories and related iconic mental pictures flooded into your mind without any need at all for jogging by checking these listings. Fine. You have *internalized* your Checklist. But such quick checking could additionally alert you to something important. You might well have very brief listings under "Attemp." for your professor's likely two main approaches to arguing it: the common law and the Model Penal Code ("c.l. & MPC"). That listing might then enable you to recall your understanding that the common law approach requires that the voluntary act must come "very near" to accomplishment (or similar language), which is easily established here by X chasing Y with knife in hand, while the MPC requires only an easy-to-meet substantial step in furtherance of X's intent to kill Y. Maybe you didn't need your Checklist to ignite your memory of these two essential approaches, but if you did, routine checking takes only seconds. Recognizing them sharpens your issue spotting and foretells strong two-way arguments that will please your professor who most likely stressed both. An 'A' grade is emerging on this issue.

> 1. Is X l. f/ attemp. purp. M. per MPC f/ chas. Y with knife & shout. "I'll kill you"?
>
> Is X liable for attempted purposeful murder applying the Model Penal Code rules for chasing Y with knife in hand and shouting "I'll kill you?"
>
> 2. Is X l. f/ attemp intent. M. per c.l. f/ chas. Y with knife & shout. "I'll kill you"?
>
> Same as above except common law rule applied

The third issue is simpler.

> 3. Is X, who flails out with knife & kills Z, a stranger, l. f/ E. R. M?
>
>   E.R.M. means, of course, extreme reckless murder

Referring to your Checklist might also remind you that your professor taught extreme recklessness murder as a twin, as many professors do, with reckless manslaughter, and emphasized how they differ in degree and also overlap, and always argued both theories in class, usually favoring one choice over the other depending on the magnitude of culpability demonstrated by the facts. Given her teaching priority, you should emulate her on the exam and spotlight a separate issue about reckless manslaughter — a disfavored issue here since these facts spell out extreme moral/legal culpability, and thus a preferred prosecutorial judgment in favor of the murder charge. In jurisprudential language, these appalling facts fit within the core of this murder rule, not at its edge or penumbra. Nevertheless, respect her practice and also frame the manslaughter.[13]

> 4. Is X, who flails out with knife & kills Y, a stranger, l. f/ Reck. Mansl [manslaughter]?

A final look at your Checklist and the fact pattern for untapped facts might channel your focus to the description of X as "in a fury" when he flails out and kills Z, and the inclusion in your Checklist under "Crim. Hom." of "Vol-Heat-Pass.Mansl," the common law approach to this type of manslaughter. But

---

[13] Without such a clear professorial practice in class, you would not argue the manslaughter charge on these egregious facts. At most, you would explain in one sentence why you are not arguing it.

even a moment's reflection should enable you to remember that this manslaughter is also a partial defense to a charge of intentional murder that is not the proper charge on these facts for the killing of Z. Thus, a negative issue arises:

> 5. Does X, who is "in a fury" when he flails out, stabs and kills Z, have the partial defense of voluntary, heat-of-passion manslaughter? No!

This final check might also spur your reaction as you note the Checklist reference under intentional murder to "transferr. Intent" — could X's earlier intent to kill Y, though thwarted, apply to X's actual killing of Z a few minutes later? Just a moment's recalling of the iconic example of this rule — A who shoots at B with intent to kill him, misses and kills C — could lead to a quick rejection of its applicability to the instant facts, since they are different (X did not miss). And his killing of Z by flailing out a few minutes later is also not intentional murder, so the partial defense is irrelevant. Another and final issue emerges:

> 6. Does the rule of transferred intent apply to X's killing of Z a few minutes after his intent to kill Y is thwarted when X cannot catch Y? No!

SPOTTING ISSUES: AGAIN A BLEND OF METHODS

It is instructive to reflect on the issue spotting methods that you may have applied as you practice with these Type One problems, and to realize explicitly how these different methods blend together. The intuitive light-bulb approach, when triggered by your successful search for red-hot facts, is the quickest initial issue-spotting method. But note that referring to your Checklist also triggered some of the issues. These include the *respondeat superior* issues in the prior negligence problem, the two approaches to attempt here, remembering your professor's twin approaches to killings from reckless behavior that you may not have initially spotted with the intuitive approach, as well as the final negative issue detailed above. In addition, your Checklist not only sparks issue spotting; it also provides confirmation of your issue spotting. You did not apply HATRI to uncover any of the issues, but it was another available arrow in your quiver if you needed it. Do not see these three methods as separate categories. Plainly, your particular path for cultivation of this critical exam skill of issue spotting is personal. The blend that works best for you may not work for your colleague. As noted, practice during the semester should reveal your own best mix of methods.

Finally, ask yourself if you've accounted for all the conflicts you have identified and mined all the untapped key facts? If not, work with your Checklist and utilize the HATRI decoder specified above. You don't want to miss any important issue(s).

Recapitulating the five issue spotting steps for Type One Problems

• THE FIRST STEP:	concentrate on the question at the end of the fact pattern (p. 57)	
• THE SECOND STEP:	quickly scan the problem to determine its type (p. 57)	
• THE THIRD STEP:	spotlight the legal conflicts by identifying the parties in conflict (p. 58)	
• THE FOURTH STEP:	add the act and the legal harm (p. 58)	
• THE FIFTH STEP:	specify the issue or issues raised (pp. 58-59)	

ISSUE SPOTTING WITH TYPE TWO EXAM PROBLEMS: UNPACKING AN ULTIMATE ISSUE INTO INTERMEDIATE ISSUES

Though not as popular as the Type One problem, you will encounter the second type of exam problem: a multi-issue problem that requires a step-by-step unpacking of a single *overall* issue into the separate, but closely related intermediate issues necessary to resolve it. It's not paragraph-based as in the Type One problem; you therefore cannot simply mine each paragraph for separate parties, conflicts and issues. This Type Two problem details facts that build up to one overall issue that is divisible into intermediate issues, and perhaps sub-issues within each intermediate issue. Truly, it's a long way from the simple issue spotting that began this Chapter. These problems present an altogether more challenging magnitude of complexity in issue spotting and in resolving these issues. With practice during the semester, however, these problems can become familiar and almost routinely unpacked on the day of the exam. As certain interrogatories signal a Type One problem, the following interrogatory signals a Type Two Problem.

A contract example

The "Olivia Warbucks" contract problem and responding argument (p. 137) aptly illustrates the structure of this Type Two multi-issue problem. The extensive factual presentation culminates in the interrogatory: "Mr. Gray [the executor of the estate of the late Olivia Warbucks, Esq.] has asked you [counsel for the estate] whether he should regard this request for payment of additional law-school tuition by Annie McArdle, the daughter of close friends of Olivia, as an appropriate expenditure [meaning legal obligation] to be paid out of the funds of the estate." In short, is there an enforceable contract obligation, so that the estate is legally bound to pay the rest of Annie's law-school tuition? The decedent (Olivia) had generously befriended Annie to redeem an old moral obligation owed to Annie's late parents, who had extended Olivia free room and board when she was a poor law student, decades before. She had, therefore, gladly paid three semesters of their daughter's tuition before her death, and had clearly promised to pay the rest. The executor, however, is obligated to pay only legal, not purely moral, obligations of the deceased.

The above issue framing presents the single overall issue in the problem. All the facts in the problem lead up to this overall issue framing that is easy to identify since it is virtually a given. Do you see how this Type Two problem differs radically from the conventional Type One problem? The latter presents a bunch of serial issues set forth in paragraph-centered clusters of red-hot facts embodying mostly separate legal conflicts. There are no such clusters in this Type Two problem. Instead, the single overall issue must be deconstructed into its major intermediate issues, all of which should be argued pro and con on facts clearly designed for that purpose. In this instance, they are the following:

- Does Annie's actual attendance for three semesters at law school at the invitation of Olivia Warbucks constitute acceptance by Annie of an offer by Olivia for a consideration-supported contract?

- Can moral obligation serve as a basis for enforcement of Olivia's promise to Annie to pay the rest of the tuition?

- Can Annie's reliance on Olivia's promise, shown in her attending law school for three semesters, serve as a basis for enforcing that promise?

- Can the written form of Olivia's promise to Annie provide a ground for enforcement?

Indeed, scrutiny of the pervasively pro and con responses to these intermediate issues by a well-known contract professor confirms that they are themselves divisible into another more concrete layer of sub-issues (see pp. 138-142). To recapitulate, the first level is the overall issue on the prior page, the second level is the four intermediate issues just above, and the third level is all the sub-issues. During the exam, frequently consulting your one-page contract Checklist categories under "Offer," "Acceptance," "Consideration and alternatives" could quickly jog your mind for the relevant intermediate and sub-issues, and related back-and-forth arguments that are essential here.[14] As noted, there are other illuminating examples for study of this Type Two issue spotting in this Book (pp. 144-149, 150-152, 152-154).

There is obviously a simple technique for verifying to what extent each of your professors utilizes and even favors this Type Two problem. Old exams provide the answer. Expect a considerable variation here. Some of your professors may favor this approach. Others may use it less or not at all. Checking old exams enables you to see the choosen signature pattern for each of your professors early in the semester. You will then prepare accordingly and avoid any exam surprises.

ISSUE SPOTTING WITH A TYPE THREE EXAM PROBLEM: UNPACKING THE POLICY ISSUE

Policy issues on law exams are plainly signaled by your professor's interrogatory at the end of her problem. Whenever that interrogatory asks whether "you agree or disagree" with an existing rule or principle of law, a policy, or a proposed new rule, principle, policy or legislation, sometimes in an imaginary jurisdiction, you have a policy issue. You are not asked simply to identify issues about applying existing rules, principles, and policies, and then to apply the rules to a fact pattern as in the first two types of exam problems. Rather, you are asked whether you agree or disagree with such rule, principle, or policy, or you are asked to argue for a new rule, principle, or policy. Thus, you are asked for your critical assessment of the soundness and desirability of such rule, principle, or policy. In addition, you likely will be asked to respond, for example, as a lawyer, judge or legislator; you then frame and argue on one of these different wavelengths. Since the policy question forges a different exam terrain, you need to traverse it with a quite different map and hiking gear. A few examples illustrate the different mapping.

In a classic criminal-law policy problem, Barbara Wooton's reasoned and appealing (to some but not to me) proposal to abolish *mens rea* as a criterion of criminal liability is set forth and is then followed by the professorial interrogatory, "Do you agree or disagree with Barbara Wooton's proposal? Please explain your reasons." (p. 133). Other actual examples include: "Should the mailbox rule for acceptance be retained (contracts)?" "What are the purposes of civil procedure? How do the rules achieve these purposes? In responding, you can focus on a specific rule, a set of rules, or on civil procedural rules as a whole." "As you know, there are both First-Amendment and Fourteenth-Amendment approaches to the problem of public racist speech. Please detail these contrasting approaches. Which do you favor? Please explain your reasons." Sometimes, the policy question is framed by presenting a problem and, as mentioned, premising an imaginary new jurisdiction, and you are asked to argue for the desirability of one or another rule as a judge. Or, you may be given a problem and be told that in an existing jurisdiction, the rule is unsettled, and you are asked to argue for it or another rule as more desirable as a lawyer. You may also be asked as a legislator to draft legislation about a topic addressed in your professor's course.

If your professor[15] stresses policy issues in class and in her assigned materials, expect them on her exam. If her old exams regularly embody such issues, part of her signature pattern, it is virtually certain that you too will see such issues on the exam. Study her past issues carefully. Are the policy issues

---

[14] Suppose the only two beneficiaries, nieces, tell you, "We know our aunt's tuition payments for Annie were very important to her and we therefore expect the rest of them to be paid from her estate. Her parents' free room and board enabled our aunt to become a lawyer." Do you see how your decision as counsel on the legal issue might be impacted, especially since the chance of challenge to an interpretation in Annie's favor is remote? Law-in-the-books is influenced by law-in-action. But it's not for exams.

[15] Law schools vary significantly. Exams in some schools incorporate a substantial emphasis on policy, others less so or not at all. Thousands of law professors, who are very independent-minded and exercise great autonomy, simply do not follow a single exam tune. Beware of any exam guru who espouses that all follow a single pattern. Individualize; check the old exams.

interspersed in the issue-spotting problem, e.g., does a Type One multi-issue problem contain one policy issue? Or, more likely, is the entire problem a policy problem (e.g., Policy Problem, p. 133). Is there a pattern to her old-exam-specified policy issues? Do some issues repeat? Policy issues are not endless, at least not in light of her priorities as revealed in class and assigned materials. You should be able to zero in on the likely policy issues. Practice writing such arguments well before the exam, especially in pro and con form, rather than discursive college-type presentations.

ISSUE SPOTTING WITH THE TYPE FOUR PROBLEM

As mentioned, the Type Four exam problem is different in that it presents a purely legal issue that transcends the triggering facts — and this issue is a given or a virtual given (pp. 49-50), so no issue spotting challenge is presented. Instead, it requires different exam writing as set forth in the next Chapter.

BEYOND THE TYPES OF PROBLEMS: SECONDARY OR SUB-ISSUES

To resolve some issues, it is necessary to identify and resolve a secondary issue inherent in the principal issue. To illustrate, in New York and some other states, the principle of equitable distribution governs the distribution of marital property in a contested divorce, and requires an approximately equal distribution of marital property, especially in a long-term marriage. Thus, if the facts in a problem detail, in part, that a judge distributed equally the $100,000 bank account of a husband and wife, but awarded sole interest in a business inherited by the wife during the marriage *to the wife*, the general issue is whether this judge's award of the couple's property, accumulated during the marriage, conforms to the requirements of equitable distribution. But the decisive sub-issue is whether the business inherited by the wife during the marriage is marital property. Do you see how the resolution of the general issue (equitable distribution of marital property) requires that the sub-issue (what ought to be considered marital property on the instant facts) must first be resolved? It is useful therefore to classify this type of issue as an *a priori* sub-issue. Look for such issues in all your subjects during the semester — and on exams. Spotlight them in your outlines.

HELP IN SPOTTING ISSUES

Spotlighting interrogatories in each course that signal issues

As you know, the classic interrogatory at the end of many exam fact patterns — What are the rights and liabilities of the parties? — signals a Type One problem but does not signal issues. But, other interrogatories do signal issues, or at least the relevant category of potential issues.

To illustrate, part of a lengthy fact pattern in a procedural problem indicated that the plaintiff was a legal infant when he suffered injuries, and included a question at the end asking whether a judge's ruling was correct in denying a defendant's motion to bar a cause-of-action for negligence, initiated years later when the plaintiff was an adult, on the basis of the expiration of the negligence statute of limitations. The fact of the plaintiff's infancy when injured, coupled with the interrogatory, gives you the issue on a silver platter: is the statute of limitations for A's negligence cause-of-action tolled by A's infancy? The issue is only the interrogatory made more specific, in light of your basic procedural understanding that infancy ordinarily tolls a negligence cause-of-action.

A tort example: the facts specify that at the end of a charge by the trial judge to the jury (as to the standard of care to be applied in determining the property owner's liability, if any, for injuries suffered by a trespasser on the owner's property) specified that the owner's behavior must be "willful, wanton, or malicious." This is the traditional, but not the modern standard, for determining a landlord's duty to trespassers. The interrogatory at the end of the problem inquired whether the judge's charge was correct. Again, these facts, coupled with the question at the end, present you with this different legal issue on a silver platter: is the standard of care to be applied in determining a landowner's liability to a trespasser, injured on the owner's property, whether the owner's behavior was willful, wanton, or malicious, or the modern standard of reasonableness?

A corporate law example: the facts specify that A, a director of X corporation, bought shares in Y corporation and then directed its sales effort, which competed with that of X corporation. The questions at the end of the fact pattern included an inquiry as to whether X corporation could recover the damages it suffered from Y corporation's competition directed by X's director. The issue is a virtual given: is A, a director of X corporation, who directs a sales effort by Y corporation, which competes with X corporation, liable for damages to X corporation for a violation of her fiduciary duty as a director of X corporation? All you have added to the interrogatory is the elementary concept in corporate law that a director of a corporation owes a fiduciary duty to that corporation. You should notice that, as always, all these issue formulations also signal the rule(s) to be applied, and thus direct your argument.

Do you see how such a specific interrogatory usually also signals its matching cluster of red-hot facts in a separate legal conflict in the larger fact pattern in a Type One problem? With each one, you search and identify the particular cluster of red-hot facts, the specific legal conflict comprised of the parties, act and harm that is relevant for each such interrogatory, often centered in one paragraph. You know that the other clusters of facts are relevant for the other interrogatories, but not for this one. You repeat this matching of relevant clusters of red-hot facts in separate legal episodes with each interrogatory at the end of the problem. The premise in this sequence, of course, is that you have correctly identified the structure of the essay as a collection of such mostly discrete legal conflicts, a Type One paragraph-based problem (p. 48). Where the exam explicitly segments the essay by specific rulings (e.g., one through four), such premise is crystal clear. Indeed, even if not segmented for you, all you have to do is to verify that the essay is not of the Type Two problem that presents one ultimate issue to be decoded into intermediate issues or a different type of problem altogether (pp. 48-49). Highlight these interrogatories, too, in your outlines.

Red-hot facts that signal issues

You have repeatedly seen the power of learning the rules with iconic examples comprised of red-hot facts. You have also seen how such facts spark issue spotting. I suggest spotlighting such facts in each course, turning them into hypotheticals that you practice daily after class and highlight in your outlines.

Some other illustrations of red-hot facts that you should be highlighting follow. Facts about a trust for several generations probably signal an issue concerning the rule against perpetuities in real property. Facts about an oral agreement to transfer real property probably signal an issue about the statute of frauds. Facts about a party to an agreement notifying the opposing party concerning difficulties in compliance (increased prices for supplies, inability to make a profit) and asking for a variation in the contract terms signal an issue about breach of contract or an issue about the requirements for a modification agreement including the Uniform Commercial Code. And so on. My examples are only suggestive: do your own spotlighting in each course outlining to dial into each professor's exam wavelength. If you perfect this skill with practice during the semester with one or two classmates, you might directly and quickly ace most issue spotting on exam day.

Legal relationships that signal issues

By now, you have gradually become sensitive to the legal relationships that signal issues. For example, all the above detailed relationships between the employee (an ambulance driver, an intern or surgeon) and his or her employers often trigger a bunch of issues (pp. 58-63). Once a product harms someone, another bunch of issues can be triggered (p. 163). And, of course, these are only illustrations. There are many other examples: e.g., facts about a trust trigger legal duties and rights between the trustor and trustee, facts about sellers and buyers of goods trigger the operation of duties and rights founded in common-law contract and the Uniform Commercial Code, and facts about one party aiding another to plan or commit crimes signal issues about conspiracy, complicity, or criminal facilitation.

The point: each course, and its old exams, is replete with a teacher's signature pattern of issues embodied in interrogatories, red-hot facts, and legal relationships, all of which signal issues. Become sensitive to them, compile and practice hypotheticals with them, highlight them in your outlines; you'll very likely see at least some of them on the exam. In addition, at least each week in your study group review for such signals and practice detailing issues raised by them. Gradually, the complete scope of professorial signals and related issues she stressed will aggregate by semester's end.

The payoff for this additional issue-spotting angle of vision in learning doctrine is clear: you sharpen your issue-spotting skill. Learning doctrine again blends with learning issue-spotting skills.

Conclusions of law as both givens and signals

Gradually, as you work with the old exam problems of your professors (and later, old bar exams), you also develop skill in extricating not only the red-hot facts and pregnant legal relationships, but also any conclusions of law specified in the problem as givens. To illustrate, a contract problem includes a specification that A, retailer, contracted with B, a manufacturer, to buy one hundred cameras. These facts spell out a conclusion of law, a valid contract, which is a given in the problem that you acknowledge. Do you appreciate that this conclusion of law provides important direction? Negatively, it tells you that there are no issues here about the formation of said contract: e.g., no issues about offer, acceptance, consideration, or capacity to contract. Instead, this conclusion of law implicitly directs you towards other issues that will almost certainly arise down the road about this given of A and B's contract. These include, e.g., modification of the original contract, breach of contract and remedies, or statute of frauds issues in enforcement of the contract. Finally, do you appreciate that it is an unlawyerly blunder. as well as a waste of your precious time, to translate this given of a contract, this conclusion of law, into an issue that you address and analyze, instead of use as a premise for considering the down-the-road issues?

Other such conclusions of law as givens may proliferate in the essay problems. For example, any use of the word "duly," or an equivalent such as "appropriate" or "valid", as in "duly called special meeting of the board of directors of X corporation" means negatively that there is no issue arising about the legality of the calling of the special meeting. But look affirmatively for a highly probable issue about the legality of some board-of-directors' action at the meeting, such as breach of a fiduciary duty by one of the directors, or an action by the board that is beyond its power, and instead requires shareholder approval to be valid.

A final example: sometimes tort negligence problems specify that one party was "negligent" in a particular situation. Negatively, there is usually no issue that needs to be raised about the liability of such party. But look affirmatively for issues that utilize such negligence as a predicate (another given) for other issues. For example, does the negligence rise to the level of gross negligence? Is an original tortfeasor liable for any ensuing ordinary or gross negligence? Is an employer also liable for ordinary or gross negligence in *respondeat superior*? Is the tortfeasor also liable for damages such as aggravation of prior injuries? May procedural issues be intended such as the statute of limitations or the propriety of personal service of such a tortfeasor in another state?

Be sure that you accept as givens or premises for your issue spotting all of the red-hot facts, legal relationships and conclusions of law set forth in the problem. Strive to hone your skill in identifying such gifts in each course, especially from your professor's hypotheticals in class and her old exams. Highlight them, too, in your outlines and study groups.

So-called "hidden" issues

If you learn and practice in ways that empower your issue spotting, the question of "hidden issues" fades in importance. As all the prior challenging examples indicate, so-called hidden issues are liberated from their refuge by such practice. Most such issues are only truly hidden to those who have not prepared to spot them. To illustrate, if you have not practiced spotting the "original tortfeasor," that issue may be hidden to you on the exam. But, as noted, if you have practiced spotting such an issue, it's not hidden at all, it should jump out at you as plainly apparent, once you see an initial tortfeasor in a problem commit negligent harm with consequent harms by ensuing tortfeasors. Your practice has made the obscure transparent. Similarly, the "hidden" negative issue about the absence of liability for the intentional tort of assault in the previously specified hypothetical (A striking B from behind on the back of his head) becomes plain as day if you have learned the rule of assault with iconic and counterexamples of its scope of application, and practiced them as hypotheticals.

Issues about claims and counterclaims or defenses

Avoid any automatic claim-and-counterclaim approach to issue spotting. At the unfounded extreme, some students believe they must routinely argue this ping-pong approach with each element in every rule they are applying. Such belief is utterly misconceived and misleading. The facts sometimes spell out a defense or counterclaim to an element and sometimes do not. You only argue such a defense or counterclaim when there are facts to support your argument, and there is nothing automatic about it. Moreover, study of countless exams over decades reveals that you generally argue only one element in the applicable rule, not every element; the remaining elements are usually not at issue. Remember always that the facts and relevant rules, considered in light of your professor's course expectations, are sovereign and determine which issues you do or do not raise.

Where the issues point to rules that are open-ended and elastic, do not be surprised that the back-and-forth arguments may resemble Republicans and Democrats in election heat. Many fact patterns that raise such claim-and-counterclaim issues can be argued both ways because of the open-ended character of the relevant rules. Examples include such rules or standards as "the best interest of the child" in custody cases, "equitable distribution" in dividing marital property in divorce cases, "reasonable accommodation" in disability cases, and, indeed, any standard, rule, test, or principle that incorporates such words as "equitable," "just," "fair," "proper," "reasonable," "undue," and other comparably open-ended terms.

Constitutional standards, usually labeled as "principles" because of their foundational status, may lead to two-way argument. Examples include the First Amendment guarantees of freedom of speech, press, assembly, association, and petition; the Fourth Amendment prohibition of unreasonable search; the Fifth Amendment guarantee of due process; the Fourteenth-Amendment guarantee of equal protection of the laws. Even if the applicable test is not open-ended but more concrete, professors in all courses can nevertheless craft the essay language so that two-way argument is expected, and you may sometimes even be asked explicitly in the interrogatory to argue two ways. Here, too, your professor's class hypotheticals and old exams should enlighten you as to her choices. And recall that these same teachers can pose emphatically one-sided facts that call only for one-sided argument. As always, be open and responsive to their priorities; go with their flow. Respect their facts, framings, language and preferred arguments.

Watch out for issue and rule relativism: the reality that issues and rules may often be argued two or more ways certainly does not mean that all arguments are of equal validity or weight. Frequently, as the examples in this and other chapters illustrate, some arguments are valid, while others are invalid or at least of lesser weight. The exam challenge includes demonstrating your legal judgment: argue which are best and which are inferior or outright wrong, given different facts, rules, principles, policies, and each professor's expectations. Your professor will decide which prevail, which get the most exam points (as later a judge determines which lawyer's arguments are best).

THE JURISPRUDENCE OF SPOTTING ISSUES

Spotting issues is not simply a technical matter requiring only technical understanding. It is also inescapably jurisprudential. From different jurisprudential perspectives, identical facts can be framed into quite different issues. The reason is that spotting issues implicitly presupposes a frame for analyzing and resolving facts, and jurisprudential wavelengths provide different frames of legal thinking for doing this formulating, arguing and resolving. Typical traditional jurisprudential frames include positivism, natural law, and policy perspectives including legal realism; modern wavelengths include law and economics, critical legal studies, critical race theory, and feminism. Issue spotting often exemplifies one or more of these or other jurisprudential wavelengths, mostly the traditional perspectives. But your challenge is gradually to become aware of the different frames emphasized by your professors and, where appropriate, to apply those frames in spotting exam issues and argument making. Examples of positivist, natural law and policy framings follow.

> **Positivism**: "The issue is whether the defendant is liable for intentional murder when he shoots and kills X while saying, 'Go to thine ancestors quickly.'"

> **Natural law**: "The issue is whether the driver who intentionally drove off the street and killed X, a stranger/pedestrian, to avoid striking a mother and child crossing the street against the light, is justified under the general defense of justification."[16]

> **Policy**: "The issue is whether it is in the best interest of the child (the controlling standard) for the divorcing mother (or father) to have custody of their child."

It is not necessary to be jurisprudentially *au courant* to recognize that these different framings resonate on diverse wavelengths of legal questioning and resulting argument. Positivist framings are more concrete while natural-law framings are both more abstract and typically pivot on ideas of justice or fairness. Policy framings, though usually broad, also vary widely since there are multiple types of policy including pragmatic, utilitarian and economic articulations.

Jurisprudential choice of issue in a landmark real property case

Consider the following facts detailed in a landmark real-property case from New Jersey, *State v. Shack*.[17] Tejeras, a health-care worker for a federally funded nonprofit group, enters the farm of Tedesco to remove twenty-eight sutures from a farmworker. Shack, a staff attorney for the federally funded anti-poverty group, accompanies Tejeras to help with "the legalities involved," and also to discuss "a legal problem" with another farmworker on Tedesco's farm. When Tejeras and Shack insist they have a right to see the farmworkers in "their living quarters and without Tedesco's supervision," the farm owner calls the State Police and executes a formal complaint charging violation of the state trespass statute. That statute specifies that "[a]ny person who trespasses on any lands…after being forbidden so to trespass by the owner…is a disorderly person and shall be punished by a fine of not more than $50."

From different jurisprudential perspectives, these facts can be framed into many issues. Let's assume that your real-property professor emphasized two or three of the following perspectives in framing and analyzing this case:

1. From a positivist perspective focused simply on the facts and the statutory words, "the issue is whether a health-care worker and an attorney, who enter a private farm to see their clients — farm workers in their

---

[16] See, e.g., Chapter Seven in my book, *Learning Legal Reasoning, Briefing, Analysis and Theory* (2011). Another vibrant example of framing on the natural law wavelength is Justice O'Connor's characterization of the individualized sentencing proceeding required in capital punishment cases as "a moral inquiry into the culpability of the defendant…" [*California v. Brown*, 107 S. Ct. 837 (1987)].

[17] *State v. Shack*, 58 N.J. 297 (1971).

private quarters — after being forbidden to see them there by the farm owner, have violated the state trespass statute." [18]

2. From a positivist perspective focused on the intention of the legislature, "the issue is whether the state legislature, in enacting the criminal trespass statute, intended to criminalize such behavior as the entrance on the farm by Tejeras and Shack to provide medical and legal services to migrant farm workers in their private quarters."

3. From a broad policy perspective, focused on the purposes of the federal anti-poverty statutes that support aid to migrant farm workers (e.g., "…to assist migrant…farm workers and their families…"), "the issue is whether under 'State law the ownership of real property' should include the right to bar access to [federal] governmental services available to migrant workers by use of the trespass prohibition embodied in the [state] penal law." [19]

4. From one constitutional perspective, focused on the supremacy clause, "the issue is whether the application of the state trespass statute to Tejeras and Shack, who by providing health and legal services to migrant farm workers, are fulfilling their duties pursuant to federal anti-poverty statutes, violates the supremacy clause of the United States Constitution…" [20]

While these four framings of the issue arising from these facts are hardly exhaustive of the possibilities, it is crucial to gradually become skilled in dialing into the jurisprudential wavelength-based framings stressed by your teachers in analyzing at least some cases, which will also reflect general course wavelengths.

Choice of issue reflects the era

These four framings illustrate jurisprudential frame shifting. Many, but not all teachers, stress frame shifting that exemplifies their preferred jurisprudential perspectives. You should not be surprised that professors committed to broad policy analysis, law and economics, feminism, or critical legal studies contrast their claimed "superior" frame for issue spotting and arguing to those of traditional and other frames. On their exams, you might expect facts that raise such policy, law and economics, feminist, critical legal studies or other issues. But an important warning here: some professors soar into the exciting heavens of their prized jurisprudential realm in class and materials, and then present you with exams that are as tightly rule bound in positivist (technical) fashion as their more prosaic colleagues. Verify their *actual* exam preferences with the old exams. There is no reason to be uncertain about these preferences, and thus about which wavelengths to apply on the exam.

---

[18] Note the case-and-fact-centered character of this concrete positivist formulation. In sharp contrast, a flexible interpretation of a statute means a focus on the statutory words in an open-ended way. In interpreting often open-ended constitutional provisions, Justice Oliver Wendell Holmes caught this emphasis: "…when we are dealing with words that are also a constituent act, like the Constitution of the United States, we must realize that they have called into life a being the development of which could not have been foreseen completely by the most gifted of its begetters… The case before us must be considered in light of our whole experience and not merely in that of what was said a hundred years ago." *Missouri v. Holland,* 252 U.S. 416 (1920)). Naturally, while interpreting the New Jersey trespass statute is different from interpreting a constitutional provision, the idea applies, though in weaker form, especially with an old trespass statute rooted in case law that is many hundreds of years old. Interpreting the trespass statute too can be "considered in light of our whole experience," including the status of farm-workers living on farms and our evolving values about their dignity and worth and our obligation to them.

[19] Since policy has diverse authors and presentations, the particular policy perspective underlying this formulation could probably be characterized as utilitarian, pragmatic, or legal realist. Clearly, it reflects more expansive currents of thinking, sensibility, and action that were influential in the 1960's and afterwards. And it is the framing *chosen* by the Supreme Court of New Jersey in *Shack.*

[20] The New Jersey Supreme Court explicitly rejected the temptation to frame the issue in this federal Constitutional form, which could have triggered a review by the United States Supreme Court with uncertain results.

These four framings of the *Shack* facts also illustrate that issue spotting is not objective, ahistorical, apolitical, or value free. Indeed, they are shot through with different values. These facts spring from the emergence of the federal anti-poverty program that authorized and funded medical and legal assistance to migrant farm workers. Remember that Tejeras is a federally funded health-care worker about to remove sutures from a farm worker, and Shack is a legal-services lawyer trying to talk to a client privately on the owner's farm. This program emerged from the tumult and struggles of the 1960s including the Vietnam War, the assassinations of President John Kennedy and later of Senator Robert Kennedy, the presidency of Lyndon Johnson, the struggles of Dr. Martin Luther King and his assassination, the murder of the four African-American children in their Birmingham church, and many other martyrs. Concern for African-Americans, Latinos, women, gays, farm workers, the disabled, the elderly, and the poor blazed forth in the 1960s and resulted in transformational changes in the fabric of American life including the anti-poverty program, civil rights legislation, Medicare, Medicaid, and aid to education.

The *Shack* facts, then, are really artifacts, powerful epiphenomena of this era, its passions, and social and political transformations. These facts, resulting issues, and cases could not have emerged in the 1950s or earlier. The history and struggles of the time are exemplified in these 1960s-forged facts and issues. The lesson: The world of fact, and hence of legal issues, arguments, and decision-making evolves with time, culture, and politics. In a democracy, the law and the Constitution are alive and crackle with the passions of the time.

Choice of issue springing from constitutional frame shifting

Since many areas of the law are increasingly constitutionalized, at least in part, special attention should be given, following your professor's lead, to the frame shifting required by any constitutional context for studying course rules. While identifying issues is ordinarily focused on discerning the legal significance of facts and which, if any, legal rule or principle applies, a constitutional perspective adds a yet different framing: does the rule that apparently applies conform to evolving constitutional principles, raising the possibility of invalidation of said rule on its face or as applied rather than the usual interweaving of the relevant rule with the key facts? Such framing arises not only in studying the basics of constitutional law, but also in studying the First Amendment, the Fourteenth Amendment, substantive criminal law, criminal procedure, family law, constitutional torts, administrative law, and "takings" in real property or environmental law.

This mid- and late-twentieth-century trend to constitutionalize parts of many doctrinal areas is manifested in landmark cases which transformed the relevant law and thus naturally trigger professorial interest. Witness *Brown, Mapp, Miranda, Escobedo, New York Times v. Sullivan, Baker v. Carr*, and many others. In *Brown*, the school desegregation decision in 1954 that is sometimes called the most important case in the twentieth century, the Supreme Court repudiated the reigning nineteenth-century principle of "separate but equal" as applied to schools as intrinsically and inevitably unequal, and thus a violation of the Fourteenth Amendment's Equal Protection Clause.

Do you understand how the principle of separate but equal in education and elsewhere becomes increasingly untenable in mid-twentieth-century America? Fifty million people were killed by 1945 in World War II in a titanic struggle against Nazi fascism, which exalted Aryans and demonized many others, especially Jews, as subhuman. In addition, the Imperial Japanese war machine justified its imperialism and widespread massacres, rape and looting inflicted upon the Chinese and others, since the Japanese claimed to be a superior race and those they victimized were inferior. Separate but equal and its odious caste presuppositions of superiority and inferiority became an acute embarrassment with the rise of the cold war. In 1952, James McGranery, the Attorney General, filed a legal brief for the plaintiffs in *Brown v. Board of Education* arguing that [r]acial discrimination furnished grist for Communist propaganda mills..." As in *Shack,* the world of fact, issues, arguments, and decision-making evolves with transformations here and in the world.[21] In studying the law, you should, therefore, not be surprised and confused to learn the law can be transformed — it is not fundamentalist religion. Since we cannot forecast the future, we do not know the scope and character of the transformations to come. But come they will.

Choice of issue from common-law frame shifting

But not all of fundamental frame shifting is rooted in the federal (or state) Constitution. An example of such non-constitutional, policy-based frame shifting in reformulating the pivotal issue follow. First, in the landmark case, *Javins v. First National Realty Corp.*, 428 F.2d 1070 (1970), Judge J. Skelly Wright substituted a contract framework in reframing the issue in a landlord-tenant case where the issue was whether a contract-based warranty of habitability, measured by housing code standards, is implied by law into leases of urban dwellings. This new policy framework and resulting reframing contrasted sharply with the historically embedded application of a real property framework in issue formulation which was based on the premise that a "conveyance of an interest in land" imposes no duty on the landlord to maintain or repair the premises. This old policy and rule was a child of the medieval common law; the new policy and rule is a product of the twentieth century and the rise of new values respecting the rights of tenants, especially in proliferating apartment buildings rented to tenants by owners. The Judge concluded that the old rule was too one-sided and made no sense in the twentieth century. The reframing struck a responsive chord among many judges and lawyers and prevailed, a vivid instance of the dynamic potential of the ancient common law to reject old policies and rules and substitute new ones.

And from professors, too

As you have surely experienced (if in law school), many professors love to press you, not only about such dramatic frame shifting as illustrated above, but also about more prosaic forms of frame shifting. For example, the relentless alteration of facts in a series of class hypotheticals from your professor sooner or later forces the facts out of the original issue-spotting frame and resulting argument into a related but different frame. The original frame cannot continue to capture the significance of the rapidly changing factual character of the hypotheticals. In addition, the frequent professorial request to students to argue as a plaintiff's lawyer, followed by a request to argue as a defendant's lawyer, illustrates another typical form of professorial frame shifting. Lastly, as noted, many professors contrast how issue framing and argument vary radically when contrasting common-law, statutory, Restatement or Model Code rules, are applied.

Expect facts in the exam essays that trigger some of these classroom priorities. Individualize your preparation. Practice in your study groups the jurisprudential, policy and other forms of frame shifting emphasized by each professor in each course, and expect considerable variation from professor to professor. Such practice develops the prized mental flexibility and judgment that you need for exams and will require as a lawyer when listening to clients, witnesses, and formulating cogent arguments for legal supervisors and judges.

THE ADVERSARIAL CHARACTER OF SPOTTING AND ARGUING ISSUES: NOTES FROM PRACTICE

As an experienced trial and appellate lawyer, I assure you that your skills in advocacy issue spotting are not just for law school and the bar exam. But there are differences in practice that should also clarify your current cultivation of this core skill. In practice, issue spotting is hostage to fact-finding, and is therefore

---

[21] The world of *personal opportunity* also evolves with time and change in values. I recently heard Colin Powell say that if he had entered the army "five or ten years earlier, I would never have become a four-star general and Chairman of the Joint Chiefs of Staff" [and Secretary of State]. The reason: Powell entered the Army after President Truman ordered the armed forces integrated in 1948. I speculate from my own experience as an Infantry Officer and Army Ranger that otherwise his highest rank would probably have been as a Colonel of a regiment of Black troops in a segregated Army.

indeterminate. Unlike law school exams where the facts are givens and where there is no fact finding, in practice, fact-finding is critical for issue spotting and is continuous during the litigation process, not a one-time event. The facts at trial in actual cases are almost always in dispute, a vital — often the pivotal dimension of the trial. The adversaries at trial, plaintiff and defendant (or in criminal cases, the prosecution and the defendant) argue their conflicting versions of the red-hot facts (their conflicting theories of the facts). They also argue their conflicting theories of the applicable legal issue(s) and related rules that govern the case (their conflicting theories of law). The fact finder, jury or judge, decides which argued version of the facts applies. And the judge decides which argued version of the law applies.

Trials also differ from essay exams in their relentless challenge to the credibility of many witnesses, as well as in their sometime morality-play drama and the haunting specter of the unexpected; e.g., most trial lawyers have experienced the suddenly disappearing key witness, the confident, credible witness who becomes a frightened and difficult-to-believe mutterer on the witness stand, or who testifies quite differently at trial from what he told you at a pre-trial phase. Surprises are a constant risk, and jury reactions to the witnesses and their often contradictory factual presentations are always uncertain. Thus, it is not the facts in themselves that mostly control decisions but rather the fact-finder's perception and weighting, none of which is neutral or value free.

Do you appreciate how success in fact-driven framing of the issue at trial and on exams ordinarily results in success in the case or exam? Framing isn't simply about the issue. It also, as noted, determines the resulting field of analysis and decisions that emerge from this field. One example: if defense counsel in a murder trial succeeds in getting the jury to focus in its deliberations on whether or not the defendant had a valid claim of self-defense, rather than on the prosecutor's framing of a culpable killing, there may be a good chance of an acquittal. All she need then accomplish is to raise a reasonable doubt about the prosecutor's case through her persistent framing of the self-defense issue. On exams, well-crafted framing of issues rightly impresses your professors, since it demonstrates that you are dialing into the right legal wavelengths.

On appeal, issue spotting is distinguished from trial issue framing since the governing principle is that the conflicting issues of fact and credibility were resolved at trial and generally cannot be rehashed on appeal. Appellate courts do not hold hearings and listen to witnesses. Thus, issue advocacy in appellate briefs and arguments, while still intensely adversarial, is typically restricted to claims that the trial judge made improper rulings concerning motions and evidentiary matters, or erred in instructing the jury as to the applicable law and related legal issues. Issue spotting on law exams is more akin to issue advocacy in appellate cases since in both instances the facts are resolved and givens.

You can also learn about the adversarial character of issue spotting by studying how judges frame issues in resolving appellate cases. Once the judge becomes persuaded by one of the issue framings urged by one of the parties or adopts another issue framing not explicitly argued, the judge become *de facto* advocate for that particular issue framing. Indeed, that formulation frames their analysis and resolution of the case in their opinion, including their reasoning, holding, and judgment. It is good judicial form to begin an appellate decision with a specification of the court's issue formulation; numerous appellate opinions so begin including those of the late Justice William Brennan.

CONCLUSION

I want explicitly to acknowledge that this Chapter, though it begins in straightforward steps, becomes quite complex and dense. That's why I frequently describe the need for "decoding", and for verifying each professor's exam choices and priorities. It's not easy. But legions of students before you have succeeded in this. You can, too. They have identified the types of problem that their professors present from studying their old exams and listening carefully in class, discovering that their professors' exams often fall into only two or three categories, rather than all four of them.

In the next Chapter, you learn the output of all this sharpening of your learning and issue-spotting skills — the writing of different types of 'A' exam arguments to resolve the issues you have spotted.

ON LOOKING BACK

First, if you are discouraged at the density and complexity in this Chapter, welcome to the club. In response, there is sometimes an understandable desire to oversimplify the formidable challenge. I've resisted the temptation, however, to engage in a misleading exam reductionism that can hurt you. Sure, it's formidable, but keep in mind also that even outstanding trial lawyers like David Boies and the late Johnnie Cochran and F. Lee Bailey were beginning law students at one time and almost certainly fumbled in their initial issue spotting and argument making. If you persist daily, the high probability is that you can certainly do it competently, and with time and practice, even excel at it. Optimism and persistence can create facts of initial success that then begets more success.

Revisit this Chapter as you proceed in the first year. There is content in it that you may quickly absorb, including issue spotting with the straightforward or surface examples. But other material, including applying the five-step issue-spotting method for dense Type One exam problems, is more difficult. It will be a challenge to learn in the abstract and for many students it requires experience with professors and their challenging materials in each course. That immersion makes your struggle come alive. If you like, e-mail me with your occasional question or comment.

Second, it may help you to understand better why well-crafted issue spotting and specifying — pinpointing the pivotal issue to be decided in one sentence — has such a favorable exam impact. The simple reason is the sharp and pleasant contrast with all the poor answers professors ordinarily see on exams that emerge in good part from so much off-base issue spotting. In contrast, apt issue spotting also promises accurate specification of the correct rule already alluded to in the issue, as well as careful interweaving with the facts. Professors know from extensive experience that this promise is often fulfilled. They similarly know that poorly crafted issue spotting is usually associated with defective and off-base statements of rules (or inapt rules) and poor interweaving to match.

Third, if you are aware that first-year professors often have intimidating piles of bluebooks to grade (I graded 120 papers for a course at the NYULS, and as many as 160 at CUNYLS), as well as pressure from the Associate Dean for Academic Affairs reminding all professors of the looming deadline for submitting grades, then the value of clearly stated issues followed by concise cogent arguments is manifest. Helping your graders get through the pile helps you.

Lastly, in addition to the four main types of exam problems (pp. 48-50) that you will likely confront by the end of first year, there is just a modest chance that you may also see one or more of a *potpourri* of problems embodying both well-justified and dubious choices. You might confront an unusual but valid inquiry about certain cases discussed in class, or asked to respond on the exam paper itself to an explicit, specified issue with extremely limited time and space.

But other exam formats might be unclear, lack sufficient facts, and be utterly unrelated to the course outline and what was discussed in class. They might raise almost endless issues in an artificially limited time. In addition, some professors give exclusively multiple-choice questions, a pedagogical choice that can be quickly and easily graded. Happily, checking your professors' old exams should reveal exactly which types of exam problems each professor chooses. If you then expect any of these formats, be prepared to identify the exact form she favors, and prepare accordingly.

CHAPTER FIVE

Outlining and Writing 'A' Exam Arguments

INTRODUCTION

Now that you know how to zero in on the relevant issues, the initial pivotal skill, how do you resolve each one with a concise, cogent argument that will earn a high grade? This Chapter shows you, step-by-step from basics to complexities, how to quickly outline and then write such arguments under severe time pressure, often just forty-five to sixty minutes for each essay problem. Take heart: with weekly practice during the semester, you can learn to quickly make arguments that standout and more than meet your professor's grading criteria.

By so doing, you are also learning how to avoid writing the answers that many students routinely write, year after year, and that dismay professors. These 'C' and 'D' type answers are illustrated later in Chapter Six. Here, again, are the grading criteria.

> ### Six Grading Criteria
>
> 1. Your lawyerly skill in extricating the key facts from the non-key facts detailed in the exam problem.
>
> 2. Your lawyerly skill in spotting and specifying the issues raised by these key (red hot) facts.
>
> 3. Your lawyerly skill in learning, recalling, and applying the applicable legal rules or principles to resolve the specified issues.
>
> 4. Your lawyerly skill in interweaving (meshing together) the key facts with the elements of the applicable rules or with the principles (or their tests or standards).
>
> 5. Your lawyerly skill in sometimes applying the appropriate policy purpose(s) to support your rule application.
>
> 6. Your performance of all these skills with concise, cogent arguments within the allocated time, sometimes arguing two or three ways as required by the facts, the rules or principles, and each professor's expectations.

As may be clear from the criteria, the goal is concise first-draft argument making, quickly produced under severe time pressure. Understand what it is by understanding what it is not. It is not literary or poetic writing. It is not reflective second-or-third-draft writing, as in carefully researched and calibrated appellate briefs with many citations. It is definitely not the expansive and often discursive writing that you see in many judicial opinions that students sometimes emulate and that entraps them. Nor is it philosophical, scientific, or social-scientific writing. And it is clearly not intrinsically superior to these writing styles. It is simply different, designed for an important but limited exam purpose. For almost all students, however, writing such cogent arguments presupposes at least brief outlining before writing.

The dilemma in writing concise, cogent arguments to resolve issues in response to complex law-school essays is that there is insufficient time to write a full outline of your argument before proceeding. Outlining a typically complex fact pattern for its flock of issues could easily consume the entire fifty or sixty minutes allotted to you. Yet, to jump immediately to writing as you identify the issues often leads to a confused, rambling, unlawyerly answer.

Even so, with much practice, some straightforward arguments can be quickly written without outlining or with abbreviated outlining. The reason is that you already have the nucleus of each argument in the issue you have formulated, and you have repeatedly demonstrated such performance in practicing the CIRI(P) formats prior to the exams. Let's illustrate the outlining and writing out process with the anchor format applied initially to basic examples.

CIRI(P) ONE: TYPE OF EXAM ARGUMENT DEPENDS ON PROBLEM TYPE

The CIRI(P) ONE writing format is a simple architecture for organizing and writing concise, cogent arguments to resolve at least some of the issues you have spotted and specified, especially in the popular paragraph-based, Type-One problem.

The application of all of the CIRI(P) writing formats presupposes that you have spotted and specified the major issues either through the intuitive light-bulb issue-spotting method, the five-step method, the HATRI decoder, or likely a blend. Remember, you cannot resolve any issue you have not spotted.

CIRI(P) is an acronym that stands for the following:

C	Conclusion
I	Issue
R	Rule (or principle)
I	Interweaving
(P)	Policy

A very simple demonstration of the application of CIRI(P) ONE follows, using the familiar factual example for intent-to-kill murder: A shoots B, who dies immediately from the shooting, while saying to B, "Go to thine ancestors quickly." The interrogatory (question) at the end of the criminal-law essay problem asks: "What are the rights and liabilities of the parties?" Applying one or more of the issue-spotting methods, you have spotted and specified this issue: Is A, who shoots and kills B, liable for intent-to-kill murder? If you used HATRI (pp. 55-56; and Appendix A, p. 159) these facts might be decoded as follows:

HATRI	Harm & Parties	Act	Topic	Rule	Issue
	A kills B	shoot	Hom.	Inten. M.	Is A, in sh. & k. B, liab. f/inten. M?

If you applied light-bulb issue spotting and/or the five-step method, you do not need this step-by-step written HATRI decoding. You might already have specified the issue in abbreviated form in the margin of the exam problem or on scrap paper. In either event, you use this issue specification to apply the CIRI(P) ONE format as follows:

First state your conclusion [C] in a brief heading:

> A liable for intentional murder.

Next pinpoint the issue [I] in one brief sentence:

> The issue is whether A, who shoots and kills B, is liable for this form of murder.

Then meticulously specify the applicable rule [R] by its elements in its logical order:

> Intentional murder requires (1) an intent to kill (*mens rea*) (2) expressed in (3) a voluntary criminal-law act (*actus rea*) (4) that causes, both factually (but-for) and legally (proximately), (5) the death of another.

The challenging next step is interweaving [I] the red-hot facts with each element of the rule, a crucial skill that takes practice. Don't make the common error of simply restating the facts instead of interweaving them. Interweaving of key facts with a relevant rule makes the facts crackle with legal meaning because it proves liability as illustrated here:

> When A shoots B, this behavior proves the criminal-law voluntary-act element (the *actus reus*); and when B dies immediately from the shooting, this plainly proves the element of factual (but-for) and legal (proximate) cause, and the death element. The intent-to-kill element, i.e. A's conscious objective to kill B (the *mens rea*), is established by a compelling inference from A's behavior of shooting and killing B while saying, "Go to thine ancestors quickly."

The final step in applying CIRI(P) ONE is to ask yourself: what is the policy purpose [P] served by the applicable rule of intentional murder, and does specifying the relevant policy strengthen the argument by adding any analytical or persuasive value? Here, one policy purpose served by the prohibition of intentional murder is the protection of human life from intentional depredation, but specifying this policy on these clear facts of violation adds no value at all to this rule application. It's too obvious. Thus, you do not specify it in this illustration. You only specify a policy purpose where it strengthens your argument; many examples of policy application and non-application follow.

Your strong advocacy argument, the simple aggregation of these parts, can be concisely written out by applying the first CIRI(P) format.

> **A liable for intentional murder**
> The issue is whether A, who shoots and kills B, is liable for this form of murder. Intentional murder requires (1) an intent to kill (*mens rea*) (2) expressed in (3) a voluntary criminal-law act (*actus rea*) (4) that causes, both factually (but-for) and legally (proximately), (5) the death of another. When A shoots B, this behavior proves the criminal-law voluntary-act element (the *actus*

reus); and when B dies immediately from the shooting, this plainly proves the element of factual (but-for) and legal (proximate) cause, and the death element.[1] The intent-to-kill element, i.e. A's conscious objective to kill B (the *mens rea*) is established by a compelling inference from A's behavior of shooting and killing B while saying, "Go to thine ancestors quickly."

Please note that this strong advocacy argument is only four sentences because the facts here are crystal clear in establishing A's liability. This argument is lawyerly because it (a) raises only the single issue posed by the red-hot facts, (b) specifies the applicable rule of intentional murder, and (c) proves that this rule applies by interweaving of the red-hot facts with each element, and why, therefore, A is liable for this form of murder. More precisely, this argument is lawyerly because it is direct, it spots and specifies the issue accurately, it applies the authoritative rule, and does all of the above in a concise organized fashion without any irrelevant and, hence, unlawyerly statements of fact, rule, or argument. Indeed, the ideal of no extra words is realized: every word counts. As is evident from this first very simple non-exam example, the CIRI(P) ONE writing format offers an elementary anchor architecture of legal argument.

What should be outlined before writing?

How much outlining you need to write this strong argument varies from student to student and depends on how much you practiced before the exam. If you have practiced the CIRI(P) formats throughout the semester, you do not need to think about how to organize and write out your argument, and that's a lot you don't have to think about. In addition, you already have specified the issue and therefore also know the conclusion; no need to outline these parts. Nevertheless, based on experience in grading thousands of exams over decades and seeing the same weaknesses each year, I suggest you might need quickly to abbreviate the elements of the intentional murder rule and the interweaving step. If you are hazy on how to do this, please review the examples on the prior page.

It is impressive to a first-year grader if you can precisely detail the elements of the rule in the proper sequence, and if you can then interweave the red-hot facts with each element. Many first-year students cannot competently perform this detailing of elements and interweaving because they have not been taught it, have not practiced it throughout the semester, and therefore do not know how to begin to do it on the exam. In contrast to these students, if you have practiced CIRI(P) format writing sufficiently, even the partial outlining of this straightforward hypothetical may be unnecessary. The bottom line: practice in writing these formats will allow you to ascertain how much exam outlining you need to resolve different kinds of issues.

Can you spot the issue and write out CIRI(P) ONE arguments to straightforward hypotheticals? It is important to verify that you can actually perform this set of basic skills before you progress to more challenging exam-type hypotheticals. The latter are, in Atticus Falcon's compelling words, "micro-exam-fact pattern(s)" that aggregate into challenging Type-One problems. Thus, test yourself by applying the CIRI(P) ONE format in writing your argument to resolve the issue posed by some of the straightforward hypotheticals posed by professors in class.

---

[1] Since the facts specify that B dies "immediately" from A's shooting, there is no causation issue raised, and thus no need here to elaborate or further define factual and legal (proximate) causation (or any other element). Remember the general rule: issues are factually grounded. No facts = no issue. Do not elaborate then on elements of rules that are not in issue given the instant facts. Such unnecessary elaboration is a version of "legal lecturing" that detracts from the argument and disquiets many professors and judges. In contrast, if the facts raise an issue about proximate causation (or other element), you might easily elaborate on it with a few sentences defining and explaining it in light of the instant facts. Many examples of both elaboration and non-elaboration follow throughout this and remaining Chapters. Nevertheless, another warning: the model exams of some professors clearly indicate an expectation of rule statements that exceeds what is technically required by the instant facts. Again, you have to individualize: old exams and any model or strong responding arguments provide direction for each professor's expectations — and her classroom practice should provide clarification. If still uncertain, ask her.

A BASIC TORT EXAMPLE OF CIRI(P) ONE

Remember the familiar and simple hypothetical of A silently approaching B from behind, and punching B on the back of his head, and the identification of one issue arising from these facts as, "Is A liable to B for battery for punching B in the head?" Your cogent CIRI(P) ONE argument to resolve this issue could be quickly written out as follows.

> ### A liable to B for the intentional tort of battery
>
> The issue is whether A, who punches B on the back of his head, is liable to B for this tort. Battery requires (a) an affirmative act (b) with the intent to touch another (c) that results (d) in unprivileged harmful or offensive contact with another. When A punches B on the back of B's head, this is an affirmative act which expresses A's intent to touch B and that results in unprivileged harm to B, the blow landing on his head. The policy purpose of this tort is to preserve respect for bodily integrity against such intrusions.

Notice that this cogent argument also is only four sentences long. These CIRI(P) ONE arguments can often be written out in four to seven sentences. Where that can be done, it ought to be done. Conciseness is a lawyerly virtue, and garrulousness a vice. Clearly, the interweaving here could appropriately have taken two sentences, but three would be unnecessary and should therefore be avoided. The specification of policy here adds little, if anything, with this iconic example of battery and should, therefore, be omitted, making the argument even more concise. Unless instructed differently by your teachers, always omit policy where it does not add to the argument. Iconic examples of liability, as here, or of no liability, are always leading candidates for omission of policy in the resulting argument. Iconic examples of liability can also often warrant just a one-sentence rule statement.

A POOR ANSWER TO THE INTENTIONAL TORT (BATTERY) QUESTION

Contrast the strong argument above with the following answer. Think CIRI(P) and you won't make this mistake.

> A is liable to B for the intentional tort of battery. The issue is whether A, who punches B on the back of his head, is liable to B for this tort. The clear policy that applies here is that the intentional tort of battery is designed to preserve respect for bodily integrity by prohibiting such intrusions as punches and slaps. Thus, when A punches B on the back of B's head, this is an affirmative act which violates this clear tort policy and that results in unprivileged harm to B, i.e., the blow landing on his head.

The mistake, of course, is that policy is applied directly in place of the rule of battery that is mentioned, but never really defined and applied by interweaving the key facts with its elements. The underlying misunderstanding centers on the correct relation between a rule and its supporting policy purpose. Where there is a clearly applicable rule, as with these facts, the rule should be specified and applied directly to the facts. Indeed, liability for violating a rule that embodies a cause-of-action requires, as you now know, that each element comprising the rule must be proved by the credible key facts at trial, or by the given key facts on a law exam. Liability is not established by directly applying the policy in place of the rule. That ignores the democratic and common-law imperative: judges and lawyers are sworn to apply the existing "laws," which include relevant case-based rules like battery, as well as legislative rules. Rules apply first.

A BASIC CONTRACT EXAMPLE OF THE CIRI(P) ONE FORMAT

A familiar and easy-to-spot legal conflict in a lengthy contract problem specifies that "A asks B to mow her lawn and promises to pay B $30 for doing so. B says nothing in reply, but mows the lawn. A refuses to pay on the basis that B never accepted her explicit offer and thus there is no contract between A and B. As judge, how do you decide?"

A liable to B for the $30

The issue is whether B accepted A's offer by mowing her lawn, even though he never explicitly replied to A. A unilateral contract is formed when an offer of one party authorizes the other party to perform an act as acceptance rather than a promise. Thus, when A asks B to mow her lawn and promises $30 for doing so, A has authorized B to accept by performing the mowing. When B does so, an act for a promise, the *unilateral* contract is complete. The fact that B did not orally promise to mow the lawn is not decisive.

How much outlining do you need for the above tort and contract arguments?

The answer might be very little. If you have practiced CIRI(P) writing formats sufficiently during the semester, you might at most need only a quick abbreviated outlining of the elements of the rule, and perhaps a matching of the red-hot facts with these elements.

A more challenging exam-type example of CIRI(P) ONE

What follows illustrates a different type of exam problem I had not seen until recent years. That is, a short problem with a direct and specific question that calls only for a Type-One super concise and one-sided argument, often accompanied by a word limit or limited, lined space for your response right on the exam paper. It is important to determine early in the semester whether each of your professors includes this type of specialized exam problem. You don't want to confront this challenge for the first time on exam day. An example in constitutional law follows.

A group of activists from the "Vigilantes Against Creeping Socialism" movement announces its plans for a two-hour public protest to "Keep Creepy Government Hands Off Our Medicare." Several hundred of its members are expected, and there will be amplified speeches at a government building at 10p.m. The building is located in a mixed office and residential area housing many families with children and older people. The president of a local residential association contacts you and asks you if the residents have any remedy to prevent such protest at that hour. Advise her.

A STRONG ARGUMENT

The First Amendment does not protect this protest at 10 p.m. in a mixed office and residential area. Generally, a protest at a government building implicates the most fundamental First Amendment interests, including here the rights of free speech, assembly, association, and petition to redress grievances. Indeed, the First Amendment, as interpreted by the United States Supreme Court, *denies* government the very power to restrict expression based on its message, ideas, subject matter or content. Nevertheless, reasonable time, place and manner restrictions may be imposed.

> Here, a large public meeting with amplified speeches at 10 p.m. in a mixed residential area threatens the interests in peace and quiet late at night of parents and children, as well as older residents. In no way, however, is this time-based regulation to be interpreted as a content regulation: the "Vigilantes" remain free to say whatever they like — but not amplified and late at night in an area with residents of all ages.

Please note that this emphatically one-sided, cogent argument is only six sentences. Such a concise argument presupposes especially careful outlining before writing. Note, too, that the rule statement here is three sentences (unlike the prior CIRI(P) ONE examples), including a one-sentence statement of the relevant First Amendment principles, an additional one-sentence elaboration, and then, as often occurs, a relevant exception to the principle(s) that applies to the exam facts. Note also that the issue statement is omitted. This argument heralds the more complex CIRI(P) THREE arguments later in this Chapter.[2] This type of problem can appear by itself, or in the midst of a Type One problem with many other issues. Of course, if the protest was instead set to begin at 6 or 7 pm, that would result in a different argument and result. If it were set to begin at 8:30 or 9 pm or so, two-way pro and con arguments would be appropriate.

Other actual examples of this type of mini-problem — with its direct question calling for a short pointed argument — include the following, all one-sided fact patterns of varying length. (1) "What damages, if any, is Builder entitled to recover from John?" (Five lines allocated for response.) (2) "Elaine wants specific performance. Is she entitled to it? Explain." (Again, five lines for response.) (3) On the basis of these figures, what, if any, recovery is Oliver entitled to?" (Seven lines for response.) This type of problem, is, I believe, one professorial reaction to grading far too many wandering, off-base student responses.

Diagnosis and correction

If in the initial weeks of your semester you have difficulty performing this CIRI(P) ONE writing format, some self-diagnosis is called for before proceeding to the more challenging formats that follow. Identify any weaknesses and take corrective action promptly, since these more complex formats build upon the CIRI(P) ONE format. It is folly to proceed to them before strengthening your grasp of this anchor format. If you interweave poorly, practice with class and casebook hypotheticals and your own exercises. If difficulty persists, go back and practice the underlying skills of legal and fact diagramming presented in pages 15-17.

If your weakness is in recalling all the core elements of rules stressed by your professors, even though you have studied intensely, ask yourself how you are learning such rules. Study and practice a few of the suggestions for learning rules specified in Chapter Two.

CIRI(P) ONE(a) Format: *A shorter version of* CIRI(P) ONE

As you know, a minority of professors specify exam essay problems that pose ten or more issues to be spotted and resolved in fifty or sixty minutes. While the issue-spotting process does not change, the writing out of your arguments must be even more concise because of the heightened time pressure. In this pressure cooker, I suggest the following changes to the CIRI(P) ONE writing format. Begin with a very brief conclusory heading [e.g., A liable to B]. Then specify the issue [I] in one sentence, follow by detailing the rule [R] in one sentence, and finish your argument with one sentence (or occasionally and at most two) of interweaving [I]. Omit policy. What you have is a shortened version of the CIRI(P) ONE format: CIRI, often just three sentences after the cryptic heading.

---

[2] As you'll see down the road in this Chapter, this argument with its three-sentence statement of the relevant principles could also fit within the CIRI(P) Three category. But including it here illustrates that the CIRI(P) One writing format includes somewhat more complex actual exam argument making than is demonstrated in the prior, very basic, and mostly non-exam-level examples.

Practice with such old problems should enable you to spot the multitude of issues posed, and to write ten or more of these mostly three-and-four-sentence arguments in fifty or sixty minutes. But you may be unable to spot the issues and then to write so many of the longer CIRI(P) ONE arguments in the allotted time. Determine whether any of your professors include such extreme issue-spotting problems by examining the old problems on file in the library early in the semester, and prepare accordingly. If unclear, talk to prior students and ask each teacher. If you do not identify this type of specialized essay on the exam, you risk writing longer arguments and running out of time without getting to all the core issues.

With this type of exam argument, beginning your argument with the issue also spotlights what the professor is initially looking for: how many of her major issues can you spot and specify? She typically has a grading sheet that lists the issues she expects to see. Make it easy for her to grade by beginning each argument with the explicitly stated issue (after the heading). She is also looking, of course, to see if each element of your rule statement is accurate and to assess if your quick application of the rule to the red-hot facts — the interweaving is terse but complete. Though the issue is the likely initial focus of her grading sheet and likely worth the most points, it isn't the only one. Incidentally, many students do not do well on these exams because they simply did not recognize this exam challenge, and did not practice this extreme version of the multi-issue-spotting Type One problem with its somewhat distinctive form of argument.

Study two examples of this more abbreviated writing. First, examine the initial argument on page 83. Shorten the heading to "A liable to B." The one-sentence issue statement should instead end with "for this battery" instead of "for this tort." The statement of the rule is already in one sentence, and the interweaving is also in one sentence. Omit the policy statement. After the cryptic heading, the argument is only three sentences. After weekly practice during the semester, you will be able to spot each such issue, outline the argument quickly and write it out, all in just a few minutes. A second example is set forth in the second argument in the "A is liable..." box on page 84. It's just four sentences, after the omission of the policy statement. Look for other examples of such super concise arguments throughout this Book.

In addition to these generally three-sentence arguments, there is a stark one-sentence reduction of this first format that has a narrow but important, use. Where the facts plainly reveal that an element or other requirement of a rule or principle cannot be established, a sweeping, one-sentence negative argument is sufficient. To illustrate, "In a private school, the student editor's First-Amendment claim of a violation of the right to free press against the principal's censorship of the school paper should be dismissed on its face since the principal of a private school is not a state actor, and the First Amendment applies only to state actors." Look too for other examples of such one-sentence negative arguments in this Book.

Common blunders in CIRI(P) ONE *exam arguments*

NO INTERWEAVING

One of the most common weaknesses in writing out arguments to resolve issues is the absence of interweaving, or plainly inadequate interweaving. Compare the excellent argument on pages 81-82 with the deficient argument that follows.

A is liable for intentional murder

The issue is whether A, who shot and killed B, is liable for this form of murder. Intentional murder requires (a) an intent to kill (b) expressed in a (c) criminal-law act that (d) causes, both factually (but-for) and legally (proximately) the (e) death of another. A did this.

Have you noticed that the statement of the conclusion, issue and rule are fine, but the interweaving step is missing altogether? The words "A did this" are no substitute at all. There is no interweaving, element by element, of the red-hot facts that prove each element of the rule. Thus, there is no demonstration that the student knows that this authoritative rule applies, resolves the issue, and that liability attaches because the red-hot facts prove, element by element, that the rule is established.

While the strong argument is at an 'A' level of grading, the answer without interweaving is probably in the 'C' range, even though this argument correctly states the applicable rule, and articulates the right issue and some of the red-hot facts. The critical distinction between the two arguments is the contrast between excellent interweaving and no interweaving at all. The first argument with interweaving is a cogent argument. The answer without it is simply not a legal argument.

Interweaving is that important. It is the law exam equivalent to what lawyers do in court when they introduce eyewitness testimony, admissions, physical evidence, etc. All these forms of evidence (facts) are aimed at proving each of the elements of the prosecutor's indictment or the plaintiff's cause-of-action (in a civil case), so that a *prima facie* case is established, and the defense's inevitable motion to dismiss for failure to establish such a case will be rejected. Understanding why it is so important may motivate you to practice it and perfect the skill.

In law exams, the facts are givens, presented to you in the problem; your interweaving emulates the trial lawyer's challenge to prove to the trial judge that the facts spell out a *prima facie* case. In contrast to the trial lawyer's duty to establish the credibility (believability) of her witnesses and other evidence, you, as a law student, have no comparable duty. The facts in the problem are all true and credible as givens from your professor. Your challenge then is to concentrate on their legal significance — i.e., do they add up to legal liability or no liability for the parties?

INADEQUATE INTERWEAVING

While the conclusory statement ("A did this") shows no interweaving at all and is a blunder, other students make the mistake of interweaving with one or more elements, but not others. To illustrate, insert the following partial interweaving into the above answer instead of the conclusory statement that "A did this."

> The facts specify that A shot and killed B, which establishes the voluntary criminal-law act requirement (the *actus reus*) as well as all the other elements needed for intentional murder.

The initial part of this sentence is apt interweaving on the voluntary act element required for intent-to-kill murder. But the rest of the sentence is next to worthless, a mere conclusory statement that does not show your professor at all that you can interweave the key facts with each of the other required elements, and, thus, that A is liable for this form of murder. Imagine how a prosecutor at trial, knowing that she is to be challenged by a defense motion to dismiss for the absence of a *prima facie* case at the conclusion of the prosecution evidence, would painstakingly prove each element by testimony and other evidence.

Some students fail to interweave key facts with each element of the applicable rule because they misunderstand a core rule of law-school exams. You only obtain credit for the skills and doctrinal understanding that you demonstrate. Your professor gives no credit for what is merely in your mind and little, if any, credit for what you merely imply. Specific demonstration is essential. Some students mistakenly believe that the professor *qua* grader naturally knows how to interweave, and that it is somehow unnecessary (or even stupid) to spell it out to such a knowledgeable person. But your professor *qua* grader knows nothing about what is in your mind and awaits your demonstration that you have both the skills and doctrinal mastery to perform a concise cogent argument — and argument is always a performance on an exam or in practice.

FAULTY RULE STATEMENT

To illustrate another common mistake, insert the following statement of the intentional murder rule into the above response in place of the existing one:

> Intentional murder requires that a person means to kill another and then actually does so.

This type of rule statement is a very rough, non-legal paraphrase of the rule. The words, "means to kill," are not a substitute for the old, entrenched *mens rea* element/language, of "intent to kill." The words, "and then actually does so," are no substitute for the elements/language of act, causation, and harm. Not at all. On exams, avoid such paraphrasing of core legal language into everyday, non-legal language. Given this faulty rule statement, the interweaving step is inevitably wrong since interweaving presupposes an accurate statement of core elements of the applicable rule. Here, not a single element is correctly stated. The result is a poor answer and a low grade, even though the conclusion and issue statement are correct.

EXPOSITORY ANSWER

Contrasting the concise lawyerly argument on pages 81-82 with the following bad answer, below, will help you to understand the strengths of the model argument and the core weaknesses of this poor one.

> In our society, murder has a variety of forms including intent-to-kill murder, extreme-recklessness murder (also known as depraved-heart murder or willful and wanton murder), and felony murder. Actually, there are, of course, other forms of murder in many states, including premeditated and deliberated murder and intent-to-inflict-serious-bodily-injury murder, but we are not presently applying those types of murder. Intentional murder, whether of the intent-to-kill type or the intent-to-kill plus premeditation-and-deliberation type, is designed to promote the policy purpose of protecting human life against different forms of intentional depredation. In contrast, the purpose of extreme-recklessness murder is to protect life against extremely reckless behavior that threatens life, and the policy purpose of felony murder is to protect life against the risk of death that is associated with the commission of dangerous felonies. Here, the given facts seem to spell out intentional murder.
>
> (no more time)

It is illuminating, and surely important, to understand why this well-written, college-essay-type response is such a poor exam answer, even though each statement of rule and policy is correct. The core reason is that it is not a legal argument. Not at all. It virtually ignores the professor's interrogatory at the end of the problem that inquires about A's liability; it displays no required legal skills such as extricating key facts, issue spotting, rule application, and interweaving. Instead, it focuses on mostly irrelevant knowledge about forms of murder. This conspicuous display of such irrelevant knowledge is called the vice of "legal lecturing," as if the exam challenge is to show off what one has learned and outlined in a collegiate, expository-writing mode.[3]

But the only knowledge that is relevant is that called for by these facts, i.e., the knowledge and understanding that empower you to make a legal argument. This requires you to apply the skills to extricate key facts, spot the issue, select and specify the rule, interweave key facts with elements of the rule, sometimes apply pertinent policy, and do all of this with concise lawyerly writing. These core skills are not displayed in this expository answer and its conclusory last sentence.

---

[3] A University of Michigan law professor defines a "good law exam answer" as one "that answers the question. Banal as that sounds, many students take the question as an excuse to write a canned answer on some area in which they've learned the black-letter law. I tell my students, 'imagine you're riding down an elevator with a boss who knows the law and who has told you the facts but wants your help in advising the client. Don't repeat the facts to him. Don't tell him the law. Apply the law to the facts.'"

Remember: law exam arguments pivot on applying the correct authority in the form of a legal rule (or principle) to the key facts to resolve the issue posed by those facts. Thus, the underlying fallacy in the above very bad answer is in the application of an expository, analytical writing style rather than making an advocacy argument. Put differently, this bad answer presents a simple exposition and comparison of homicide rules and policy, rather than the persuasive writing that scans your knowledge, your criminal-law "mental rolodex," to select the intentional murder rule that, when applied in lawyerly form to these red-hot facts, authoritatively decides the issue posed.

A far less egregious form of this expository writing style is shown below. It adds irrelevant exposition to the cogent argument specified on pages 81-82.

A is liable for intent-to-kill murder

The issue is whether A, who shoots and kills B, is liable for this form of murder. Intentional murder requires (1) an intent to kill (*mens rea*) (2) expressed in (3) a voluntary criminal law act (*actus reus*) (4) that causes, both factually (but-for) and legally (proximately) (5) the death of another.

When A shoots B, this behavior proves the voluntary criminal-law act element (the *actus reus*), and when B dies immediately from the shooting, this proves the element of factual (but-for) and legal (proximate) cause, and the death element. The intent-to-kill element (the *mens rea*) is established by a compelling inference from A's behavior of shooting and killing B while saying, "Go to thine ancestors quickly."

The policy purpose served by the prohibition of intentional murder is the protection of human life from intentional depredation. This policy purpose should be differentiated from the policy purposes of the felony murder statute, which is to discourage the commission of dangerous felonies that sometimes result in accidental killings, and from the purpose of the prohibition of extreme-recklessness murder, which is to discourage extremely reckless behavior that risks the death of another.

The long last sentence in the argument is patently irrelevant and unlawyerly; it actually weakens the strong prior argument. If you have trouble understanding why, imagine yourself as a lawyer arguing before a judge; or yourself as the judge listening to such an argument. The engine that drives the argument is the set of red-hot facts at issue in the case: A intentionally shooting and killing B. Thus, felony murder and extreme-recklessness murder have nothing at all to do with these facts. Hence, their policy purposes are completely irrelevant.

If after practice you still engage in such unlawyerly legal lecturing, try to understand why. Remember that in class, on exams and in practice, lawyers argue to judges and supervisors; they do not simply engage in a show-off-type display of their doctrinal knowledge. Contrast a lecture with an advocacy argument. Judges and professors appreciate cogent arguments — but hate to be lectured.

CIRI(P) TWO: THE TWO-RULE FORMAT

In law practice it is often necessary, in arguing a motion or ruling at a hearing, during trial, or on appeal, to deal with two closely related rules. You probably have encountered examples of this two-rule approach in cases, in classroom discussion, and in other materials. Later, in clinics, in working part time or in the summer in law firms, you will see many examples of it.

In typical multi-issue exam problems, there are often occasions where the two-rule architecture is required. Some of the fact patterns in the essays are specifically designed to raise an issue that requires the application of two rules. Why? Because two causes-of-action arise from the identical fact pattern and issue, or because to resolve a particular issue, the red-hot facts require the application of majority and minority rules that you have studied.

But there are, as you may know, many other examples of relevant professorial emphasis. These include the common law rule, sometimes called the traditional rule, contrasted with the modern statutory rule; the common law rule contrasted with the Restatement rule (e.g., in contracts, real property, torts, or with the Model Penal Code rule in criminal law); "facial analysis" versus "as applied" analysis of a statute with facts impacting the First-Amendment area; common law contract rules contrasted with Uniform Commercial Code rules; the rules for the closely related intentional torts of trespass to chattel and conversion; the rules regarding negligence and strict liability. Sometimes, the question posed at the end of the essay problem will even explicitly require two-rule application, e.g., "In responding, please apply both the common-law and the Restatement rule."

Even if you do not see such plain direction in a question, it is important to apply both rules on any exam for a course where the professor or the assigned materials have presented two related rules, and the facts in the problem raise an issue about such rules. As you study appellate cases and listen carefully to your professor in class (including her reactions to student responses and comments), you will likely hear numerous examples of issues in all your subjects that require you to apply two or more rules to resolve them in a lawyerly manner. Listen especially for her particular focus, e.g., does her pedagogic approach stress a comparison of the common-law rule with the Restatement or modern statutory rule (in torts, contracts, real property, etc.)? As you work with your professors' old exams, you will likely see iconic examples of clusters of facts in problems that require the application of two or more rules.

Your professors seek to demonstrate the pervasive jurisprudential truth that legal argument is not simply straightforward, as illustrated in the anchor legal architecture embodied in Format One. In many fact situations, both those presented on law-school exams and in practice, a lawyerly response requires that you see at least two possibilities for arguing from the identical facts. Your professors also seek to show you that liability often attaches with the application of one rule, but not with the application of the other. The two-rule format enables you to organize and write such lawyerly arguments, usually *pro* and *con,* which embody a different mode of legal argument, a quite different legal architecture.[4]

Basic illustration of two-rule format

You recall the simple hypothetical of "A silently approaching B from behind and punching B on the back of his head." We have already (p. 53) demonstrated the lawyerly specification of the first issue: Is A liable to B for the intentional tort of battery for punching B in the head? But there is, as you know, a second issue arising from these identical facts: is A who punches B on the back of his head liable for the intentional tort of assault?

STRONG ARGUMENT APPLYING CIRI(P) TWO

A is liable to B for the intentional tort of battery but not for assault

The issue is whether A, who punches B on the back of his head, is liable to B for this tort. Battery requires (a) an affirmative act (b) with the intent to touch another (c) that results (d) in unprivileged harmful or offensive contact with another. When A punches B on the back of B's head, this is an affirmative act which expresses A's intent to touch B and that results in unprivileged harm to B, the blow landing on his head.

---

[4] Please spotlight such two-way arguments for each course in your outline where the professor stresses such arguments, and practice them in your study group. A common exam blunder here is to argue only one way instead of two ways.

> **A, however, is not liable for the intentional tort of assault**
>
> This tort requires an *apprehension* by the victim of an imminent battery. Thus, when A approaches B from behind and punches B on the back of his head, there is no factual basis for inferring that B experienced an apprehension of the imminent battery by A. Indeed, A's battery here was entirely unexpected. The policy purpose served by prohibiting such apprehensions is the protection of our emotional and mental tranquility, and is *inapplicable* on these facts.

Do you notice that only eight sentences in two concise paragraphs were needed to resolve the two issues raised by this hypothetical? With practice, you too can write out such no-extra-words arguments.[5] Notice also that the argument in the first paragraph results in a finding of liability, while the argument in the second paragraph results in a finding of no liability — a frequent juxtaposition. Raising this second negative issue is not a "red herring", since the facts of A silently approaching B from behind and punching B on the back of his head might at first blush appear to spell out assault in addition to the manifest battery.

Indeed, since the battery here is an iconic example of this intentional tort (A punching B), the challenge here is to spot and resolve the obvious issue about battery, and then the somewhat less obvious negative issue about assault. Your professor is also challenging you to see that the usual pattern of assault and battery going together like "ham and eggs," in Prosser's words, does not apply to these facts. You are often asked on exams about such exceptions to basic patterns. Notice that the sophisticated negative deployment of policy here supports the non-application of the assault rule on these facts, and shows your teacher that you understand that the inapplicability of the rule here is well justified.

A POOR EXAMPLE OF A CIRI(P) TWO TWO-RULE ANSWER

To appreciate the lawyerly quality of the arguments applying CIRI(P) TWO (the two-rule format), contrast them with the following unlawyerly presentation that professors often see in one version or another.

> When A strikes B on the back of his head, A has committed an illegal act. The act seems to be unjustified, or in the jargon of tort law, "unprivileged." In any event, it seems probable therefore that A can impose tort liability on B for this punch to the back of his head. A good theory might be battery, which is an unprivileged striking of another that is harmful or offensive. Surely, A's assault on B is a good example of this intentional tort of battery. But it is not clear that A can also succeed on the theory of assault, a type of fear or apprehension that someone is going to strike or punch you — a slap in the face, or someone spitting in your face (not harmful but surely offensive). The difficulty that the jury as fact finder would probably encounter in finding A liable here is that B did not appear to realize that he was about to be beaten. Therefore, A may not succeed on this theory, the intentional tort of assault. In contrast, the facts, as mentioned above, of the battery, A punching B on the back of his head, are much clearer and the jury should have no difficulty in finding liability. Of course, there is also a crime spelled out, at common law the crime of battery, and in many modern statutes, the crime of misdemeanor assault. We are not, however, dealing with crimes in this tort exam.

This 'C' range response reflects good issue spotting (though not issue specifying), and it is also doctrinally knowledgeable, but it is woefully weak in lawyerly form though each statement in the answer is correct. It would be a good exercise for you to contrast the strong arguments embodied above in the two

---

[5] A Stanford University law professor said: "A good law exam answer…is like a poem. Every word is there for a reason."

separate paragraphs with this jumbled, meandering presentation. Its weaknesses are: first, that there is no interweaving of the red-hot facts, element by element, with the rules; second, there is no specification, in fact no mention, of the helpful policy; third, the rambling away in the final two sentences about criminal liability is totally irrelevant and a waste of scarce time in a tort exam; fourth, the focus on the jury's fact-finding joined with the tentative language such as "appears," "seems probable," and "might be" are not germane here, given the crystal clear character of the facts spelling out liability for battery, but no liability for assault.

A STANDOUT ARGUMENT APPLYING CIRI(P) TWO

Suppose the facts in a much larger multi-issue problem in criminal law specify, in one legal conflict, that Harry, who does not know Jack, enters Jack's barn through the open door in the daytime to steal a valuable horse. The question at the end of the problem explicitly asks you, among other matters, about criminal-law liability given the common-law and modern statutory rules (your professor had compared the common law and modern approaches in teaching burglary). Your cogent argument here on the issue of burglary embodies a "standout version" of the CIRI(P) TWO writing format.

Harry is not liable for burglary given the common law rule

The issue presented is whether Harry, in entering the barn through the open door in the day to steal a horse, is liable for this form of burglary. The common law burglary rule requires (1) a breaking and (2) entering of the (3) dwelling of another (4) at night (5) with the intent to commit a felony therein. Here, the facts specify that Harry entered through an "open door" (no breaking element) of a "barn" (no dwelling element) during the day (no night element). Three elements are missing; one would be enough to deny liability. Moreover, the policy purpose of common law burglary — to protect dwellings and their occupants from certain threatening crimes committed at night — is obviously inapplicable.

Harry is liable, however, for burglary under the modern rule

Influenced by the Model Penal Code, many states have broadened the scope of their burglary rules beyond dwellings to include other structures, and have eliminated the breaking, night, and felony elements. Thus, a typical modern burglary statute authorizes a finding of liability for one form of burglary if a person (a) knowingly (b) enters or remains in (c) a building (d) without license or privilege and (e) with intent to commit a crime therein. Thus, when Harry enters Jack's barn in the daytime to steal a valuable horse, Harry is knowingly entering a building without Jack's permission (he doesn't know Jack) to steal the horse therein (larceny). The far broader scope of modern burglary statutes is properly designed to protect diverse farm structures, offices, and many other structures that have proliferated in modern times in addition to dwellings. [Clear liability for larceny not detailed].[6]

Do you notice that the second paragraph applying the modern statutory rule mainly varies from the CIRI(P) ONE writing format in that it omits the specification of the issue? The reason why the issue can usually be omitted in applying the second rule in the second paragraph is that it ordinarily is virtually identical to the issue specification in the first paragraph. Do you notice, too, that there is a finding of no liability in applying the common law rule, but there is a finding of liability in applying the modern statutory

---

[6] A separate and concise detailing of Harry's clear liability for common-law larceny may or may not be required. It depends on the professor and whether she covered common-law larceny in class or materials, and her resulting expectation. The point here: sometimes, the two-rule format becomes the three-rule format, all from a single legal conflict. As always, emulate your professor's practice.

rule to the identical facts? Often, even usually, the two-rule approach results in contrasting findings — no liability and liability, or the opposite. Note also that the apt specification of contrasting policies in the arguments illustrates how policy can sometimes add depth and texture and help you make standout 'A' arguments. Note, too, that evolving legislative policy choice determines the correct rule now.

Professors (but not bar examiners) present you with many such two-rule challenges. Their inclination is well grounded in the theory and practice of legal argument. They are testing your skill in distinguishing the contrasting legal significance that follows the application of changing legal policies — and, hence, rules — to the identical set of facts. Understanding and performing the two-rule approach is also foundational for understanding and performing more complex architectures of law detailed in CIRI(P) THREE.

CIRI(P) TWO(a): *"It might be argued..."*

A slightly different presentation of this two-rule architecture is contained in Format Two(a), which should generally be modestly applied, where one rule is preferable but the other rule is arguable, and therefore should be raised (at least briefly) and then rejected (often quickly). With this type of facts, proceed as follows.

Begin with the rule that you believe to be preferable. Apply this first rule on these facts, usually with the anchor CIRI(P) ONE format. In the next paragraph, make brief argument for the application of the other rule; then concisely explain why your first choice embodied in your initial paragraph is either clearly or arguably preferable. Organize the following paragraph in the usual CIRI(P) TWO format for the second paragraph (see above), with one exception. After stating the conclusion [C] followed by the second rule [R], and interweaving the key facts with the second rule [I], concisely explain why you have decided that the first rule is either clearly or arguably preferable. This last step is the rebuttal step.

An illustration of the CIRI(P) TWO(a) *variation*

A more complicated fact pattern includes the following fact cluster concerning one legal conflict:

> E, an enforcer for a loan-shark ring, severely beats D, a delinquent debtor, for two minutes, and then breaks both of D's legs. D dies from shock. E says, "As a professional enforcer, I'm truly appalled and repentant. Since the courts do not favor our legal actions to collect from the estates of dead debtors, I meant only to teach D and other delinquent debtors a lesson: a little individual and general deterrence, mob style." (The interrogatory at the end of the overall problem inquires about the "charges that should be initiated by the local prosecutor.")

STRONG ARGUMENT APPLYING CIRI(P) TWO(a)

> #### E is clearly liable for intent-to-inflict-serious-bodily-injury murder (manslaughter in some states)
>
> The issue is whether E, in severely beating and breaking D's legs, is liable for this form of murder. This theory of murder requires (a) an intent-to-inflict-serious-bodily injury (*mens rea*) that is (b) expressed in a (c) voluntary criminal-law act (*actus reus*) that (d) causes, both factually and legally, the (e) death of another. When E "severely beats D for two minutes" and "breaks both of D's legs," for the purpose of "teaching D a lesson," E's intent-to-inflict-serious-bodily injury is established beyond quibble. This same behavior also establishes the voluntary act element. When D dies from shock resulting from this attack, the causation element, both factual (but-for) and legal (proximate), and the harm element of the death of another, are also established.

It might be argued, however, that E is liable instead for intent-to-kill murder, whose elements differ from those specified above only in requiring a different form of *mens rea*, an intent to kill. When E "severely beats D…for two minutes" and then "breaks both of D's legs," these shocking facts arguably establish an intent to kill that arises *during* this vicious "two-minute beating" (though the mob enforcer did not begin with this intent); or in the secondary sense that such a beating is "substantially" or "virtually" certain to cause the death of D and, hence, an inference of intent to kill may be drawn. Nevertheless, though the facts are extreme and the inference easily arguable, it is not persuasively clear that the difficult standard of proof beyond a reasonable doubt of intent to kill (i.e., a conscious objective by E to kill D), would be met. In contrast, this standard of proof applied to the serious-bodily-injury *mens rea* is persuasively clear.

For the slice of students who believe that a good argument is mainly the right conclusion, imagine that you have written this two-paragraph argument, with one deviation: your conclusion was exactly the opposite. You believed in and argued well for the intentional form of murder as the preferred charge. Let me assure you that you would still have done as well on this argument because your argument is lawyerly, meaning that the issue spotting, rule application, and interweaving are all well done.

The truth is that in practice rule application is indeterminate because fact-finding is uncertain. Indeed, it is hostage to variable fact-finding. In addition to fact-finding, assessing the legal meaning of facts is often very uncertain. Here, for example, different judges and jurors would inevitably make different legal/moral judgments about the *degree* of culpability spelled out by these facts: they are not heartless and soulless machines and many facts, as here, are open to varying weightings. In fact, some prosecutors would likely prefer vigorously arguing the intentional murder charge against this thug, especially on these appalling facts, as an imperative of moral and legal justice. As you now well know, on law-school exams professors often craft facts in problems that can be interpreted and argued two or more ways. They thereby challenge you to see the two or more possibilities that can be plausibly argued. If they do it in class, as is typical, expect it on the exam (but always check their old exams to verify what they actually do).

Some students strew their arguments with this (and other) two-rule versions. They make a good thing a bad thing by overuse. With lack of confidence, most issues can appear uncertain, so the adaptive mechanism is to apply this "it might be argued" technique incorrectly to issues that, given the facts specified in a particular legal conflict and the relevant rule, can only plausibly be argued one way. With practice in issue spotting and writing arguments, however, confidence will accumulate and the unfounded use of two-way arguments abates.

How much outlining do you need for these CIRI(P) TWO *arguments?*

Since these contrasting two-way arguments are somewhat more challenging than the CIRI(P) ONE argument, you may well have needed additional brief outlining focused on exactly how each varied from the other. Thus, you might have listed the elements for battery and assault (especially focusing on the element of apprehension); the contrasting elements of burglary (the common-law versus the modern versions); the contrasting *mens rea* (intent-to-inflict-serious-bodily injury versus intent to kill (meaning a conscious objective to kill) in the two closely related murders.

Depending on the level of your practiced skill in interweaving, you might or might not need to match up relevant red-hot facts with elements of the corresponding battery, assault, burglary or murder for each argument. In particular, the marked contrasts between the common-law burglary rule and the modern rule may well need more attention since, as you can see, the multiple differences in rule result in very different interweaving.

As to organizing the two-way argument, the application of the two versions of the CIRI(P) TWO writing formats should require only a short reflection to decide how you will present it. If you find that you need more detailed outlining when you practice writing these formats early in the semester, seize the time; that's much better than discovering that need on the day of the exam.

With practice, you'll likely find that your outlining of arguments will shrink and your use of stark abbreviations will increase (e.g., l. for liable; A. f/ assault; B. f/ battery; c-l b. for common law burglary; mod. R. for modern rule; I-K for intent to kill; I-inf.-ser.-bod.-inj. for intent-to-inflict-serious-bodily injury, and so on).

From the above strong arguments, you should be able to practice brief outlining, matching up the relevant red-hot facts with the corresponding elements of assault, battery, and common law and the modern version of burglary.

Common errors in CIRI(P) TWO *arguments*

In addition to the above listed errors, there are two common errors that students commit in writing Type Two Arguments. The first is failing to recognize that two (and sometimes three) arguments should be written out in response to the issue, given the facts, the rule(s), and your professor's expectations. It's a significant error to miss the second (and third) argument(s) that your professor expected. The second common error here for many students is to fail to indicate which of the two arguments is better — and why (see last argument above). It's impressive if you can spot the issue, argue two (or three) ways and also concisely explain why one is the better argument.

CIRI(P) THREE: MORE COMPLEX RULE STATEMENTS

The presentation of the prior CIRI(P) formats presupposes that the rules you apply are divisible into specific elements that can often be articulated in one or two sentences; for example, trespass to real property, trespass to chattel, a unilateral contract, and many crimes and defenses. The elements of these rules, usually causes-of-action, crimes, or defenses, are then directly interwoven with key facts to establish a *prima facie* case.

While many rule statements do fit into this simple foundational model, many do not, especially in constitutional law, civil procedure, and contracts. The specification of many rules and principles requires three or four sentences including their relevant standards, tests or factors, and occasionally an additional sentence or two, depending on the instant facts. The CIRI(P) THREE formats aid you in organizing and writing lawyerly arguments incorporating these more complex rule statements, yet another architecture for framing and argument.

> ### CIRI(P) THREE *is the same as* CIRI(P) ONE *with two important elaborations*
>
> 1. The statement of the rule [R] in one, two or more sentences is followed by a definition or elaboration of all or some of the elements contained in the rule or its derivative standards, tests or factors, and
>
> 2. Key (red-hot) facts are interwoven directly with the elements or its standards, tests or factors as so defined or elaborated.

But the other parts of the CIRI(P) THREE formula remain the same: the statement of the conclusion [C]; the specification of the issue [I]; the occasional, brief statement of policy [P]. Hence, see CIRI(P) THREE as simply an extension of CIRI(P) ONE and CIRI(P) TWO, rather than as a completely separate organizing and writing format.

AN INITIAL TORT EXAMPLE OF CIRI(P) THREE MORE COMPLEX RULE STATEMENTS

The cause-of-action of tort negligence cannot be stated in good lawyerly form in one or two sentences. True, the skeletal outline of elements can be summarized in one extended sentence:

> The cause-of-action of tort negligence requires
> 1) a duty owed by the defendant to the plaintiff
> 2) to exercise an applicable standard of care, usually the reasonable person standard,
> 3) with behavior that breaches this standard and that
> 4) causes, both factually (but-for) and legally (proximately),
> 5) actual harm to the plaintiff

But this skeletal outline of elements, while fine as a foundation, is not in itself an adequate lawyerly statement of the rule for most professors. Why? You must demonstrate to your grader that, more than merely parroting this skeletal outline of the core elements of every tort-negligence cause-of-action, you understand what you have written. The challenge is to then perform this elaboration in concise lawyerly form, in a few sentences, avoiding discursive amplification and wasting time. An example follows in a motorist context.

> Motorists owe an objective duty of reasonable care to other nearby motorists. Breach of this duty by the defendant's behavior must cause actual harm to a motorist/plaintiff. The causal element includes a but-for requirement — but for the defendant's behavior, the plaintiff would not have been injured, and a proximate-cause requirement — a sufficiently close causal link between the defendant's behavior and the plaintiff's harm.

This three-sentence elaboration demonstrates that you understand the rule of tort negligence that you have already written out in your first skeletal sentence (above). The initial sentence in this elaboration specifies the first two elements in the context of motorists. The second sentence explicates the element of breach and actual harm. The final sentence, which could be two shorter sentences, explicates both parts of the causal element. Notice that there is no unlawyerly nonsense: no puffing, no rambling, and no expository showing off of irrelevant knowledge.

You are now ready to interweave the key facts with the elements as defined. For example:

> Thus, when the defendant, D, turned her head to engage the rear-seat passengers in an animated conversation while driving on the parkway at sixty miles per hour, she breached her duty of reasonable care owed to the plaintiff, P, a nearby motorist. A driver exercising reasonable care in these circumstances would not have taken her eyes off the road to talk to the passengers in this manner. When this breach results in collision with P's car and physical injury to P, D's behavior has caused actual harm to P, both in the but-for sense that without the breach P would not have been injured, and also in the proximate sense of a clearly close causal link between D's breach and P's harm.

Thus, the complete strong argument here would simply combine these parts and precede them with the statement of the conclusion and the issue statement as follows:

> ### D is liable to P in tort negligence
>
> The issue is whether D, who takes her eyes off the road to talk to a back seat passenger thereby injuring P, is liable to P for this form of tort.
>
> The cause-of-action of tort negligence requires (1) a duty owed by the defendant to the plaintiff; (2) to exercise an applicable standard of care, usually the reasonable-person standard; (3) behavior that breaches this standard; and that (4) causes, both factually (but/for) and legally (proximately); (5) actual harm to the plaintiff. Motorists owe an objective duty of reasonable care to other nearby motorists. Breach of this duty by the defendant's behavior must cause harm to such a motorist/plaintiff. The causal element includes a but-for requirement — but for the defendant's behavior, the plaintiff would not have been injured, and a proximate-cause requirement — a sufficiently close causal link between the defendant's behavior and the plaintiff's harm.
>
> Thus, when the defendant, D, turned her head to engage the rear-seat passenger in an animated conversation while driving on the parkway at sixty miles per hour, she breached her duty of reasonable care owed to the Plaintiff, P, a nearby motorist. A reasonable driver in these circumstances would not have taken her eyes off the road to talk to the passenger in this manner. When this breach results in collision with P's car and physical injury to P, then D's behavior has caused actual harm to P, both in the but-for sense that without the breach P would not have been injured, and also in the proximate sense of a clearly close causal link between D's breach and P's harm.
>
> [Note the omission of the policy purpose(s) for tort negligence. Little is added by such specification of policy here with this very plain example of tort negligence.]

This argument illustrates the more complex rule statement that is typical of CIRI(P) THREE and the resulting interweaving with the key facts.[7] Once you have stated the basic negligence rule in an argument, do not repeat it. Since you have demonstrated to your professor that you know it in a lawyerly sense, one detailing is ordinarily sufficient. Indeed, you have no time to waste in doing so. If you need the rule again, refer to it later in the same argument by stating — "See basic negligence rule above."

EXAMPLE OF OMISSION OF PREVIOUSLY SPECIFIED RULE

Suppose that P in the above hypothetical, after being struck and injured by D, is further injured when a slightly drunk ambulance driver, A, who works for the Acme Ambulance Company, does not notice a car stopped directly in front of the ambulance at a red light and collides with it, thereby aggravating P's injuries. A model argument to this portion of the essay problem, the second legal conflict (or episode), follows:

> ### A liable to D for tort negligence
>
> The issue is whether A, a slightly drunk ambulance driver who collides with a car stopped at a red light thereby aggravating D's injuries, is liable for this tort. See basic negligence rule above. Thus, when A, while slightly drunk, fails to notice in time that a car is stopped at a red light, A breaches his duty, that of a reasonable ambulance driver, owed to D to drive while sober and to

---

[7] An important caution here: in resolving issues in the most extreme time-pressured problem with a multitude of issues, there is almost certainly insufficient time to do the above detailed and very lawyerly elaboration of the rule. Your professor probably does not even expect it in this context (or at most may expect its detail only once in a problem). Check the old exams and see the "Mary Lee" argument in Chapter Six. You need professorial individualizing here as elsewhere. Tailor your response to the specific professor; if still uncertain, ask.

> watch for stopped cars. When A then collides with said car thereby aggravating D's injuries, A's breach of his duty to D has caused harm to D, both in the but-for sense that such harm to D would not have occurred without A's breach, and also in the proximate cause sense of a close causal relationship between A's breach and the harm to D.

This strong argument resolving the initial issue arising from the second legal episode in the essay problem has only four sentences. Do you notice how this concise cogent argument builds upon the prior argument? As noted, the elaborated statement of the basic negligence rule resolving the first issue should not be repeated here. Even a shorter statement of the negligence rule is unnecessary. A brief reference to the statement of the basic rule in a prior paragraph in the same problem is enough for most professors. To verify, check any old exam answers, talk to prior students who did well, and, if still unsure, ask your professor.

Additional rules

You also apply, in addition to this core rule, a variety of other supplementing rules to resolve most issues arising from fact patterns spelling out negligence. The basic negligence rule, set forth above, is necessary but insufficient to deal with most such issues. Additional rules further elaborate and specify core elements of negligence. They are aids in applying the core rule, in determining whether particular facts spell out, or fail to spell out, liability.

These additional rules have crystallized from countless cases over many decades and apply to injuries that are proximately caused by negligent behavior in a variety of contexts. Moreover, there are countless basic rules in all areas of our law that are particularized by additional elaborating rules, including consideration in contract, the rule against perpetuities in real property, and equitable distribution in family law. In addition, elaborating rules (often called standards) typically are necessary in applying any broad principle of law or constitutional provision such as due process, equal protection of the laws, freedom of speech, press and assembly, and the prohibition against cruel and unusual punishment.

The best direction for you as to how elaborated your exam rule statement should be is found in those old exams with a model or strong student response. If not obtainable, follow their professorial practice in class; if still obscure, ask each teacher.

A TORT EXAMPLE OF AN ELABORATING RULE

The second legal episode gives rise to another issue that illustrates the application of an additional elaborating rule.

> ### D's further liability to P
>
> D is also liable to P for the aggravation of his injuries by A, the ambulance driver. The issue is whether D, as the original tortfeasor, is also liable for A's aggravation of P's injuries. The additional rule required is that the original tortfeasor is also liable for *ensuing negligent aggravation* of a victim's injuries by others, including ambulance drivers and medical personnel. Thus, when A negligently injures P (see above), D, as the original tortfeasor, is also liable for this ensuing ordinary negligence of A that follows from his breach.

The brevity of this strong argument is enabled by the first argument containing the basic negligence rule. The words "additional rule" implicitly refer back to this basic rule and analysis, so that this strong argument is also derivative of that initial response. Both this argument and the prior argument, totaling nine sentences in two paragraphs, illustrate again that very lawyerly responses can often be concisely written, and that there is enough time to write such arguments, if you know what to do and have regularly practiced the skills to do so.

A FINAL STANDOUT TORT ARGUMENT FOR AN ADDITIONAL RULE

The one-sentence fact statement comprising the second legal episode in this essay problem triggers yet a third issue; its resolution illustrates the application of a different type of additional rule.

The Acme Ambulance Co. also liable to P

The issue is whether this Co. is liable to P when its employee, A, negligently collides with a stopped car, thereby aggravating P's injuries. The doctrine of *respondeat superior* imposes strict vicarious liability on an employer whose worker negligently causes harm *within the scope of his employment*. Thus, when A, the employee of the Co., negligently causes harm to P (see second argument above) while driving P to the hospital (within scope of employment), the elements of *respondeat superior* are clearly established. The policy purposes served are to provide a plaintiff recourse against a defendant who has deep pockets; who can pay for insurance against such risks; who can guard against such risks by careful recruitment, training and supervision; who therefore can fairly be held responsible in addition to the driver.

Do you see that this rule of *respondeat superior* presupposes the prior application of the basic negligence rule and whatever additional rules were required? The rule only applies to an employer if one of its workers is liable for a tort. The worker's liability invokes the company's vicarious liability (distinguish such strict liability imposed on an employer from the imposition of negligent liability arising, for example, from an employer's failure to supervise workers reasonably). Note how the concise specification of relevant policies here adds depth and analytical power to your argument. You can clearly see that the relevant rule is best understood as a policy writ concrete, and why it is wrong to encapsulate rules as your single learning focus. Indeed, as you now know, all rules you study in any subject are also policies and principles writ concrete and should be understood as such.

Have you noticed that these last three arguments resolve three issues arising from the facts spelled out in one sentence? They illustrate the general exam maxim that you already know: a single legal conflict, though by definition containing a minimum of one legal issue, may also give rise to two, three, or more issues and related arguments. Practicing with hypotheticals and each professor's old exam problems refines your skills in spotting all such issues, and in resolving them with cogent arguments by applying one or more of the CIRI(P) formats.

How much outlining do you need for these CIRI(P) THREE *arguments?*

It varies. You might need to do considerable abbreviated outlining of the negligence argument (p. 97). This eight-sentence argument, after the heading, is not only longer. It is also more complex than the arguments presented so far in this Chapter. Its enumeration of the five elements of tort negligence with brief definition of certain core elements, followed by somewhat dense interweaving, requires at least terse outlining of the elements as well as the definitions and perhaps the interweaving.

In contrast, the need for outlining the four-sentence argument on the prior page might well be limited to briefly listing the elements of the rule of *respondeat superior*. It's a straightforward CIRI(P) ONE argument that relies on the prior CIRI(P) THREE argument. Since this argument rides piggyback on the prior one establishing the negligence of the ambulance driver, there is no need to repeat any of that and no need to outline it. You've already demonstrated that you can do that. Remember that CIRI(P) THREE arguments sometimes lead to CIRI(P) ONE and TWO sequels.

CIRI(P) THREE(a): *Elastic standards and tests or factors*

Many rules and principles require a different statement in the form of broad elastic language. To illustrate, in criminal law, the standard (or rule) is that a killing is sufficient for felony murder if "the killing was committed in, about and as a part of the underlying transaction" or in "immediate flight" from it. In family law the principle that "the best interests of the child" is the legal standard to apply in determining custody issues. In election law, the principle that the "intent of the voter" should govern the counting of disputed ballots. In constitutional law, the Eighth Amendment principle that prohibits "cruel and unusual punishments".

These broad elastic statements illustrate a more expansive panoply of rules and principles that cannot be applied directly by interweaving key facts with elements. Rather, rules and principles of this type require standards and tests or factors whose application determines if abstract rules and principles do apply in a specific case. Rather than interweaving key facts with elements, the key facts are interwoven directly with the relevant tests or factors as illustrated below.

AN INTENTIONAL TORT EXAMPLE OF CIRI(P) THREE(a)

A straightforward example is provided by the intentional tort of conversion. That tort is defined very broadly as (1) the intentional and unprivileged exercise of dominion and control over a chattel that (2) so seriously interferes with the right of another to control it that (3) the actor may justly be required to pay the full value of the chattel. This vague, elastic standard can be applied, however, since the case law also supplies numerous tests or factors that help to define and clarify the malleable language, especially which behavior "seriously interferes" and the meaning of the elastic language "may justly be required." These tests are as follows:

---

a) the extent and duration of the actor's exercise of dominion and control;

b) the actor's intent to assert a right in fact inconsistent with the other's right of control;

c) the actor's good or bad faith;

d) the extent and duration of the resulting interference with the other's right of control;

e) the harm done to the chattel;

f) the inconvenience and expense caused to the other (Restatement of Torts 2d, 1965, §222A).

The following strong argument resolving a basic conversion issue illustrates the concise application of the relevant tests or factors to an elementary fact pattern, a single legal conflict. These limited facts detail that "Straight lends his car to Hot Dog to go for a drive in the country on a sparkling spring afternoon. Instead, Hot Dog drives to Alaska, four thousand miles away. As a result, Straight has to buy another car."

Hot Dog liable to Straight for conversion

The issue is whether Dog's driving of Straight's car to Alaska, after borrowing it for an afternoon drive, spells out this intentional tort. Conversion requires (1) an intentional exercise of dominion or control over a chattel that (2) so seriously interferes with the right of another to control it that (3) the actor may justly be required to pay the full value of the chattel. Here, Hot Dog's 4,000 mile excursion to Alaska deprives Straight of his car and thus *completely* interferes with

---

Straight's control of his car for a substantial period. Dog's outrageous act is an assertion of control exhibiting bad faith and causing Straight inconvenience and the cost of another car. Thus, it is *just* to require that Dog pay the full value of the converted car.

Do you notice that the relevant tests or factors are interwoven directly with the red-hot facts? The tests or factors are not separately specified after the statement of the rule of conversion. While it is entirely proper to separately state each relevant test or factor before the interweaving step of your argument, it is also very lawyerly to blend them together with the red-hot facts in your interweaving. There is, of course, a real advantage in this more sophisticated approach: your argument is more concise. You have saved precious time without any sacrifice of lawyerly quality.

At first, when you practice writing such cogent arguments, you should separately spell out the relevant tests or factors after the statement of the rule and before the interweaving step.[8] As soon as you feel that you can do so, however, practice this blending together in your interweaving of the relevant tests or factors with the red-hot facts. The more you practice, the more skilled you'll become at this advanced lawyerly blending which will impress your professor and serve you well in the decades of your practice.

The use of the adjective "relevant" may pique your legal curiosity. Since tests or factors are guidelines for applying a broad rule, here the rule of conversion, you only apply those guidelines that aid you in applying the rule to the particular fact situation. For example, all the tests or factors are relevant except (e), harm to the chattel/car. Contrast how this highly flexible, fact-adjusting use of tests or factors differs markedly from the invariable need to establish each element of a cause-of-action (here, conversion) or a defense in order to establish liability or a defense to such liability.

Do you clearly understand then the difference between tests and factors as guidelines in applying a broad rule, principle or standard in contrast to the elements of a cause-of-action or a defense, all of which must be specified? It is a bad error to omit any one of the three elements set forth above to establish liability for the cause-of-action of conversion, but you should omit all irrelevant tests or factors (unless you are instructed otherwise). Always keep in mind in any course that relevant tests or factors are vital in applying broad rules, but they are not elements of rules that must invariably all be applied in each case. Unlike rules, they have only derivative and instrumental value.

How much outlining do you need for this CIRI(P) THREE(a) *argument?*

The need to perform more detailed outlining escalates as the complexity of the rules and accompanying tests increase. Given the stepped-up complexity of the last argument, it's almost certainly better for you briefly to detail the elements of conversion and corresponding tests. Using your own abbreviations, this can be done quickly. Before writing out your argument, match the appropriate red-hot facts with their corresponding tests. Incidentally, I recall elements not abstractly, but by thinking of iconic mental pictures of conversion. Pictures enable me to recall the elements. My mental pictures for conversion include the shoplifter (thefts are also conversions), and the "friend" who borrows your car for the afternoon and drives to Alaska. Though this conversion rule with its tests is somewhat complex, please notice that the interweaving in the strong argument above is only a few sentences.

---

8 As you may have noticed from many prior arguments, the magic word "Here" signals the end of the rule statement and the beginning of your interweaving of key facts with the elements, tests or factors. The words "In this instance" or "On these facts," also signal this end and beginning.

A CIVIL PROCEDURE EXAMPLE OF CIRI(P) THREE(a)

The "minimum contacts" standard for acquiring personal jurisdiction in one state over a person or corporation in another state or country provides an example of use of standards, as well as tests or factors. As set forth later on pages 150-152, the purpose of minimum contacts is to ensure that the exercise of such jurisdiction does not violate the Due-Process-based standard of "traditional notions of fair play and justice" required by the Fourteenth Amendment. This standard is explained and specified by tests or factors set forth in a number of landmark Supreme Court cases and their progeny. These include balancing the actual burden on the defendant in defending the litigation in the forum state, the strength of the forum state's interest in adjudicating the dispute, the plaintiff's interest in obtaining convenient and effective relief, the court's interest in economy in judicial proceedings, and the interests of the states in promoting certain social policies. These vital tests or factors are applied in part of the excellent argument in response to a civil-procedure exam problem set forth in Chapters Six (pp. 150-152). A relevant part follows:

The Fairness standard is not met

Even if "minimum contacts" are found to be present, D [the defendant] could object that the separate fairness standard of *Asahi, International Shoe* and related cases have not been met. These cases require the court to balance the burden on the defendant in defending the suit in the forum state, the forum state's interest in adjudicating the dispute, the plaintiff's interest in obtaining convenient and effective relief, the judicial system's interest in economy, and the interests of the states in furthering certain social policies (see *Kulko*).

Here, the burden on defendant, a municipal utility with primarily local functions, may be presumed to be great. New York's interest in asserting jurisdiction (and the interstate social policy interest) may also be great because of the nature of the pollution interest discussed above. Tipping the balance may be P's interest in a local forum and the question of judicial economy. It seems unusual that P who has always lived in northern N.Y. would be bringing suit in the southern, as opposed to the northern, district [court], especially since the facts indicate the pollution was brought into the [upstate] area in which P "lived and worked." Unless there is some compelling reason why suit in the southern district seemed more reasonable, P has little legitimate interest in this choice of forum. Similarly, judicial economy would argue against asserting jurisdiction, since the trend seems to be to transfer cases out of the [crowded] southern district whenever possible. Thus, without more information about P's interest in this choice of forum, I would have to conclude that this issue should be resolved in favor of D, and the court should dismiss for lack of personal jurisdiction.

Do you notice the three sequential levels in the statement of the relevant law? First, the Due Process principle as the foundation; second, the standard of "traditional notions of fair play and justice" required by the foundational principle; and third, the various factors for determining whether the standard is violated by the instant facts. Do you notice, too, that both the fairness standard to be applied and all the factors are also quite broad? You should therefore not be surprised then that application of such a standard and its related tests or factors usually leads to expansive pro and con arguments on exams and in practice. Indeed, your professor is probably testing you to see if you understand the almost inevitable *pro* and *con* texture and breadth of this legal language, and typically will give you facts that necessitate such back-and-forth argument. As always, of course, the basis for your grade is the quality of your advocacy argument, not the conclusion alone. I hope it is apparent now that there is another important scaffolding of legal language illustrated here that you will apply in your courses, i.e. various levels of abstraction and concreteness.

A BASIC CONTRACT EXAMPLE OF CIRI(P) THREE(a)

In a Type-One paragraph-based multi-issue problem, the facts in one of the legal conflicts specify that A, the president of a carpet company, agrees to level the floor and carpet the office of B company for $30,000. But A, who performs the work over a weekend when B's office is closed, instructs her workers not to in a manner that hides the failure to do so. B company, nevertheless, discovers A's failure to have the floor leveled. When A submits her bill for the agreed $30,000, B company refuses to pay. The value of the leveling is $10,000 of the $30,000 contract. A initiates a cause-of-action for breach of contract against B company for non-payment, and argues that A has substantially performed its obligations under the agreement with B company. B defends by claiming that A has materially breached its contract with B. As a judge, how do you decide?[9]

> ### A does not succeed on theory of substantial performance of her contract with B
>
> The issue is whether A, who intentionally fails to fulfill her duty to level B's floor worth $10,000 of a $30,000 contract, may recover on a theory of substantial performance. This doctrine provides that "where a contract is made for an agreed exchange of two performances, one which is to be rendered first, substantial performance rather than exact, strict or literal performance by the first part of the terms of the contract is adequate to entitle the party to recover on it." In applying this doctrine, factors to be considered include whether the breach was willful and its extent.
>
> Here, A willfully breached her duty to level B's floor in accordance with the agreement by instructing her workers to carpet the office in a manner that hides their failure to level the floor. This breach is a conscious and intentional variation from the contract and is therefore willful. It is also a substantial breach, not insubstantial, since the cost of the leveling is $10,000, one-third of the total contract price of $30,000.

How much outlining do you need for these latter two arguments?

In the prior minimum contacts argument (there with five tests or factors and here with only two in the argument immediately above), I suggest the obvious: specifying and then interweaving with five tests or factors requires more careful detailing and then matching of the corresponding red-hot (key) facts with each. For writing out the substantial performance argument, quickly abbreviate the elements of the rule (the "doctrine") and the easier two tests or factors; you might also need only briefly to match each test or factor with the corresponding red-hot facts.

Caveats for all CIRI(P) THREE Formats so far

1. Please reflect on these diverse illustrations of different kinds of exam scaffolding for abstract and elastic standards, and their related and usually more concrete tests or factors. Your initial objective is to understand this particular architecture for performing such advocacy arguments. You have probably seen it many times in cases, heard it in class, perhaps applied it in case briefs and elsewhere. You will use it many more times on law school exams and will frequently apply it in practice.

2. Don't be confused by the varying language used to describe these abstract elastic rules, sometimes also called principles, standards, or doctrines. The tests used to explain and specify some of these rules are usually called factors, or guidelines. Other rules, such as the basic tort negligence rule, have elements that

---

[9] These facts and the resulting issue appeared at least twice on New York State Bar Exams, illustrating that issues and even an entire problem can frequently have a second or third life on both law-school and bar exams.

require elaborating definition. These brief elaborating definitions are sometimes also called additional rules. While language varies, there is no need to be confused. Simply use the language that your professor uses, or the language in her assigned cases. Law is not science. Be flexible and individualize as always.

3. Don't slight the basic standard (e.g., "conversion," "fairness") that is explained and specified by the tests or factors, or the basic rule (e.g., the elements of tort negligence) that often requires additional rules elaborating on some of the elements. Remember that the objective in interweaving red-hot facts with such tests or factors is to determine whether or not the basic standard is established.

4. Keep in mind that some professors, following your technical legal argument, may expect you to briefly explain whether you agree with the argument you just presented. And some don't.

CIRI(P) THREE(b): *The multi-step approach*

Another genre of this more complex exam writing is multi-step argument. In contrast to the Type One problem with paragraph-based, multiple legal conflicts and matching issues, a Type Three(b) problem focuses on one overall issue that is then unfolded into its multiple parts. The following facts from a short criminal-law problem and the standout responding argument illustrate this unfolding succinctly.

> A lends her car to B, a friend, who fails to return A's car even though A repeatedly asks B to return it. One night A goes to B's house, sees her car on the street and decides to reclaim it. As she unlocks and opens the car door, B bursts out of her house, grabs the open car door, and remonstrates with A about everything B has done for A in the past. Since B continues to hold the open door, blocking A from getting into her car, A gently shoves B away. Unhappily, B falls, hits her head and dies. The police arrest A for felony murder for an accidental killing during the commission of dangerous felonies, stealing the car and robbery. The district attorney asks you, an intern, to analyze A's liability on these facts.

A STANDOUT ARGUMENT APPLYING CIRI(P) THREE(b)

> #### A not liable for felony murder
>
> The main issue is whether A, who "gently shoves B" to regain her car, is liable for this form of murder when B falls and dies. Felony murder requires a killing, intentional or accidental, in furtherance of the commission of a dangerous felony or in immediate flight therefrom. Larceny, the claimed "stealing" of the car, is not such a dangerous felony that triggers felony murder liability when B accidentally dies. In addition, robbery, which is such a dangerous felony triggering felony murder liability for an accidental death in furtherance of its commission, does not apply. Robbery is the use of actual force, or the threat of force, in the commission of common law larceny ("forcible larceny"). This form of larceny requires a trespassory taking of the property of another with the intent permanently to deprive the owner of possession. Here, A cannot steal her own car (it is not the property of another) and thus there cannot be any trespassory taking of it. Without these elements, there is no larceny, and without the larceny, there is no robbery. Without the robbery, there is no felony murder. The additional required rule is that A can use reasonable force to recapture her property — a "gentle shove" easily qualifies, and the fact that death results does not retroactively transform it into a culpable use of force. B's death is a tragedy but not a murder or manslaughter.

Note how this step-by-step unfolding contrasts both with the first category of complex rule statements requiring defining and elaborating rules (pp. 93-94), and the second category requiring the use of tests or factors (p. 102). In sharp contrast, there is here an unpacking of closely related rules that are dependent on one another, e.g., no felony murder here without robbery, no robbery without common-law larceny, and no such larceny in recapturing your own car. All courses have the potential for exams that require different forms of step-by-step unpacking. For a classic constitutional law example, see the 'A' student argument in "Let Them Eat Cake" (pp. 153-154). For a challenging contract example, see the 'A' argument in "Olivia Warbucks" (pp. 138-143). And for a civil procedure example, see "Blowing in the Wind" (pp. 151-152).

How much outlining do you need for this step-by-step argument?

It varies, of course, from person to person, and depends on the complexity of each argument. I suggest you at least briefly detail each step. Otherwise, you might omit one of the steps even though you "know" it and have processed it in your mind. I recall many such omissions in student exam arguments. As you now know for sure, outlining and writing arguments is different from just expounding on your understanding — exam performance is much more than that.

Common exam errors in CIRI(P) THREE *arguments*

Common errors here include stating rules only in one sentence when some of the rule elements should be elaborated upon, given the facts, rule(s), and your professor's expectation. Other errors include interweaving directly with elements of the rule instead of the relevant tests or factors, or omitting a relevant test or factor, or a step in multi-step argument making.

CIRI(P) FOUR: INVALIDATING THE RULE (LEGAL PROBLEMS)

In all the prior CIRI(P) formats, the challenge, after spotting the issues, is to apply the relevant rules and interweave the red-hot facts with the rules (or standards, tests or factors). But in the contrasting CIRI(P) FOUR architecture, the challenge is to decide if the red-hot facts raise an issue(s) that calls not for application but, rather, for invalidation of the seemingly applicable rule since it conflicts with a constitutional principle. Remember that all rules, whether statutory or case based, must not violate constitutional principles, with the final meaning of the federal Constitution determined by the United States Supreme Court, and that of state Constitutions determined ordinarily by the highest court in each state.

In our jurisprudence, the federal and state constitutions are our fundamental charters of liberty and government, specifying our rights, the grant of governmental powers, and the checks and balances inherent in our federal system of separated, divided and checked powers. These powers are distributed among the legislature, executive and judicial branches at both national and state levels. The rule of law forbids any exercise of state power outside of our constitutions. You study this constitutional invalidation of rules in Constitutional Law courses, and many others, including criminal law, criminal procedure, civil procedure, domestic relations, and conflict of laws.

A straightforward example from juvenile delinquency (family) law

The following problem poses a constitutional issue about the facial invalidation of a statutory rule in the realm of juvenile delinquency. The trial court convicted the appellant, a twelve-year-old boy, of juvenile delinquency for entering a locker room and stealing $112 "from a woman's pocket book." Counsel for the boy argued to the [trial] court for the application of the standard of proof of beyond a reasonable doubt, even though then section 744(b) of the New York Family Court Act imposed the standard of proof of "a preponderance of the evidence" for a determination that a juvenile did "an act or acts."

Counsel: Your Honor is making a finding by the preponderance of the evidence.

Court: Well, it convinces me.

Counsel: It's not beyond a reasonable doubt, Your Honor.

Court: That is true… Our statute says a preponderance [of the evidence] and a preponderance it is.

On appeal by the boy, how do you argue?

A STRONG EXAM ARGUMENT APPLYING CIRI(P) FOUR

> ### The statute mandating a preponderance standard of proof in a delinquency proceeding is unconstitutional
>
> The issue is whether this lower evidentiary standard of proof comports with the Due Process requirement of fairness. In the landmark *Winship* case, the U.S. Supreme Court explicitly held that the Due Process Clause, applicable to the states though the Fourteenth Amendment, protects the accused against conviction except upon proof beyond a reasonable doubt of every fact necessary to constitute the crime with which he is charged, and this holding applies to juveniles as well as adults. Thus, the lower standard of proof mandated by the statute of a preponderance of the evidence is unconstitutional. Here, the boy's acts must be judged by the reasonable doubt standard. In its reasoning in *Winship*, the Court stressed that the reasonable-doubt standard vindicates the presumption of innocence, that bedrock principle animating the administration of our criminal law.
>
> [The last sentence, the policy statement, linking the Supreme Court's holding here to the "bedrock" principle of presumption of innocence, clearly deepens and strengthens the argument.]

Do you understand how this concise five-sentence argument demonstrates the facial invalidation of a rule, here of statutory origin, since the Court holds that the Due Process Clause mandates the stricter reasonable-doubt standard of proof for juvenile as well as adult defendants? The argument differs from all prior arguments in this Book because the statutory rule is not interwoven with the red-hot facts, but rather it is invalidated for this and all future cases: it is null and void. The argument illustrates a different legal type of problem that you will likely encounter in the first year.

Please also note that the *Winship* holding above (called "a principle," not a rule) is broad and sweeping and applicable throughout the country to all criminal trials. Since the Supreme Court articulated it as an interpretation of the Due Process Clause, the principle has constitutional dimension and, therefore, a fundamental status in our legal system.

This example of constitutional invalidation is simple and straightforward (after you study the principle). But many constitutional arguments are much more complex and, hence, more challenging. For one illustration of this complexity, see the standout student argument in Chapter Six in "Let Them Eat Cake" (pp. 153-154). The application of "strict scrutiny" in that argument also illustrates the multi-step approach, CIRI(P) THREE(b). Finally, remember that state courts may also invalidate court-made, common-law rules (see, e.g., *Woods* in my *Learning Legal Reasoning*, p.77) that do not implicate constitutional principles and decide that an old rule should be replaced.

Common errors in CIRI(P) FOUR arguments

The most common error here may be failing to understand the different exam architecture. This difference applies not only to issue spotting but also in exam writing that focuses on the purely legal issue to be resolved, rather than the usual application of a rule to the given facts of the case.

Applying the formats in battle conditions

Practicing ideal presentations of these diverse CIRI(P) writing formats may differ from their application on actual exams. As you scrutinize the strong arguments in Chapter Six, you will notice both adherence to these formats as well as deviation from them. This gap is akin to that between the planning taught in military schools and practiced in military maneuvers, and the actual implementation of such plans in wartime. In fact, this training makes battlefield deviation and improvisation possible. Similarly, vigorous practice of the various formats throughout the semester enables you the freedom and mental flexibility to deviate when necessary to write strong arguments on exams.

Informed deviation is a world away from "winging it" on the exam day. With practice, you will know how to organize and write your arguments in the allotted time. One deviation may be omission of the specification of the relevant policy [CIRI(**P**)], which is not routinely applied anyway. A second may be the omission of the specification of the issue [CIRI(P)] where the rest of your usual CIRI(P) argument clearly, but implicitly, affirms that you are right on target on the issue. The occasional omission of these steps does not mean that they are unimportant. Rather, the strong argument that omits these steps makes clear to an examiner that the student is aware of the issue and the policy that underlies the applied rule.

Another battlefield deviation can occur when you know you can write out separate arguments posed by a legal conflict, but are uncertain that you can competently write out the multi-step argument that you sense is the ideal response to an overall issue. For example, the elegant felony-murder argument on page 104 does an impressive job of resolving one overall issue with the multi-step argument. But if exam pressure causes you to pause about spelling out such an argument, there is an easier way to argue that should get you equal credit. As previously noted (pp. 85-86), simply translate each step into a separate, short CIRI(P) ONE(a) argument. After a brief heading (A is not liable for larceny), specify the one-sentence issue (Is A, who reclaims her own car from B, liable for this crime?). In one sentence, specify the absence of part of the larceny rule (Larceny requires a trespassory taking of the property of another). Interweaving is easy (thus, A cannot steal her own car).

Immediately go to the second step and convert it into a separate, short CIRI(P) ONE argument. You might practice doing it in a few sentences (the heart of it, of course, is that without larceny, there is no robbery). Also, practice writing out the final step with your third short CIRI(P) ONE argument (the heart of it is that without robbery or other dangerous felony, there is no felony murder). The three steps have become separate short arguments that may be easier for you to argue under acute time pressure and exam fatigue. However, use these as occasional field expedients, and not a substitute for any of your usual CIRI(P) writing formats.[10]

Arguing the policy problem: A quite different architecture

The first thing to know here is that you may not see such policy problems on exams. While many professors (including me) routinely include a policy emphasis in their exams, others do not. Professorial choice varies widely here. Again, check the old exams of each of your professors. Don't rely on classroom practice: a substantial emphasis on policy in class may not be replicated on the exam. Even if old exams

---

[10] I am indebted to Christopher Byck, an insightful and able law school graduate, for suggesting this occasional approach.

do not include such problems, I still recommend quickly examining what follows so that you'll be prepared for any surprises.

Let's assume some of your professors include policy issues, either as an entire problem or part of a predominantly issue-spotting problem. As noted, the way you frame, organize, and write out such argument responding to a policy problem differs markedly from the above formats. The format you apply in arguing the policy question is a highly systematic version of the college-essay-type answer. The better grades will go to the argument in response to the interrogatory that is cogent and concise: no nonsense, no meandering, and no regurgitating of irrelevant knowledge. See the exemplary student response to the Policy Problem (pp. 133-135) and contrast it with the poor response (pp. 135-136).

More specifically, it is important to address relevant perspectives and arguments, both pro and con, that your professor has discussed in class or in assigned readings. In your advocacy argument, you do not have to agree with them, of course, but don't blatantly disrespect her by just ignoring them. Indeed, if you can utilize some of her discussion as part of your lawyerly argument against her preferred position, you may trigger a professorial smile and even an 'A' grade.

Many students believe these problems are easier because they are more familiar, more akin to college essay problems. If you have been sensitive to your professor's signals in class, materials, and old exams, you should be able to perform acceptably. But the challenge is to excel. And you can, since most such questions can be anticipated and thus your arguments can be prepared in advance.[11]

You may also see a mixed rule/policy problem. To illustrate, many criminal law professors stress the contradictory consequences and policy justifications underlying the defenses of mistake of fact, mistake of law, voluntary intoxication, and involuntary act. This emphasis leads to a mixed rule and policy question that asks you to state these rules and to contrast their results, if the defense is successful, and their contrasting policy justifications. You typically also are asked whether you agree or disagree with these varying consequences and rationales, and which you prefer. While this mixed rule/policy problem is challenging, it is a joy to see if you have prepared your argument before the exam because your professor gave obvious priority to this area in class. Illustrations of policy problems in other areas follow.

> In a civil procedure class: What is the purpose of civil procedure rules, in whole or in part? Do you agree or disagree with these purposes?
>
> In a First Amendment class: Do you agree or disagree with proposals for vouchers for students to attend private and religious schools? What are the best First-Amendment rationales for and against such vouchers? Which arguments do you prefer? Explain your reasons.

Don't expect to anticipate policy problems exactly. Your preparation, especially outlining, discussion in study group, and writing of arguments, should serve you well if there are problems even on the edges of what you have prepared. Even if no such problems appear on the exam, your preparation should deepen your understanding, aiding you in issue spotting and argument-making in a more typical rule-based problem. However, unless your professors are clearly stressing such matters as measured by their assigned materials, class discussions, and their old exams, don't make this a major focus.

---

[11] I've seen it suggested that students respond to a policy problem with a relevant hypothetical. I suggest caution. If such hypothetical leads you to address her pertinent pro and con perspectives and policy-level arguments from class and materials, it may work. But the danger is that such a hypothetical may not engage her arguments and is therefore seen as yet another illustration of student denial and evasion, avoiding the exam problem in favor of a made-up student substitute. Keep in mind that all professors emphatically prefer that their problems be answered, not avoided, and in the form they prescribed in their interrogatory.

Summary of CIRI(P) Writing Formats

• CIRI(P) ONE	Foundational format for resolution of mostly straightforward issues
• CIRI(P) ONE(a)	For pressure-cooker essays with ten, twelve or more issues
• CIRI(P) TWO	Applied when resolving one issue requires two (or more) rules
• CIRI(P) THREE	Applied when resolving an issue requires more complex rule (or standard) statements with elaborating definitions
• CIRI(P) THREE(a)	Applied when resolving an issue requires standards or tests or factors to apply a rule, or requires unfolding an overall issue into intermediate and more specific issues
• CIRI(P) THREE(b)	Applied when resolving an issue requires unfolding a multi-step argument with closely related rules
• CIRI(P) FOUR	Applied when resolving an issue requires invalidating or replacing of "applicable" rule

Conclusion

The CIRI(P) formats for exam writing embody some of the different architectures of legal argument that you gradually absorb in your years of law school and eventually practice. Contrast the earlier non-exam-level examples of the formats with the complexities of the latter exam-level examples. Please note the scaffolding of language in both issue spotting and argument making, from concrete to very abstract.

See all these CIRI(P) formats not simply as organizing and writing formats for exams, but as reflections of the deep structure of law. All forms of lawyerly performance, including exams, elaborated legal memoranda, appellate briefs and oral arguments, exemplify this deep structure. Though presentation varies sharply, all incorporate conclusions, issues, legal authority, interweaving, explicit or implicit uses of policy, and advocacy writing or oral argument. In contrast to the CIRI(P) formats for quick first-draft exam writing of three or four essay problems in three or four hours, legal memoranda and briefs are usually prepared over days or even weeks. There, conscientious lawyers engage in meticulous research and a considered, detailed appraisal of the most relevant and persuasive legal arguments, citing all relevant legal authorities in carefully crafted writings. In contrast, exam writing is not so elaborated but very direct and concise. As you know, do not emulate the discursive arguments in many appellate cases on your exams.

On Looking Back

These writing formats remain useful in many ways. They direct your analyses towards cogent exam argument and away from writing out canned, outline-based mini-lectures triggered by the exam facts. They minimize meandering, disorganized writing. Both rob you of any chance for an 'A' or 'B+' grade, even though you may know a great deal. Practicing the formats during the semester should also relieve anxiety and make you much more confident on the day of the exam. With practice, and after issue spotting and brief outlining, you could almost automatically write out the varied CIRI(P) formats to resolve exam issues in a manner that meets each professor's identified expectations.

The CIRI(P) formats also improve on the older IRAC format (Issue, Rule, Application, Conclusion) that is often recommended. First, as this chapter details, the simple, one-size-fits-all character of the IRAC formula misses the complexity of modes of legal argument — the different architectures — that you need to apply for exams and practice. Moreover, all other substitutes for IRAC that I have seen also miss this patent complexity.

Second, remember that, unlike IRAC, models for writing legal memoranda and appellate briefs direct you to begin with the conclusion. For example, appellate briefs begin each argument with a heading/conclusion (Point One, Point Two, etc.) so that the judge can immediately begin to assess whether or not your detailed argument on that "Point" supports your stated conclusion. Imagine yourself as a judge. You would want to know up front, not later, what a lawyer is seeking, i.e., what the objective of her argument is. Remember, the "C" in CIRI(P) stands for "Conclusion". Professor Karl Llewellyn, one of the giants of twentieth century jurisprudence, in his legendary *The Bramble Bush* (p. 105), also "insists," in his usual vivid and compelling language, that students "begin with a conclusion. If you do not know where you are going, it is damnably hard to get there. It is even harder for the instructor to see how you got there… But if you know where you are going, you can get there."

Third, the IRAC formula could imply that you routinely reason to your conclusion as you write your argument. Don't do this, not on exams,[12] and not in practice. This process can easily lead to unfocused writing instead of the concise, focused result that you need. In a legal context, your writing should present your prior figuring out of the key facts, issue, legal authority, interweaving, and conclusion. Before beginning to write a judicial opinion, good judges know their conclusion, and at least the outline of how they will argue to that conclusion.[13] Before writing a legal memorandum, good lawyers know their conclusion and at least the skeleton of their argument. Legal scholars do voluminous research, reflection and outlining before writing. I know: I've done it. The purpose and end result of most legal writing is advocacy writing, a form of normative rhetoric, an applied ethics, rather than a discovery process akin to a scientific hypothesis with a verification procedure. Advocacy is normative rhetoric, not science. Conclusions go first.

Lastly, bar examiners in New York — and I suspect elsewhere — understandably direct you to begin each essay argument with your conclusion so that they too can immediately begin to assess the details of each argument you make. Partners in law firms and other legal supervisors also want your oral or written conclusion up front for the identical reason.

POSTSCRIPT: NOTES FROM RECENT COACHING EXPERIENCE ON INDIVIDUALIZING IN EXAM ARGUMENT

Diagnosing the instructor is as important…
as diagnosing a judge will later be.
Karl Llewellyn

My internet coaching of students from law schools throughout the country has underlined and dramatized the central importance of dialing into each professor's exam wavelength and particularizing

---

[12] There is an exception where the problem is completely indeterminate in conclusion, and your entire exam effort is all back-and-forth argument. In this category of problem, the conclusion could be inserted at the end of your argument, and is usually not important since it could go either way. Even here, however, your back-and-forth argument should be carefully outlined *before* you write. See, e.g., the "Olivia Warbucks" problem and the responding strong professorial argument in Chapter Six.

[13] Sometimes appellate judges comment privately that "the opinion did not write," meaning that the writing revealed another path or difficulty with the intended analysis and conclusion, and a resulting redirection, including even a different conclusion than originally contemplated. Writing a legal brief or memorandum after much preparation can also expose such a problem or new path. That could happen to you, too, on exams but, unlike the writing performed by judges and lawyers, exam writing under intense time pressure discourages such re-envisioning. The remedy again: relentless practice during the semester to reduce these troubling occasions on exams.

your response on that wavelength. Consider, for example, a student whose model exam answer from his tort professor featured framing of each issue triggered by his essay fact pattern with an explicit use of the name of a class-discussed case and its relevant principle or rule — an exceptional framing indeed. Contrast this emphatic professorial direction with the same student's civil procedure professor whose model answers featured no such direction, only scant reference to class-discussed cases for his single exam Type One issue-spotting problem, and who also consistently chooses policy-type problems for the remaining sixty percent of his exams.

Compare this student's experience with another student at a different school whose tort exam is mostly multiple-choice questions that reputedly are copied from bar review materials. Consider also a paragraph-based, issue-spotting problem in any course with four or five issues contrasted with such a problem with eight, nine or more issues without much more time allotted. There's also the Type Two multi-issue problem whose fact pattern poses a single overall issue that must then be deconstructed into a series of sub-issues. In addition, many professors routinely expect you to respond to a single issue with two (or more) arguments; others only sometimes expect them. There are those who expect you to "get to maybe"; most, I believe, expect you to construct the best argument given the facts, relevant doctrine, and the professor's expectations while also explaining, of course, why it is superior to alternatives. In recent years, I have also been somewhat surprised to see exam fact patterns that ask you to respond directly to specific questions without any issue spotting needed, and which rigidly limit you to a number of lines on the exam paper or very brief allotted time for responses.

Manifestly, preparation for each of these exams (and many others) must include the implicit direction from each professor's preferred exam choices. To illustrate, for any mostly multiple-choice exam, preparation is straightforward: the student should mainly systematically practice with multiple-choice questions from that professor's old questions and explanations, if available, and if not, with many hundreds or more of such tort (or other) questions and explanations from other sources (e.g., BarBri and PMBR, bar review groups). For the professor whose old exams reveal that he routinely presents Type-One, paragraph-based multi-issue problems as well as the Type-Two, single overall multi-issue problem that must be deconstructed into sub-issues, practice both forms weekly during the semester. For the professor who routinely expects two (or more) responses to each issue, practice accordingly.

For any professor who routinely poses a predominately policy-type problem or more, you prepare by practicing such problems for a proportionate preparation time. For the problem packed with issues, you practice especially concise argument making; this contrasts with the relatively more elaborated arguments necessary in resolving the problem posing four or five issues. And so on for each professor. Indeed, to seal the point, please review the striking variety of 'A' arguments in Chapter Six to appreciate fully the need to individualize for each professor.

From my coaching as well as decades-long experience in teaching, it is clear that the frequent advice that "all law professors want the same thing on their exams — issue spotting and lawyerly resolution of each issue" — is too simple and misleading, and any related advice to sometimes disregard the particular professorial interrogatory in favor of a standardized form of response is highly risky. Life varies, professors vary, and continuing study of their actual exams and 'A' responding arguments confirms extensive variation in their expectations. As noted, there simply is no one-size-fits-all approach or form for these exams. Don't be misled. Early in each semester you should identify each professor's signature pattern of exam problems, what their interrogatories require and the related argument making. Then, practice accordingly throughout the semester.

Hopscotching arguments

My continuing study of law exams also reveals occasional so-called "strong" arguments, distributed to students or on file in the library, that are plainly dubious. The most common such argument is a hopscotching style in which arguments for liability are often embodied in one sentence or so, and the next sentence claims to establish a different liability. My own trial and appellate experience, as well as my study of leading jurisprudential thinkers, leads me to brand such exam writing as conclusory and thus unlawyerly. It reminds me of the legion of weak lawyers who often engage in versions of such argument making. It simply takes more than a sentence to construct a legal argument for liability. In sharp contrast, a legal argument rejecting liability may sometimes be performed in one sentence as illustrated in the school paper censorship example (p. 86). Sometimes, too, these so-called "strong" arguments contain outright, even embarrassing, errors. If a professor's sample "strong" exam argument exhibits these weaknesses, I recommend that you still emulate it — but only for that professor's exam. Your role on an exam does not include correcting any professor. Perhaps you may do so later in an anonymous evaluation.

Standout exam writing

Lastly, my coaching experience has also led me to focus on the ingredients of "standout" exam argument making that calls for 'A' grading even among a cohort of strong exams and a curve imposed restriction on the number of 'A' grades that may be given. A student in one of the nation's most highly ranked law schools contacted me after his straight B+ grades in each of his first-semester exams placed him in the "middle" of his class. Clearly, his exam practice was thorough and his skills strong. But, in a class of very strong exam-takers, his exams did not earn the 'A' grading. My coaching focused on identifying the ingredients of standout exam argument making particular to each of his professors, as revealed by their exam priorities on old exams and in the classroom.

To that end, imagine yourself as each of your professors. You inevitably taught at several levels. Even if you gave priority to legal rules in your course, the reality that rules are policies writ concrete compelled you to explain rules in light of their policy purposes, and overwhelmingly, professors do so, though in sharply different degrees. Or perhaps you stressed policy as the priority but you almost certainly illustrated how contrasting policies drive contrasting rules, and the resulting need for choice and justification of such choice. Or you stressed theory, but that entails implicit policy that should be understood as theory writ concrete at two levels. During the semester as a student, do your best to get inside their heads: cultivate an exam blend for each professor in your framing and argument making. The 'A' grades go to those who aptly embody their blends — their voices in impressive arguments.

Candidates for such "standout" arguments include the two-way arguments detailed on page 92. Of course, the basics are all there, including the issues, contrasting rules, interweaving and conflicting policies (and thus earn the B+ grades). But it's all performed in such a focused, concise and impressive manner, without any of the usual off-base embellishment in discursive writing. There is power in such cogent argument making. Judges admire it, and it commands 'A' grading. Another illustration is set forth on page 104, detailing a multi-step argument unpacking a general issue into closely related rules that are hostage to one another. Indeed, the ideal of no-extra-words accomplished there is another marker for standout arguments, and yet nothing in pertinent doctrine is omitted: no step is missing or truncated, as is often seen in grading these or other complex arguments. For a classic Constitutional law example of such argument, see the 'A' student version in "Let Them Eat Cake" (p. 153) For a strong contract example that comes close, see "Books, Books, Books" (p. 145). For a policy example, see the "Policy Problem" with its compelling argument. (p. 133).

All these arguments are relatively concise. They are also cogent and persuasive in their advocacy for liability or against it, or for or against a policy position. Even their rule-level argument exemplifies deep multi-level understanding rather than simply surface knowledge, copying relevant mini-sections from an outline, or college-type regurgitation. Strive to write such cogent advocacy arguments every week throughout the semester, carefully fine-tuned to each professor's expectations, and you should be able to produce them on exams. They are certainly the ideal for weekly exam writing practice.

Sample Exam Problems and Arguments

INTRODUCTION

The diversity and challenges detailed in the following exam problems and arguments are in response to the types of exam problems that you will likely confront. These arguments also illustrate that law exams are commonly about core rules—and exceptions to such rules.

They also illustrate three levels of exam performance: an 'A,' 'A-' or B+ argument; a mediocre argument (roughly a 'C+' or 'C'); and a poor argument (a 'C-' or 'D'). The comments on the left side of some pages portray the reactions of a professor in applying the six criteria for grading (p. 97). Note that most arguments have explicit or implicit issue spotting, specification of the applicable rule or principle, and the interweaving of rule elements with the red-hot facts (or with relevant principle-derived standards, tests or factors).

Law-school professors prepared the tort and contract 'A' arguments to "Mary Lee" and "Olivia Warbucks." Do not be discouraged if you feel that you could never write such an argument. I believe that no professor or student can do so in the allotted exam time. You can do very well without matching the quality and scope of such arguments. The two criminal-law 'A' arguments responding to my "Speluncean Explorers" problem are actual student responses completed within the allotted exam time. Please note that there are two different ways of arguing: the first 'A' argument is the conventional prose style; the second 'A' argument is a more concise and unusual detailed outline. The 'A' arguments to the criminal law "Policy Problem," the contract "Books, Books, Books" problem, the civil procedure "Blowing in the Wind" problem, and the constitutional "Let Them Eat Cake" problem, are also student responses.[1] Notice, too, the markedly different frequencies for arguing: e.g., from relatively concrete, as in "Mary Lee" and the "Speluncean Explorers," to more elaborate and even more intricate, as in "Olivia Warbucks," "Books, Books, Books," "Blowing in the Wind," and "Let Them Eat Cake."

On the pages immediately following, before the "Mary Lee" tort exam argument is set forth, the art and craft of a quick exam-outlining process is illustrated. This includes the detailing of the five issue-spotting steps previously explicated (pp. 51-53) and then brief outlining of the exam arguments.

---

[1] Editing has not perfected these various arguments. Even 'A' arguments can be far from perfect. As noted, the hurried, first-draft writing required in law exams is not the detailed writing of a carefully edited memorandum of law or appellate brief typical in law practice. Nevertheless, strive to follow all grammatical and writing protocols on exams. Failing to do so, especially if the errors are numerous or glaring, can distract the grader. Remember: an 'A' paper also looks like an 'A' paper.

It was 5:30 p.m. on a weekday. Mary Lee was at the West 4th Street stop of the Eighth Avenue (IND) subway. She got off the A (express) train and walked quickly across the platform to catch the local (AA) train, which was waiting in the station.

Just as Lee got near the door of the AA train, a passenger (later identified as Frank Meyer) ran out of the train without looking around him, tripped Lee, and caused her to fall. She landed half in and half out of the crowded AA train.

Susan Barr, a passenger on the train, helped Lee into the train just as the subway doors were closing. However, when the doors closed, Barr's handbag was caught on the outside of the door, except for the straps, which she still held in her hand. A purse-snatcher tugged hard on the handbag; Barr lost her grip on the straps, and the handbag was stolen.

Lee's ankle was badly broken, and her knee was sprained from the fall. She hobbled off the train at 14th Street on one foot and took a cab to St. Luke's Hospital, where the intern alone on duty in its emergency room who was inexperienced, but who used all the skill he had, misset her ankle. It never properly healed and she has a limp for life.

Barr's handbag contained $300 in cash and a valuable ring.

Meanwhile, back at the scene of the accident in the West 4th Street Station, a police officer who saw Meyer trip Lee took his name and address. He learned that Meyer is the 18-year-old son of wealthy parents.

Assume that Lee and Barr can locate any potential defendant.

What are Lee's remedies? What are Barr's remedies? What is the likelihood of success of each?

(55 Minutes)

Mary Lee After a Quick Reading

It was 5:30 p.m. on a weekday. Mary Lee was at the West 4th Street stop of the Eighth Avenue (IND) subway. She got off the A (express) train and walked quickly across the platform to catch the local (AA) train, which was waiting in the station.

Just as Lee got near the door of the AA train, a passenger (later identified as Frank Meyer) ran out of the train without looking around, <u>tripped Lee, and caused her to fall</u>. She landed <u>half in and half out</u> of the crowded AA train.

Susan Barr, a passenger on the train, helped Lee into the train just as the subway doors were closing. However, when the doors closed, Barr's handbag was caught on the outside of the door, except for the straps, which she still held in her hand. A <u>purse-snatcher</u> tugged hard on the handbag; Barr <u>lost her grip</u> on the straps, and the <u>handbag was stolen</u>.

<u>Lee's ankle was badly broken</u>, and her knee was <u>sprained</u> <u>from the fall</u>. She hobbled off the train at 14th street on one foot and took a cab to St. Luke's Hospital, where the intern <u>alone on duty in its emergency room</u> who was <u>inexperienced</u>, but who used <u>all the skill</u> he had, <u>misset her ankle</u>. It never properly healed and she has a <u>limp for life</u>.

---

[2] Mary Lee" is a tort example of the popular Type-One law-exam architecture—the multi-issue problem with many mostly paragraph-based issues (p. 48), and a more challenging example of the CIRI(P) ONE writing format (pp. 80-89).

Barr's handbag contained $300 in cash and a valuable ring.

Meanwhile, back at the scene of the accident in the West 4th Street Station, a police officer who saw Meyer trip Lee took his name and address. He learned that Meyer is the 18-year-old son of wealthy parents.

Assume that Lee and Barr can locate any potential defendant.

Interrog. √ What are Lee's / remedies?   √ What are Barr's / remedies?
√ What is the likelihood of success of each?

(55 minutes)

Applying the Five Issue-Spotting Steps for Type One Problems

The first step (p. 51) is to go right to the question at the end that inquires about the "remedies" of Lee and Barr. You immediately have a riveting focus: the parties and behaviors that inflicted harms on Lee and Barr.

The second step (p. 51), determining the type of problem, should be evident at a glance after semester-long practice: it's a classic Type-One, paragraph-based, multi-issue problem (p. 48). You can therefore expect that there are likely to be many issues—and there are. It explodes with issues.

In the third and fourth steps (p. 52), you spotlight each legal conflict in the problem by identifying the serial parties in conflict, and then adding the act and the legal harm. With semester-long practice, you should be able to apply both steps together. In the fifth step (pp. 52-53), you capture the legal meaning and resulting issue(s) posed by each such conflict, aided by light-bulb issue-spotting and your Exam Checklist. Do not apply the safety net here, the HATRI decoder, for a simple reason: you do not need it.

1) Lee v. Meyer: Meyer, not looking, ran out of train and trips Lee whose ankle is broken → Neg

2) Lee v. Subway: Conductor closed door while Lee laid half-in & half-out of train → possible Neg but no harm & thus no Neg

3) Barr v. Purs. Snat: Purs. Snat. pulls handbag from Barr's grasp → conversion and battery

4) Lee v. Intern: Intern missets Lee's broken ankle with limp for life → medical negligence

5) Lee v. Meyer's parents: 18-yr.-old Meyer has rich parents, so what! Meyer is adult → no liability

So far, you have identified five legal conflicts with their parties, behavior and clear and not-so-clear harms. Assuming you have studied these topics, you should have Exam Checklist categories under "Neg." (negligence), for "Resp. Sup." (respondeat superior), and "Duty to Super" (supervise). Just seeing those category listings should jog your memory (light-bulb issue spotting) that employers, including hospitals, are strictly liable for the negligence perpetrated by an employee (here the intern) in the course of performing his or her duties. You also note that the "inexperienced intern" was working "alone" in the Hospital's emergency room, a glaring breach of the duty to supervise such an intern. You have quickly decoded the sixth and seventh legal conflicts, and two more issues then burst forth.

6) Lee v. Hosp. → *resp. super*

7) Lee v. Hosp. → failure to supervise

Scan your Checklist categories again under the topic of "Neg." You should see a category listing for "Orig. Tortf." (original torfeasor). The light bulb should ignite: Meyer, of course, is such an original tortfeasor.

8) Lee v. Meyer again: Meyer as original tortf → liable for all consequent neg. torts but not intent. tort and theft of purse snatcher

Note that with constant practice throughout the semester, the use of your own abbreviations should also mean less writing than above.

If your light-bulb issue spotting is strong after semester-long practice

Rather than applying the systematic five-step process, do your light-bulb issue spotting right on the exam problem as follows. If you can do it, you save time. Note the underlining of the red-hot facts that spell out the parties, their behaviors and harms that spell out the legal conflicts.

Mary Lee After Second Meticulous Reading

It was 5:30 p.m. on a weekday. Mary Lee was at the West 4th Street stop of the Eighth Avenue (IND) subway. She got off the A (express) train and walked quickly across the platform to catch the local (AA) train, which was waiting in the station.

Stage setter only

Neg. & Orig. tort-feasor

Just as Lee got near the door of the AA train, a passenger (later identified as Frank Meyer) ran out of the train / without / looking / around / him / tripped/ Lee, and / caused her to fall. (She landed half in and half out of the crowded AA train).

Susan Barr, a passenger on the train, (helped Lee into the train just as the subway doors were closing.) However, (when the doors closed,) Barr's handbag was caught on the outside of the door, except for the straps, which she still held in her hand. A / purse / snatcher / tugged / hard/ on the handbag; Barr lost her grip on the straps, and the handbag was / stolen /.

Subway liable?

Theft= Conversion/ Battery

Intern liable: -Med. neg.

Lee's ankle was badly broken, and her knee was sprained from the fall. She hobbled off the train at 14th street on one foot and took a cab to St. Luke's Hospital, where the intern alone on duty in its emergency room who was inexperienced but who used all the skill he had, misset her ankle. It never properly healed and she has a limp for life.

Hos. l.: Neg; & res. super.

Barr's handbag contained $300 in cash and a valuable ring.

Parents liable?

Meanwhile, back at the scene of the accident in the West 4th Street Station, a police officer who saw Meyer trip Lee took his name and address. He learned that Meyer is the 18-year-old son of wealthy parents.

Assume that Lee and Barr can locate any potential defendant.

Interrog.

√ What are Lee's remedies? √ What are Barr's remedies?
√ What is the likelihood of success of each?

(55 minutes)

From issue spotting to brief outlining of your exam argument

As you know, spotting the issues is the *sine qua non:* you obviously can't resolve an issue that you have not spotted. But as you also know, a lawyerly argument requires more: an accurately stated rule (by elements), and then interweaving with the red-hot facts. To accomplish these tasks, concise outlining that drives your exam writing is necessary. Again, use of your own abbreviations should greatly shorten this outlining; with the amount of detail varying sharply from person to person.

Meyer	Intern	Hospital
Liable for negligence to Lee Duty (Passenger) Reasonable Care (Meyer) Breach (Trips Lee) Causation (but for) (proximate) Harm (broken ankle)	Liable for Medical negligence to Lee Doctor's Test: customary & usual, minimum competency skill	Liable to Lee for failure to supervise "Alone in emergency room" and Liable for negligence of intern—*Respondeat Superior* (within scope of job)

Snatcher	Meyer as Original Tortfeasor for ensuing torts

Liable to Barr for battery
 	
  Harmful touching without permission —handbag tugging is battery
 	
  and
 	
Liable to Barr for conversion: dominion and control over goods against plaintiff's rights
 	
  Theft = conversion
	Liable to Lee for all ensuing
	
	—ordinary negligence of hospital and intern
	
	But not for snatcher's intentional torts:
	
	battery and conversion (not foreseeable)

Subway	**Parents**
Not liable—insufficient facts	Not liable—Meyer is **adult**

VOILÁ!—THE 'A' ARGUMENT TO MARY LEE

COMMENTS	LEE'S REMEDIES	
Brief overall topic sentence to specify sequence of arguments.	Lee has remedies against Meyer, the intern, and St. Luke's Hospital.	
	Meyer liable to Lee for negligence	**C**
Begins with statement of conclusion as the heading and then specification of issue. Concise statement of negligence rule with all elements. Good, quick interweaving of red-hot facts with elements of negligence. Please notice that the interweaving also includes fact-specific elaboration of core elements of negligence rule, a sophisticated blending that requires much prior practice during the semester.	The issue is whether Meyer is liable to Lee for this tort arising from his careless running from the subway, thereby injuring Lee? A cause-of-action in negligence requires that the defendant breach a legal duty owed to the plaintiff with the breach causing, both factually (but for) and legally (proximately), actual damage to the plaintiff. In running out of the train without looking around and by tripping Lee, Meyer is *breaching* the duty of reasonable care that he owes (the duty of one subway passenger to another passenger) to protect Lee against unreasonable risk creation when leaving a subway train. When his conduct then causes her immediately to fall, break her ankle, and sprain her knee, his conduct is both the factual (but for) and legal	**Is** **R** **In**

This strong argument is five sentences. This level of legal writing springs from gradual attainment of a zeroing-in understanding.	(proximate) cause of her injuries. Her injury was either actually foreseeable, or should have been foreseeable, and was as *closely connected* in time and space with Meyer's breach of his duty as is possible.	
	Intern liable to Lee for medical negligence	**C**
Also begins with conclusion and issue. Relevant rule specified and elaborated. There is a terse but effective blend of key facts and rule elements in interweaving. Note that the entire argument, after the heading, is only six sentences. During the semester, practice writing weekly these concise, cogent lawyerly sentences and arguments.	The issue is whether the inexperienced intern, who missets Lee's ankle while alone in the emergency room, is liable for this tort. Using "all the skill he had" is no defense. His judgment violated the objective standard: whether a reasonable intern in these circumstances would have so acted (as a doctor, the intern is held to the standard of what is *customary and usual medical practice, at least the minimum common skill*). A reasonable intern would recognize his inexperience, seek more expert assistance and wait for it. Lee's broken ankle and sprained knee were not life threatening—no emergency existed. His failure to wait and his faulty setting of Lee's ankle directly caused, both factually and proximately, her "limp for life."	**Is** **R** **In**
	St. Luke's Hospital liable to Lee for negligent failure to supervise intern & in Respondent Superior	**C**
Good issue statement and specification of St. Luke's duty to supervise its inexperienced interns Basic negligence rule stated above need not be restated. Conclusory statement at end of argument about factual and proximate causation is terse but adequate here on these clear facts. Vicarious liability theory, which imposes strict liability, is raised and quickly argued. Keep in mind that this particular liability of the hospital is separate from its negligent failure to supervise, which was argued in the prior paragraph. One-sentence policy statement strengthens the argument by adding analytical and persuasive value. It is also one compelling illustration of when policy should be specified on exams (and in practice).	The first issue here is whether Lee has a negligence action against St. Luke's for failing to reasonably supervise an "inexperienced" intern working alone on an early weekday evening in its emergency room. It's a classic "failure to supervise." If supervisory personnel were actually aware of what this intern was doing, they failed to stop the medical negligence. If they were not aware, they breached their duty of reasonable supervision. *Either way,* St. Luke's is liable to Lee for the harm. Their failure is also the unmistakable factual (but-for) and legal (proximate) cause of the aggravation of Lee's injuries. The second issue here is whether the negligence of the intern renders the hospital strictly liable on the theory of vicarious liability. The intern on duty in the hospital's emergency room is patently acting "within the scope of his employment," so the doctrine of *respondeat superior* applies: the intern's negligence (see above) is imputed to St. Luke's. The employer is therefore *strictly* liable for the negligence of its employee. The policy reason for this rule is that the employer with "deep pockets" can better absorb such expected costs, acquire insurance, and also take precautions (e.g., supervision) designed to prevent such employee negligence.	**Is** **R** **In** **Is** **R** **In** **P**

	Meyer also Liable for the Intern's and St. Luke's Negligence	C
Negligence by intern and St. Luke's is deemed foreseeable and thus not a superseding cause. Good analysis in well-focused sentences with no extra words. Meyer's added liability here flows easily from prior analysis of his original liability as well as the analysis of the liability of the intern and the hospital.	The additional rule is that the original tortfeasor is liable for ordinary forms of ensuing negligence that *aggravate* the victim's injuries. Such ordinary, not gross, negligence is deemed foreseeable, and the factual and legal causal chain from Meyer's negligent conduct to Lee's injuries remains unbroken. Her injuries were plainly aggravated by the negligence of the intern and St. Luke's.	R In
	Conductor and Subway Co. not Liable	C
Again, the negligence rule is not restated. Negative issue raised and quickly resolved. Recall the underlying, fundamental and pervasive principle that the absence of one required element means there is no cause-of-action [or crime], and it applies to all subjects.	There is an issue raised by the conductor closing the doors on Lee. The facts are *unclear* and *insufficient* as to whether he did not see her when he reasonably should have, or he did see her and closed the doors on her, or he reasonably did not see her. But in any event, *no injury resulted to Lee* because Barr pulled her inside. No actual harm, a required element, means there is *no* cause-of-action for negligence, no remedy at all.	Is In
	The Wealthy Parents not liable	C
Another quick raising and resolution of a negative issue.	Lee has no remedy against Meyer's "wealthy parents." On these facts, the parents have no duties here. Meyer is an adult and responsible for his own torts.	R In
	BARR'S REMEDIES	
Topic sentence indicates sequence of this segment. Remember any potential defendant was available.	Barr has remedies for battery and conversion against the purse snatcher.	
	Purse Snatcher Liable to Barr for Battery	C
Explicit issue specification. Correct statement of black-letter rule. Good, quick interweaving of red-hot facts and elements. Do you appreciate that the terse and conclusory interweaving here is permitted because the facts are so compelling in establishing liability? Such competent argument making also predisposes graders in the student's favor whenever there is any doubt as to completeness.	The issue is whether the snatcher, who tugs hard on Barr's handbag while Barr tugs on the straps on her side of the subway door, is liable to Barr for this intentional tort. Battery is the intentional and unprivileged offensive or harmful touching by the defendant against the plaintiff without the plaintiff's consent. The purse snatcher's tugging hard on the handbag on one side of the door while on the other Barr held the straps demonstrated both intent to inflict a *harmful touching* as well as the act, causation, and harm requirements. The battery is complete.	Is R In

Note the application of the additional-rule form of argument (p. 98). Note also the one-sentence raising of secondary issue—a quick but lawyerly response to unclear facts.	The additional rule required is that the touching need not be against the person; tugging on the handbag whose straps are in Barr's hands is sufficient. The rule is that a battery may be completed if a person's handbag, cane, hat, or clothing, etc., is struck. If, in addition, Barr suffered apprehension of such a touching—not clear at all on these facts—there would also be an assault, an intentional infliction of an apprehension of a battery.	**Add R.** **In**
	Purse snatcher liable to Barr for Conversion	**C**
Correct statement of black-letter rule in two sentences illustrating again the additional rule form of argument. These rules emerge from embedded tort cases. Apt and quick interweaving. Note the reference to the description ("tugging hard…") just above in the prior argument. But as a general rule, be cautious in such reference. For example, don't ask your grader to search for it a page or two back.	The issue is whether the snatcher's theft of the handbag is also a conversion? Conversion is the intentional and unprivileged exercise of dominion or control over goods completely inconsistent with the plaintiff's rights, so that it is just to require that the converter pay the full value of the goods. The additional rule required is that a *theft, as here, is also always a conversion.* When the purse snatcher manages to tug the purse from Barr's grip as described above, his intent to seize possession is clear, as are the act, causation, and harm elements; Barr loses her handbag and its contents of $300 and the ring.	**Is** **R** **In**
	Barr has no remedy against Meyer for battery and the conversion of the bag, ring and money.	**C**
Good issue raising and statement of general rule and then the additional rule that follows and results in no liability for Meyer arising from these particular facts. The last sentence here is an explanation of the general rule stated just above in the third sentence. It's a kind of policy justification for the rule and demonstrates to the grader that you know both the rule and understand its rationale and application here. Impressive and illustrates what is meant by a standout argument that mandates the highest grading.	The issue is whether Meyer is liable to Barr for the snatcher's battery and conversion. "Peril invites rescue," is a tort maxim and thus Meyer owes an independent duty to the rescuer as a foreseeable plaintiff and would be liable if she, e.g., were injured in rescuing Lee (the rescuer doctrine). But an intentional tort or crime *breaks the chain of causation* unless the crime or tort was foreseeable. There are no facts here to support a finding of foreseeability. Factual (but for) cause exists, but Meyer's legal causality is ended. The intentional tort or crime is ordinarily a *superseding cause* because it operates so directly, immediately, and completely as to become the new and effective cause of the ensuing harm.	**Is** **R** **In** **P**

The relatively terse style illustrated in this mostly paragraph-based, Type-One argument is driven by the multitude of issues to be analyzed within the fifty-five minute time frame. Additional time or fewer issues would result in a more elaborated response. This form of problem is sometimes aptly called a "racehorse."

Do not be intimidated by this very strong argument. You do not have to attain this strength to get an 'A' or 'B+.' No one can write such a response in fifty minutes. But it does demonstrate what you should be aspiring to with your semester-long practice. The very poor argument below illustrates what you should avoid. Contrast both arguments.

A VERY POOR ARGUMENT TO MARY LEE

An unfocused, meandering way to begin.	There are many causes of action here in this story.
The issue is misconceived. Meyer violates his duty to act reasonably in these circumstances, i.e., not to run "out of the train without looking around him," thereby tripping Lee. It's irrelevant that Mary is a stranger. We all have this general duty to act reasonably in different circumstances that pose a risk of harm to others.	Initially, Meyer should have looked before he ran. If he had, he probably would not have knocked Mary Lee down and injured her. It looks on the surface like negligence, a breach of duty causing actual harm, but Mary Lee is a stranger to Meyer and he has no duty to aid her. It is not true that every accidental harm gives rise to a cause-of-action. These facts illustrate one such instance: no breach exists because there is no duty to be breached.
Confused. The student is pursuing a completely wrong path for formulating and analyzing these facts. If the negligence rule had been defined into its five elements, that detailing instead would drive the argument down a lawyerly path.	It is true that there are exceptions to this general rule that there is no duty to aid—e.g., if there is a special relationship between the parties, such as parents and children, husband and wife, lifeguard and swimmer, etc. These facts, however, do not fit within these exceptions and hence there is no duty to aid. The fact that Meyer knew she had apparently fallen and kept going is troublesome from a moral point of view but tort principles and moral principles are not interchangeable.
These facts do not spell out a "regrettable accident." Negating an intentional tort issue here is also entirely misconceived. Avoid such gross category mistakes. Facts, instead, spell out negligence.	Nor is there any intentional tort here. It's true that there is a harmful contact as required for battery and there is surely an actual harm—Mary Lee's broken ankle and sprained knee. Nevertheless, the intentional tort of battery requires an intent to do a harm and these facts show a regrettable accident.
Peril indeed invites rescue and such rescue is deemed foreseeable, but a crime and intentional tort are ordinarily not foreseeable. Unnecessary to simply state what the question postulates, a waste of time. No interweaving of key facts	If Mary Lee is a legal stranger to Meyer, he is certainly a stranger to Susan Barr, the rescuer. Barr had no duty from any legal source to help Mary Lee. However commendable her act is morally and socially, this act is legally gratuitous. "Peril invites rescue" but the rescuer cannot create a legal duty where none exists. Of course, Barr has a cause of action against the purse-snatcher for conversion. It should be remembered that

with elements of rule. Conclusory last sentence is definitely not interweaving.	the question postulates that "any potential defendant" can be located. Conversion is the intentional and unprivileged exercise of dominion or control over goods inconsistent with the plaintiff's rights. The purse-snatcher certainly did this.
This exam is torts, not criminal law, and the question therefore asks about tort remedies, not crimes. This is irrelevant, unresponsive, a waste of precious time, and hence very unlawyerly.	In addition, this purse-snatcher has committed a robbery. Robbery is a forcible larceny. As to larceny, the purse-snatcher did engage in a trespassory taking and carrying away of Barr's handbag with the intent to steal (keep) it. He also used actual force to pry the bag from Barr's hands (though threats of force would suffice). Hence, there is a robbery.
Incorrect rule statement. An unfocused beginning is compounded by a discussion that quickly veers away from the main issue of the intern's medical negligence to the irrelevant issue of punitive damages. This student never returns to the main issue here.	The intern at St. Luke's misset her ankle, but the facts show that he "used all the skill he had." It is too bad that she has a "limp for life." The intern has a duty to exercise reasonable care toward Lee in these circumstances. The issue is whether he fulfilled his duty to Lee. In arguing this question, the fact that he "used all his skill" is relevant but not decisive. It is relevant on a possible issue of punitive damages that might be raised by Lee against the intern. For punitive damages, the fact that the intern did the best he could is relevant on the test of whether or not his conduct was "malicious" or "outrageous." It is not necessarily dispositive on these issues, but it is relevant.
This presentation implies, without explanation, that if Meyer is liable, the parents may be liable. Wrong.	The wealthy parents of Meyer are not liable. Meyer is not liable so they are not. They cannot be liable without their son being liable. Their liability is derivative.
A good discussion in part of this secondary issue. The mistaken issue statements in this answer illustrate the centrality of correct issue spotting.	The subway company is not liable. The conductor owes a duty of reasonable care to Mary Lee in not closing the doors on her. He breached this duty but caused no actual harm to her because Barr, the rescuer, managed to pull Mary Lee into the car just as the subway doors were closing. No actual damages, an essential element, means there is no cause-of-action for negligence.

Additional Comments

This poor argument responding to the "Mary Lee" problem, *inter alia*, misses major issues about Lee's causes-of-action against St. Luke's for failure of supervision and for vicarious liability (*respondeat superior*), the absence of superseding causes in the negligence of the intern and St. Luke's, and Meyer's liability as an original tortfeasor for the subsequent negligence of the intern and the hospital.

THE SPELUNCEAN EXPLORERS PROBLEM[3]

In a classic law-review article, Lon Fuller, a noted jurisprudential analyst, created a group of cave explorers—The Speluncean Explorers—who, after being trapped in a cave-in, ate Roger Whetmore, one of the explorers. As a result, the other Explorers survived to be rescued. The surviving Speluncean Explorers were convicted of Whetmore's murder and sentenced to death. That conviction and sentence was affirmed.

Happily for the defendants, the Chief Executive had his regular semiannual astrological consultation shortly before the scheduled execution. The astrologer advised the Chief Executive that the stars were not right, and the latter pardoned all of the defendants.

After their release to great popular approval, the Explorers discussed new vistas for exploration and decided to explore some challenging caves on the moon discovered by the first astronauts, and entitled their new effort, "the Roger Whetmore Memorial Expedition." With NASA's help, the Explorers were transferred to the moon on the spaceship Enterprise.

The Explorers entered a deep lunar cave, which had an intricate series of passageways. On the first night in the cave, Happy, one of the explorers, resolved to kill another of the explorers (his wife Pollyanna) because of festering anger over certain personal slights. Happy and Pollyanna were on a separate side exploration apart from the other Explorers. Happy set his wristwatch alarm for 3:00 a.m., figuring that he would awaken and kill Pollyanna by disconnecting her oxygen supply. Happy then fell into a deep sleep. Unpleasantly, Happy had a nightmare in which appeared the ghost of Roger Whetmore, who was eaten during the immediately prior exploration on earth. In Happy's vivid and horrid nightmare, the ghost of Roger Whetmore approached Happy with a devilish grin and with knife, fork, and saltshaker in hand, muttering something about "just desserts." In a frenzy of fear, Happy grabbed his ray gun and fired at Roger's ghost. Happy then awoke to find the ghost "gone" but noticed that the ray gun had fired and accidentally severed the oxygen supply for Pollyanna. Pollyanna was flailing about trying to repair the severed oxygen supply. Happy watched contentedly as Pollyanna slowly expired (though he could easily have fixed the break). Happy returned to the main group of Explorers and recounted a tragic tale of how Pollyanna had fallen off a cliff and had been killed.

Happy, somewhat grief-stricken at this deed but emboldened to settle other old scores, resolved to kill Darth Vader, another of the Explorers, who was a chronic critic of Happy's Speluncean skills. Happy decided to kill Darth by emptying Darth's sole spare oxygen tank shortly before Darth was to embark on an exploration with Hopeful (another Explorer) into one of the side passageways. Happy secretly emptied Darth's spare oxygen tank while Darth was sleeping. The next morning, Darth and Hopeful departed on their side exploration. While taking a break for lunch, Hopeful, who had her own grievances against Darth, decided to kill Darth by hiding Darth's spare oxygen tank (which Hopeful believed to be full of oxygen). Darth died from lack of oxygen. Hopeful returned to tell Happy and the other Explorers that Darth had committed suicide.

After her return, Hopeful was suspicious of Happy's story as to the death of Pollyanna. Hopeful taunted Happy with accusations that Happy had been unfaithful to Pollyanna, that Happy was probably negligent in allowing Pollyanna "to fall off the cliff," and that in any event

---

[3] "The Speluncean Explorers" is another Type-One problem with many paragraph-based issues but additional time and another more challenging example of the CIRI(P) ONE writing format (pp. 80-89).

Happy's Speluncean skills were better exercised in Central Park, not in a lunar cave. Hopeful persisted in these taunts and finally, Happy, pretending to be in a frenzy but actually "cucumber cool," decided to kill Hopeful because he believed that Hopeful's taunts masked her suspicion that Happy had murdered Pollyanna. Happy fired his ray gun at Hopeful, missed and accidentally killed Vivian, the Enterprise's official guru and personal adviser. As Happy fired at Hopeful, Captain Kirk, the captain of the Enterprise, appeared and saw Happy firing his ray gun at Hopeful. To help Hopeful, Captain Kirk fired and missed Happy and killed Mr. Spock, another member of the Enterprise crew. Captain Kirk then disarmed Happy and left the moon for the return trip to the earth with the surviving Speluncean Explorers.

On the way, Captain Kirk piloted and also assumed the navigational duties usually fulfilled by the late Mr. Spock. Kirk was not a qualified navigator on the moon-earth shuttle but nevertheless declined to assign Dr. Strangelove, another crewmember and a qualified navigator, to this task. Captain Kirk said: "I need the experience." When informed by the celestial radar operator of a meteorite shower in the path of the Enterprise, Captain Kirk replied, "Onward meteor show." When the co-pilot excitedly suggested that a slight detour could easily avoid the shower and all risks, Captain Kirk replied, "Who's in charge here anyway?" and sniffed more celestial dust (a derivative of angel dust). Captain Kirk succeeded in piloting the Enterprise through the meteorite shower, but a tiny meteor pierced the Enterprise and killed Buck Rogers IV and Nena, two more of the fast-dwindling number of Explorers. Nevertheless, displaying extraordinary piloting ability, Captain Kirk managed to bring the damaged Enterprise safely home.

A resourceful squad of detectives has reconstructed the above events. You are a local prosecutor. What charges, if any, would you bring against Happy, Hopeful, and Captain Kirk? Please explain the applicable theories of criminal liability and any appropriate defenses that may be relevant. Please assume that U.S. law applies. (In this jurisdiction, there is no premeditated and deliberate murder.)

(75 minutes)

AN 'A' STUDENT ARGUMENT TO THE SPELUNCEAN EXPLORERS

First sentence is unnecessary and a waste of time. Second sentence is lawyerly as a statement of initial conclusions.	As a local prosecutor, I would like to thank the detective squad for the exceptionally fine work. I will first take up the case of Happy and charge him with intent-to-kill murder in the death of his wife Pollyanna, Darth Vader, and Vivian.
Do you appreciate how this analysis quickly cuts to the heart of what is at stake here: the significance—the legal meaning—of these bizarre facts. It's all about satisfying the act requirement (the *actus reus*) in an unusual way—by a culpable omission to act. Usually of course, this *actus reus* requirement is established by the defendant's positive	Happy maliciously willed the death of his wife. I will demonstrate the requisite elements for the murder. While the *mens rea* of intent to kill is clear, the act requirement poses a hurdle. Happy had intended to disconnect her oxygen supply. However, he can be indicted under the theory of "omission to act." When he awakened from his appetizing nightmare, he contentedly watched his wife fail to repair the oxygen and breached his legal duty to help her. Omission to act has three crucial components: 1) existence of legal duty 2) physical capacity for performance and 3) awareness of situation surrounding duty

act: shooting, knifing, beating, etc. But here it's established (as an exception) by the husband's omission to act that breaches his duty to save his wife.	Happy's conduct surely fits the paradigm situation: his legal duty was clearly established not only by the fact that the two were married but also because he was the actor who originally had placed Pollyanna in her helpless state. Further, it is concluded that he had the capacity to save her life and repair the line. Finally, he was clearly aware of the gravity of the situation and approved its conclusion: thus, his "omission to act" to save his wife serves as the act requirement.
The requirements of intent to kill, concurrence, causation and harm are not really at issue on these facts and can therefore be quickly presented, as here. In each cluster of facts, each legal conflict, ask yourself: what is really at the heart of it? That's always the cogent question in any exam.	The concurrence between his *mens rea* and the omission can easily be shown in this case since his intent (to kill) actuated the conduct of letting his wife die. There can be no question either of the harm or the causation.
	The only defense that Happy can muster is to attack the act requirement: that he cannot be responsible for the severing of the oxygen supply since he did it unconsciously in his sleep. As I have mentioned, the "omission to act" theory quashes that defense.
Avoid florid language ("in its infinite wisdom and perspicacity.") Again, the student focuses on what is at stake on these facts: who caused the death of Darth Vader? The other elements of intentional murder are not really at issue.	I further charge Happy with the death of Darth Vader. From the outset I concede that Happy's defense may be more valid in this instance because what we are dealing with is an unsettled question of law. But I suggest that the court in its infinite wisdom and perspicacity will find Happy guilty. Again, there can be no question of *mens rea*. Happy intended to kill Darth by means of emptying Darth's oxygen tank. The crucial element to decide is one of causation. I maintain that Happy can argue in his defense that his act was irrelevant. He will suggest that there was no "but for" causation between his conduct and the death.
The argument shows awareness that there is no single definitive or "right" response here and then makes one lawyerly argument. Though my preferred argument is to the contrary, it's an analytical argument: and that is all I am looking for here.	Happy might say that Hopeful's action in cutting the tank was the true cause and he, therefore, should be exculpated, since her act cut off his conduct as a cause of death. Yet I would urge the court that our notion of causing death can be equated to extinguishing life. Even though the manner of Darth's death may have been unforeseeable, his eventual death was. Thus, since Hopeful's intervening action did not alter the foreseeable consequences of death, Happy's conduct was the cause-in-fact and legal cause of Darth's death. Therefore, Happy should be convicted.
Transferred intent quickly raised and decided, the pivotal issue here. "He faked his frenzy": no manslaughter (wonderfully vivid, concise language). These facts illustrate a negative issue that should be raised and can be rejected in two sentences. Model Penal Code test for	Finally, I have a tight case in charging Happy with the death of Vivian. It is a clear-cut case of transferred intent. Happy had the *mens rea* in regards to Hopeful, and the law transfers the intent as a legal fact. Thus, the five elements, *mens rea*, act (shooting Vivian), concurrence, causality, and harm, can be easily proven. In his defense, Happy might maintain that he attempted to kill Hopeful in the act of passion, and that, therefore, his intent transferred to Vivian should only be commensurate with manslaughter. However, we know from our researcher that he faked his frenzy, so murder stands. One of the essential elements of manslaughter (actual heat-of-passion) is missing. Thus, I would charge Hopeful with attempted murder of Vader (after indicting Happy). She had the requisite *mens rea*, and she committed an

attempt focuses mainly on intent; the act requirement is only required to corroborate the intent to kill rather than being a separate, autonomous requirement. This argument is terse but sufficient for most professors.	overt act corroborating it (removed the canister). She could raise the defense of impossibility, but our jurisdiction follows the Model Penal Code guidelines, which have abolished impossibility as a defense. Further, even with the objective standard, an actor should not be relieved of culpability for a mistake in fact; she should be treated as if the oxygen were there. Thus, although Hopeful can claim that she did not cause the death, she is guilty of attempted murder.
A bit of confusion here. Criminal-negligence manslaughter and extreme-recklessness murder have different forms of *mens rea*.[4] Even a strong overall exam response can have weaknesses.	Finally, I would charge Kirk with criminal negligence manslaughter in the deaths of Rogers and Nena. He is responsible for gross or criminal negligence in steering the ship through the meteor shower. He did not have the ability to navigate the ship correctly and yet refused to ask assistance from a competent crewman. Thus, he negligently subjected the crew to an unjustifiable risk. The *mens rea* for this crime is to be supplied by the extreme-recklessness form of *mens rea*.
The sophisticated analytical level continues with this issue.	In this jurisdiction we follow the Model Penal Code approach to assess culpability: in the situation as the actor believed it to be, *should* the actor have been aware of the risk to the life of the crew? Our answer is yes; the co-pilot warned him that all that was necessary was a slight detour around the meteor shower. He persisted and must pay the price. Therefore, he not only "should" have been aware of the risk, evidence points to the fact that he "was" actually aware. Thus by the objective Model Penal Code, and subjective standards, Kirk had the requisite *mens rea*. In deciding that Kirk should be prosecuted under a theory of criminal manslaughter I decided that his conduct was greater than mere tort negligence (which follows the paradigm of driving an earthly car at reckless speed).
This part of the argument illustrates how a student received credit though I intended extreme-recklessness murder as the "right" conclusion. Why? It recognizes issues, argues well, and shows knowledge of the relevant rules.	However, I decided that his conduct did not approach extreme-recklessness or depraved-heart murder, whose paradigm is dropping a boulder from a bridge with cars passing beneath. His conduct did not seem as culpable or as extremely indifferent to human life as that. Any defense that Kirk may attempt to make to the effect that he was a novice navigator, didn't know about meteor showers, that he had tried to the best of his ability, will fall on deaf ears. The essential element is that he negligently subjected the crew to the unjustifiable risk of which he "should have" been aware.
This analysis is cryptic and not well developed.	I might add that I have decided not to press charges on Kirk for the killing of Spock. As a citizen, Kirk was entitled to use deadly force in the midst of a commission of a violent felony (Happy's attempt to kill Hopeful). It is defense of another. Our modern trend is to exculpate if his conduct was "a reasonable reaction to his perception of the situation." On these extreme facts, Kirk's reaction was "reasonable," and the simple fact he missed Happy and killed Spock does not change the result.

---

[4] The course did not focus on reckless manslaughter, which is, of course, easily arguable here.

Additional Comments

Have you noticed that this exam argument does not specifically articulate the issue in each legal conflict? That omission here in this powerful argument does not detract from its lawyerly quality: the well-focused arguments make the issues implicitly clear. For ordinary human beings, however, I recommend one-sentence detailing of the issue in the analysis of each conflict (See Chapters Four and Five). Certainly, in your exam-writing practice during the semester, you should follow and apply the appropriate CIRI(P) format (see Chapter Five).

A SECOND 'A' STUDENT ARGUMENT TO THE SPELUNCEAN EXPLORERS

Overall sequence specified. It's a short road map for the grader.	I shall first discuss the charges against Happy, then Hopeful, and lastly against Kirk.
	CHARGES AGAINST HAPPY
Sequence of this segment specified.	Happy is involved in three homicides: those of Pollyanna, Darth and Vivian. I shall discuss them in that order.
	Pollyanna

Given of intent to kill is noted in nine words. Correct specification of other elements of intent-to-kill rule.
 	
Initially, I react here that there could be a bit more interweaving at times, that the response is cryptic—but overall the argument is pointed and it impressively and systematically decodes the issue.
 	
In short, the argument cuts to the heart of what these facts trigger in legal significance. And that is what most graders are looking for in order to award an 'A' for an exam segment. Contrast it with the unfocused poor argument which follows this example.
 	
The two separate bases for duty to act are set forth in the context of Happy and Pollyanna as husband and wife and Happy's creation of a peril for Pollyanna.
 	
A few inserts are acceptable but do not lace your response with them.
	We are informed that Happy has intent to kill. The remaining elements of the crime of intent-to-kill murder are 1) conduct 2) accompanying intent to kill, which 3) causes the death of another. I will begin with conduct.
	
	A. Conduct. There are *two issues* for exploration here: the act of firing the gun, and the omission to act upon awakening.
	
	    1. Affirmative act of firing the gun. Two points are to be made here:
	
	        a. The act is not legally sufficient. It is not a voluntary act: the defense of unconsciousness would be available.
	
	        b. There is no concurrence: the act that is intended to kill is not the act that kills. The problem is analogous to that of A, a gunman, who intends to kill B. On her way to buy a new gun for the occasion, she accidentally runs over B and kills him. No concurrence.
	
	    2. Omission to act. The omission to act is legally sufficient only if there is a duty to act. The *issue* is, therefore, one of whether there is a duty. Duty to act may be provided by a number of sources. The two that are relevant here are (1) the husband-wife relationship and (2) duty based on the creation of peril. Each individually is sufficient to impute a duty to Happy. The act requirement is therefore satisfied.
	
	A comment added by student insert: I note in passing that there is a prerequisite that completion of the omitted act must be possible; a father who cannot swim has no duty to save his drowning child. Here, however, "he could easily have fixed the break."

127

Powerful last sentence gives conclusion on this issue. Obvious and resolved in one sentence. This type of conclusion is not essential—but it is not harmful.	B. Concurrence. The earlier concurrence problem has now been solved. The omission intended to kill does indeed kill. C. Cause. The omission is both the cause-in-fact and the proximate cause of Pollyanna's death. Pollyanna, therefore would have reason for optimism: Happy is susceptible to a charge of intent-to-kill murder.
	Darth

Charges triggered by the facts are specified as conclusions.
 	
Systematic analysis with macro decoding patterns for core crimes (*mens rea*, concurrence, act, causation, harm) frames issue at stake.
 	
Analytical discussion. No definitive response exists.
 	
Demonstrates awareness of contrary analysis and gives good reason for rejecting it.
 	
Permissible to refer to later discussion in same response. Avoids repetition.
 	
A "legally sufficient act" is a lawyerly reference to a series of closely related common-law tests in different jurisdictions, including "unequivocal act," defining how close behavior must be to completion to establish the *actus reus* required for attempt liability.
	Again, Happy has intent-to-kill *mens rea*. The applicable charges are, therefore, intent-to-kill murder and attempted murder.
	
	A. Intent-to-kill murder. The act is, of course, the emptying of the spare air tank, and it indeed concurs with the intent-to-kill. The *issue* is one of causation. Cause requires both cause-in-fact and proximate cause.
	
	  1. Cause in fact. There is no "but-for" cause here; but for Happy's act, Darth [would have] died anyway. However, "but-for" cause is a sufficient, not a necessary, condition. If the act is a "substantial" factor in bringing about the harm, it is also sufficient. It is arguable, however, that the act of emptying the cylinder was not a substantial factor. Indeed, the sole substantial factor is Hopeful's intervening act.
	
	I am aware it has been argued that the intervention should be irrelevant. Thus where A poisons B's water canteen in the desert, C subsequently steals it and B dies of thirst, it has been argued A is susceptible to a charge of murder. I do not accept this argument on the grounds of lack of cause in fact and proximate cause.
	
	  2. Proximate cause. Hopeful's intervention is in this case a superseding cause (see discussion of charges against Hopeful below).
	
	B. Attempted murder. Attempted murder requires (1) the intent to cause a criminal result and (2) some legally sufficient act toward the end. The *issue* is whether the act is legally sufficient. The relevant test is that of the unequivocal act: here the act is an unequivocal manifestation of Happy's intent. (It is in addition the last act necessary.) The defense of impossibility is not available. Therefore, Happy is susceptible to the charge of attempted murder of Darth.

	Vivian
Issue of transferred intent is raised and resolved. Example shows relevant knowledge, uses paradigm example, and applies relevant brief policy purpose for rule of transferred intent.	Again, Happy has the requisite intent to kill; it is, however, directed at Hopeful and not Vivian. The *first issue* is, therefore, one of transferred intent. Where A, with intent to kill B, hits C, A is deemed to have intent to kill C; an unintended victim does just as well. The law transfers A's intent to kill B to C, even though C is a stranger. It's a legal fiction designed to prevent A from escaping liability for murder because his aim was bad. The

	remaining elements of the crime are satisfied.
No heat of passion in fact means no manslaughter. No further discussion of manslaughter is necessary or lawyerly.	There remains the *issue* of whether the mitigating (partial) defense of heat-of-passion manslaughter is available; it is not, and the question is quickly disposed of by noting that Happy must in fact be in a heat of passion, one of the elements of manslaughter. He is not. He is "cucumber cool."
	CHARGES AGAINST HOPEFUL
	Darth
Given of intent to kill is noted. Correct focus on causation issue.	We are informed Hopeful has intent to kill *mens rea*. The act of hiding the air tank and the intent to kill concur; Darth indeed dies. The *issue* is one of causation.
Subtle analysis: causation exists, though "but-for" does not.	A. Cause in fact. Note that Hopeful is not a "but-for" cause; there is, however, an exception for the killing of a person. If A is a substantial factor in hastening the death of B, A is a cause in fact. Here Hopeful is such a substantial factor.
Lawyerly argument.	B. Proximate cause. Hopeful's intervening act is arguably a superseding cause; her act was both unforeseeable and abnormal, sufficiently so, I would argue, to make it superseding. Therefore, Hopeful may be charged with intent-to-kill murder.
	A comment added below by student insert: Hopeful's mistaken impression that the air cylinder was full has no bearing on her culpability.
	CHARGES AGAINST KIRK
Immediate focus on issue: no intent to kill; question is whether there is extreme- recklessness murder or criminal- negligence manslaughter.	There is no intent-to-kill here; the relevant states of mind are extreme recklessness or criminal negligence. Although there are no firm guidelines for drawing the line between them, there are a number of classic illustrations of conduct sufficiently reckless to constitute "extreme recklessness."
Citing illustrative examples demonstrates relevant knowledge.	Among them are firing into a crowded room that one knows is occupied by several people; playing "Russian roulette"; and dropping boulders onto a crowded street from an overpass. It is certainly arguable Kirk's conduct is equally reckless. The following factors are important considerations:
	A. Kirk had subjective knowledge of the danger—he was told of the danger of the meteor shower and that a slight detour could avoid all risk.
Lawyerly marshalling of reasons for conclusion that Kirk's behavior is similar to egregious culpability in classic examples and hence the rule applies.	B. An experienced alternative was available; Dr. Strangelove. Hence the conduct was unjustified.
	C. Kirk was sniffing celestial dust. Note that the defense of voluntary intoxication is not available in a crime with the mental element of recklessness. See e.g., Model Penal Code.
Factual and legal cause.	The *remaining question* is one of cause. Generally, the risk must be within the range of foreseeable risks and the victim must be a

All elements satisfied.	foreseeable victim. Here both are true. Since there is in addition a but-for cause (but for Kirk's action, Buck Rogers and Nena would not have died); all of the elements of the crime of extreme recklessness murder are satisfied.
	Spock
Another lawyerly example of a "negative issue: raises the issue and explains why there is no liability.	Finally, no charge is brought against Kirk for the killing of Spock. It is valid defense of another (though tragic in the death of Spock). The traditional rule places Kirk in Hopeful's legal position (the alter-ego rule). If Hopeful had valid self-defense (necessary and proportionate force in the circumstances, resisting deadly force with deadly force), Kirk has the same rights and his defense of another is legally correct. In addition, it is also reasonable (the modern test) on these facts. Either way, Kirk has a defense. The fact he missed does not prove criminal negligence and the above analysis stands.
Not essential. If time, a short summary is fine.	In conclusion, Happy may be charged with the intent to kill murders of Pollyanna and Vivian, and the attempted murder of Darth. Hopeful may be charged with the intent-to-kill murder of Darth; Kirk may be held to extreme recklessness murder of Buck Rogers and Nena.

Additional Comments

Have you noticed that these arguments embody responses that do, and do not, require back-and-forth analysis, a typical pattern for responding to many exam problems? Note, too, that conclusions can vary—e.g., the embracing of extreme recklessness murder for Kirk here while the first response rejects it—and both conclusions are well argued and receive full credit.

MEDIOCRE TO POOR ARGUMENT TO THE SPELUNCEAN EXPLORERS

This argument is based, in part, on an inaccurate reading of the facts (Happy did not awaken and then sever Pollyanna's oxygen supply) and, in part, on reading into the facts what is not there: a "proclivity to 'vivid and horrid' nightmares."	First, Happy has clearly committed a murder here and it appears to be extreme recklessness murder. When Happy goes to sleep with his ray gun at his side, and with a proclivity to "vivid and horrid" nightmares, he is creating a risk, a very serious one, of harm to anyone in the vicinity. This risk and harm is then realized when Happy has the nightmare, "sees" Roger Whetmore, awakens and then "accidentally" severs Pollyanna's oxygen supply. Either he was subjectively aware of this risk and did not prevent it or he should have been aware of the risk. Either way, he is liable for this risk creation.
The language "looks very much like…" is unlawyerly and is no substitute for the utter absence of interweaving; correct statement of black-letter rule. Incorrect statement of this form of rule.	This looks very much like extreme recklessness murder. This crime has two definitions: i) Act "committed recklessly under circumstances manifesting extreme indifference to value of human life" and which "causes death of a human." ii) Unjustifiable act creating an illegal risk and which causes

	death.
Purpose of giving these examples is unclear, and last example is wrong: it is an illustration of criminal-negligence manslaughter.	Some of the common examples of this form of murder are shooting into an occupied house or car, or driving over the speed limit while intoxicated.
"Could perhaps be prosecuted" is unlawyerly language. No explanation of why "intent-to-kill" theory and "extreme-recklessness" theory are both applicable. Factual mistake is repeated ("when he awakened"). No interweaving at all (which might have revealed mistaken view of the facts). "He did this" is no substitute.	Next, Happy could perhaps be prosecuted too for intent-to-kill murder. He did intend to kill her, although he did not actually kill her in the way he intended. Instead of "disconnecting her oxygen supply," he severed it with a ray gun when he awakened from his nightmare. Happy can't just watch Pollyanna die. They are husband and wife and he has a duty to help her if he is able to do so. He did not fulfill his duty here—he breached his duty and this breach, both legally and factually, caused her death. He could therefore be charged with intent-to-kill murder whose elements are intent to kill manifested in an act that causes death. He did this.
Begin with legal conclusion, not a statement of confusion.	Liability for the death of Darth Vader is a tough one. Both had the intent to kill. That's clear. Both did their best to kill him and subjectively believed they had done all that was necessary. Darth died. The question is who is responsible for Darth's death. Both can be held liable. Both contributed to this death: Happy by emptying the tank, Hopeful by hiding it. Both had intent to kill, performed the act manifesting this intent that caused the death.
This part is an excellent analysis of an issue without a definitive response.	The better argument, however, is that Hopeful actually killed him. Why? When Darth needed the spare oxygen tank and looked for it, he did not find it and died from lack of oxygen. That is the cause of death. It is true of course, that had he found it, he would have died anyway because Happy had emptied the oxygen. But that is a "would have been." The act must cause a death of another. Hopeful's act did, not Happy's.
No explanation of elements of rule of attempt and application to murder. No interweaving with key facts.	Happy, however, does not escape liability. Happy is guilty of attempted murder. He did all that was necessary for the murder. Fortunately for him, however, his act did not cause Darth's death. Hence, there is only an attempted murder.
All of this is true and a waste of precious time. It's a striking example of the vice of "legal lecturing"—a conclusory argument to be avoided. Happy not actually provoked by Hopeful's taunts, and thus there is no manslaughter. Essential element is missing. This is all that is necessary to state here.	The next issue invokes the murder to manslaughter reduction. Manslaughter is an intent to kill homicide, too, and it requires an act manifesting the intent that causes death. In addition, manslaughter requires provocation. Provocation is not only a factual issue—it is also normative: certain kinds of provocation are legally sufficient. If every kind of provocation were deemed sufficient, in effect each person would determine for himself what provocation was valid to reduce murder to manslaughter. That would be a

	"hot-head" rule: those easily provoked because of short tempers would be in no worse position than those who exercise great restraint and then succumb to extreme provocation.
	Not every form of provocation is sufficient but certainly the accusation that Happy had been unfaithful to his wife is sufficient. The difficulty here, however, is that Happy is actually not provoked. This element is not met and therefore there is no manslaughter. The charge is murder.
Not well-based in facts. Why is "missing" his target, and nothing more, evidence of criminal negligence. "Due care" is language and standard of torts, not crimes. Confused.	Captain Kirk gets off, I think, initially—he's defending Hopeful though he kills Mr. Spock accidentally. It appears that he was negligent in missing Happy. If he aimed more carefully, he probably would not have missed. This appears to be criminal negligence manslaughter. This negligence is often described as culpable criminal negligence, worse than tort negligence. The duty of due care is breached thereby causing, legally and factually, harm. All of this applies here.
Another confusing, unlawyerly beginning. "Malice" has technical meaning not explained and apparently not intended. The word "intentionally" as in "intentionally piloted" is confusingly used to indicate a voluntary act. It is a term typically meaning a *mens rea* requirement, not a voluntary act. The use of the word "responsible" is confusing too, without specification or coherent development.	Captain Kirk certainly performed irresponsibly here, though he managed to get the Enterprise back to earth "displaying extraordinary piloting ability." This display of "extraordinary piloting ability," nevertheless, did not prevent the death of Buck Rogers IV and Nena who were victims of Captain Kirk's malice. Captain Kirk intentionally piloted the ship through the meteor shower. He knew what he was doing even though he was taking "celestial dust." He is therefore responsible for his actions. Kirk should have assigned the qualified navigator, Dr. Strangelove. His failure to do so created a severe risk of harm.

Additional comments

This response also largely misses the following issues: the absence of a voluntary act by Happy in severing Pollyanna's oxygen supply and transferred intent in Happy's killing of Vivian. The response is also incomplete on the final issues concerning Captain Kirks' liability for the deaths of Buck Rogers IV and Nena. It's typical for weak responses to miss important issues.

POLICY PROBLEM[5]

As we have seen throughout this course, *mens rea* or criminal intent of some degree is considered an all but absolute prerequisite to criminal liability. There are certain "strict liability" crimes, but these are exceptions, and occur in relatively tangential areas. It has been suggested, however, by responsible observers that strict liability should be the rule and not the exception in the criminal law. One such observer is Lady Barbara Wooton, whose proposal may be summarized as follows:

Barbara Wooton argues for the elimination of the *mens rea* element in our concept of crime. The mental state of the defendant would have no bearing in determining liability for the crime. There would be no focus on whether the act was committed intentionally, knowingly, negligently, or recklessly. The victim, after all, is just as dead, the family just as grieved, whatever the defendant's mental state.

Instead, the focus in a criminal trial would be first on whether or not the defendant committed the prohibited act, e.g., killing, arson, robbery. Once it is judicially determined that he did so, the focus would then change to disposition, i.e., what should be done with him. On this question, all relevant information would be collected and analyzed about the defendant's family, psychological state, work history, etc.

The guiding standard in choosing a disposition for the defendant would be whatever will best protect the public from the defendant's future criminality. This might be imprisonment, job training, psychiatric care, whatever. The length of confinement, or other treatment, would be for so long as the defendant continues to demonstrate a threat to the public, as determined by the best professional judgments of psychiatrists, psychologists, and social workers. If the defendant poses no threat to the public, no imprisonment or other treatment would be imposed. Scientific rationality would replace a medieval, past-obsessed retributivism. Protection of the public would replace metaphysical and other obscurities.

Do you agree or disagree with Barbara Wooton's proposal? Please explain your reasons.

(45 minutes)

STANDOUT STUDENT ARGUMENT TO THE POLICY PROBLEM

Begins with the conclusion. It's a lawyerly start to the argument and alerts the grader to your slant.	I disagree with the Wooton proposal. Although the use of intent as a factor in sentencing fulfills one objective of the present role of *mens rea* in our legal scheme, it fails to meet several others.
This critique is very sophisticated and demonstrates a penetrating understanding of the role of *mens rea* in our criminal law and in our society. It was clearly thought through before the exam and written out from an exam outline.	One purpose of *mens rea* is to serve as a guideline for the grading of punishment according to the relative culpability of the actor's intent. This function would be fulfilled in Wooton's plan by the consideration of intent in post-trial sentencing. However, Wooton ignores the fact that conviction itself is a social assignment of legal and, usually, moral blame.

---

5 This Type Three "Policy Problem" illustrates an exam architecture that contrasts sharply with other types of problems (p.49).

Each aspect of the critique is systematically presented and related to Wooton's proposal, Two vivid images reinforce the student argument	Historically, our culture has decided that we not only want to punish malicious wrongdoing more severely than negligent or even unconscious illegal acts, but further, that we wish to assign the stigma of conviction based on a similar hierarchy of moral culpability. This distinction, I believe, is worthy of preservation, but Wooton's scheme would abandon it. Presumably, whether you struck another for the purpose of saving the President from assassination or whether you did it with intent to murder your mother, you would be convicted of the same offense—battery. Only your post-trial disposition would differ.
The routine application of *mens rea* is linked to broad societal values. Judgments about magnitude of culpability in specific cases all reflect such influential currents in the culture. Once again in applying law, the "cosmos is in a grain of sand."	Related to this hierarchical theory of assignment of moral blame is a function of law as a reflection of society's values. This reflection of values is accomplished by linking intent to act and then linking act and intent (crime) with sentence before the act is committed. In this way society tells us that carelessly running a traffic light is considered less culpable than deliberately (or even carelessly) setting a house on fire. In eliminating this intent/act/crime/sentence structure, an important function of law is lost under the Wooton proposal.
This argument shows that policy arguments are not occasion for "throwing the bull." These policy points are well established in our law. The argument reflects an insightful understanding of general and individual deterrence, one of the major justifications for our criminal law. The general and individual deterrent impact of laws also reinforces social norms, which arguably would be undermined by Wooton's proposal.	Along the same lines, notice to potential criminals is undermined. Granted potential criminals will be told what to do or not do, but they will not be warned in advance of the significance the law attaches to their acts. Since most of us violate the law in some ways during our generally law-abiding lives, we have made our decisions about what laws to break (e.g., jaywalking) and what laws to abide by (filing tax returns) at least in part because of notice the present legal structure gives us concerning the seriousness with which various infractions will be viewed. Not only does the Wooton scheme eliminate this notice, it also undermines a correlative deterrent function of the law. Some people refrain from doing some very bad things only because they know in advance what is likely to happen if they do them.
The present extensive discretion of police and prosecutors would be enhanced. To preserve the rule of law, state officials, including police, prosecutors and judges should exercise discretion bridled by a constrained discretion guided by legal rules.	Finally, the proposed system is extremely susceptible to arbitrary and abusive enforcement. Since any infraction will be considered a strict liability offense (with potentially indefinite sentence attached), a tremendous amount of discretion will be placed in the hands first of police, who decide who will and will not be arrested, and later in the courts who will have unlimited discretion in sentencing.
Officials are supposed to exercise not ad hoc, unfettered discretion, but a well-cabined discretion guided by legal rules.	Our present sentencing system should have taught us the dangers of even limited discretion being used abusively; this proposal would give corrupt policemen and judges free reign. Even judges who act with integrity would receive no guidance from society as to what punishment suits what crimes or intents—they would be left to their own prejudices and idiosyncrasies.

Keep in mind that an 'A' argument could certainly come to an opposite conclusion.	A society that wishes law to reflect, at least to some degree, the value judgments of the community, rather than the value judgments of individuals in authority positions, would be compelled to reject the Wooton proposal.

A MEDIOCRE TO POOR ARGUMENT TO THE POLICY PROBLEM

"I think I disagree" is an unlawyerly start. Be responsive to the question asking you to "agree or disagree." Lawyers qua advocates take a stand and make their best arguments.	I think I disagree with Lady Wooton's proposal to abolish *mens rea* in criminal prosecution. But I must acknowledge that her proposal has, not only surface, but also real strengths.
Beginning with a detailed unpacking of the strengths of the proposal you oppose is misguided advocacy. Instead, begin with the best arguments you can muster for your position. Later you can deflect, minimize or rebut opposing arguments in light of your best arguments.	First, the criminal trial is greatly simplified: the focus would be where it should mainly be: on the D's destructive behavior, killing, robbing, stealing, etc., and not on the vagaries of D's subjective mind. What did Shakespeare say: Who knows the mind of man (and woman, I might add), whereas in principle behavior can be absolutely verified—did A shoot and rob B or steal his wallet (recognizing, however, that problems of proof do occur).
Actually, many homicide detectives, prosecutors, defense lawyers and judges would disagree. The grief of families may vary if the victim/pedestrian was killed by a stray bullet in a gang shootout, contrasted to a killing by torture arising out of a falling out of drug dealers. Indeed, capital punishment is supposed to be reserved for the most shocking murders.	Second, the public, I believe, would prefer the focus on behavior. Isn't there a lot to Lady Wooton's statement that the "victim, after all, is just as dead, the family just as grieved, whatever the D's mental state."
Avoid juvenile humor. There is something to this argument, but it's not clear why a judge's choice here is a "bias" while other choices presumably are not.	Third, the doctrine of *mens rea* is a bloody (ha!) mess! Witness all the words of *mens rea* or intent found in the cases—e.g. intent, willful, culpable, blameworthy, evil, etc. The meaning of all these terms depends solely on the individual choices (biases) of different judges and jurors. I have to admit, however, that the Model Penal Code attempts to reduce the confusion by explicating only four categories of *mens rea*—intent, recklessness, criminal negligence and knowing.
Provocative and worthwhile but needs at least a couple additional sentences to coherently focus the insight on *mens rea*. Are they only ancient beliefs?	Fourth, the great emphasis on mind in calibrating fault seems a triumph of Platonic and early Christian beliefs. Why should intention be regarded as more culpable than recklessness or negligence simply because the mind is regarded as the highest human faculty, closest to God? Why should our criminal law continue to be a prisoner of those ancient beliefs?

Assumes that "moral notions of culpability" are only religious. While of religious origin, most prosecutors and lawyers who argue for and against culpability would deny they are engaged in a religious exercise. Most judges, too. Origin determinism is implied. Witness Sunday as a holiday. Initially, of religious origin, but today it's not only that: it also has a secular function as a day of rest for many.	Fifth, in a scientific era, it is somewhat undermining of the majesty of the law to dwell in the criminal law on moral notion of culpability. Shouldn't all of that be a private matter? Our religious beliefs, in a pluralistic society should be private, not public, and we should not impose our beliefs on others.
A powerful argument that undermines the core of Wooton's proposal. Its power comes in part from its conciseness—only four well-focused sentences. This argument lifts the overall grade from a D range to at least a C range. A generous grader might give a B- because of this argument and despite the poor quality of most of the rest of the response.	Nevertheless, there are real problems with Wooton's proposal. First, it is naïve to believe that the best professional judgment of psychiatrists, psychologists and social workers has the base of scientific knowledge and insight to enable them to predict accurately who will harm the public and who will not. The truth, attested to by many such professionals, is that they *cannot predict future behavior*. Indeed, if you postulate that behavior flows from interaction of people in sharply varying and unpredictable contexts and situations, it may be *impossible* in principle ever to make such predictions for the persuasive reason that such contexts and situations are endless and *cannot be anticipated*.
Argument is too sweeping and would bar any basic change. The Common Law is saturated with history but, as courts stress, is not its prisoner.	Second, *mens rea* is embedded in our laws and the consciousness of lawyers, judges and even jurors. It could be confusing to introduce such a radical change in a historically drenched criminal law.
True but far too sweeping and applies to all new proposals in every area of life. The student does not at all particularize this general and valid insight in light of Wooton's proposal.	Third, such radical changes usually produce harmful unintended consequences. True, we can't predict what they will be, but we can be confident they will occur. On balance, and reluctantly, I oppose her proposal.

OLIVIA WARBUCKS PROBLEM[6]

You are an attorney who has been retained to represent Harold Gray, the executor of the estate of Olivia Warbucks. Ms. Warbucks, herself a New York City attorney, recently died at the age of sixty-two, leaving an estate consisting mainly of stocks and bonds valued in the aggregate at roughly $550,000.00. Her will provides that her entire estate, after payment of her debts and estate taxes, is to go to her two nieces, the daughters of her sister who died some years ago.

During most of her adult life, Ms. Warbucks was a successful and prominent member of the New York Bar. She had attended N.Y.C. Law School, which is part of N.Y.C. University, a large private university located in New York City. While attending N.Y.C. Law, she had lived in the home of Josephine and Andrew McArdle, close friends of her own parents (who lived at that time in Chicago). The McArdles had provided her with room and board throughout the three-year period of her attendance at law school, free of charge. (During the summers she returned to Chicago where she worked for her father in his tailor shop.)

Ms. Warbucks learned that the McArdles' daughter Annie had been accepted for admission into the N.Y.C. Law entering class for the fall of 1998. Annie McArdle had at that time already been living for several years in Manhattan, where she was working as a paralegal at the large law firm of Aspen, Punjab, and Sahib. Ms. Warbucks called Annie and invited her to lunch, at which time they talked of Annie's plans to study law and her ambition for a career as an entertainment lawyer in New York (Ms. Warbucks' own field of practice, as it happens). That evening Ms. Warbucks wrote and mailed to Annie the following letter:

> Dear Annie:
>
> I enjoyed very much our chat today, and was impressed with your ambitious plans for the future. As you know, I went to law school at a time when many schools did not welcome female students; in fact, some did not even accept women as students. N.Y.C. may not have been the best or most prestigious school in the world when I went there (I understand it is very well regarded today), but I've always been grateful for the education I received there, and proud to be a N.Y.C. graduate. If you do go ahead with your plans to enroll at N.Y.C. Law, I will be pleased and proud to pay your full tuition for the three years of law study. I have never felt that I could adequately repay your wonderful parents for the kindness they showed me as a young student struggling to make ends meet; this way I can at least share some of the financial rewards of my practice with their daughter.
>
> We'll talk again soon, I hope, but I wanted to write you now so that you could know my intentions in making your own plans.
>
> With great affection, (signed) Olivia Warbucks

It appears from Ms. Warbucks' financial records that she did in fact provide Annie with the funds to pay her law-school tuition at N.Y.C. Law for the 1998–1999 academic year and for the fall 1999 semester. Mr. Gray, the executor of the Warbucks estate, has just received the following letter:

(over)

---

[6] This problem illustrates the different Type-Two, multi-issue problem with only one overall issue that is unfolded into many sub-issues (pp. 48-49) that are argued back and forth—and without definitive conclusions. Issue spotting here is *not* paragraph-based. The problem and its response was provided by Professor and former Associate Dean Charles Knapp of the New York University Law School.

Dear Sir:

Enclosed is a Xerox copy of my law-school tuition bill for the spring 2000 term. I will appreciate you sending me a check for the appropriate amount, payable to the order of N.Y.C. Law School, so that I can register for the spring term. As you probably know, Ms. Warbucks, before she died, had committed herself to paying my law-school tuition (see the enclosed copy of her letter to me), and I am sure that you will want to honor that commitment.

Sincerely, (signed) Annie McArdle

Mr. Gray has asked you whether he should regard this as an appropriate expenditure to be paid out of the funds of the estate. How would you advise him?

(90 minutes)

AN 'A' ARGUMENT TO OLIVIA WARBUCKS

In this practice contract exam, this well-known professor authorizes both an outline form and the more usual prose form. If you believe you might use an outline form, check with your professor before the exam. The exam is contract, not wills and estates.	PROFESSORIAL NOTE: This answer has been written in outline form to indicate the logical relationship of its parts. An answer could well be written in that form. Occasionally it expands into more elaborate prose-style; that too is acceptable, and sometimes better to express a more complicated argument. The answer assumes that the principal point of the question is to test the student's understanding of the legal rights of the parties in contracts, and that discussions of the laws of wills and estates beyond the rudimentary points discussed in our class is neither expected nor particularly germane.
Notice that in this practice exam, this professor specifies no conclusion. You provide the conclusion here. Resolution of the ultimate issue depends on resolution of intermediate and more concrete issues that are systematically raised, argued and (where possible) resolved.	Since the executor of the Olivia Warbucks (W) estate is presumably bound to honor the legal obligations of the estate out of estate property, but is not free to give away estate assets, the question of how to advise my client will turn primarily on whether there is any legally enforceable obligation to Annie (A) on the facts given. The following points would be relevant to that question.

Note the broad issue formulation to the right and above, a virtual given from the problem. No challenging issue spotting here. It's simply, as stated, "whether there is any legally enforceable obligation to Annie on the facts given." It's therefore a quite different	I. *Consideration*: Does A's attendance at NYC constitute acceptance of an offer by W for a consideration-supported contract?
	
	A. The consideration rule stresses "benefit" to the promisor and "detriment" to the promisee as constituting consideration.
	
	  1. "Benefit" to W?
	
	    a. On the facts stated, no direct benefit to her.
	
	    b. Possibly she seeks a benefit to NYC (consideration may be given to someone other than promisor).

138

type of multi-issue problem. Note the professor's description of the intermediate or sub-issues as "points."

First intermediate or sub-issue is then specified.

Revealingly, "benefit" means legal, not moral, benefit. Thus, a moral payback by W for generosity of A's parents decades ago is not a legal benefit to W.

Issues of benefit to W and detriment to A are systematically raised and explored.

Legal meaning of "bargained-for exchange" is explicated and applied to facts.

This "gift-on-condition" construction of the instant facts is analyzed in light of similarities and differences with several cases discussed during the course.

Professor signals here and elsewhere that references to names of key cases and their rationales that were stressed in class are invited, and could enhance the value of your response. But don't assume all graders want such references. Individualize for each professor here as always. Any model or "sample exam" answers from a professor tell you what he or she expects. Search for such exams in each course.

A contrasting construction is assessed in light of equivocal facts.

c. Possibly she foresaw an eventual benefit from A's services as a NYC grad.

d. Can her desire to benefit A serve as consideration?—cf. *Hamer*, where the court relied on "detriment" (below)

2. "Detriment" to A?

a. In not attending another law school instead? (Fact not supplied—we don't know whether she *could* have attended any other school. Would she have been accepted elsewhere?)

b. In not pursuing some career other than law? (Facts do not suggest she had any interest in doing so.)

c. Could argue there is no detriment to A, because she is better off having attended NYC for three semesters than if she had not.

d. But "detriment" in the legal sense need not be substantially injurious to the promisee; it can consist of doing something the promisee is not otherwise legally bound to do. Her attendance at NYC clearly could be consideration, if bargained for (see below).

B. Was there a "bargained-for exchange"?

1. Seemingly there was no "bargaining" in the sense of "negotiation," but this element seems to look rather to the requirement that the transaction be in substance an *exchange*.

2. A's detrimental action can be consideration if sought by W in exchange for her promise and given by A in exchange for that promise. Was it?

3. In form, this can clearly be an exchange transaction—"If you will do X, then I will do Y in return."

4. However, in substance this could be merely a "gift-on-condition."

a. This is not so clearly a gift as was the promise in *Ricketts*, where the promisor may have hoped that the money would be used in a particular way but did not make that a condition to his promised performance.

b. But it is also different from *Hamer*; there the promisor's promised performance (payment of $) had no direct relation to the acts bargained for in return (not smoking, etc.). Here if one views the promised performance as being in substance a payment of law-school tuition, it has a direct relationship to the acts that A must perform in order to receive it.

c. One could also say that this is like *Kirksey*, or the "tramp" example: it is merely a gift of law-school tuition, and one that the promisee therefore cannot avail herself of unless in fact she does attend law school.

d. Or, one could say that the promisor is in fact seeking to *induce* A to perform her promise, and that it is indeed in

139

	substance the "price" of that promise.
	i. Williston suggests a "benefit to promisor" (see above) test may be useful.
	ii. We don't know if A had decided to attend NYC before her lunch with W, before she got W's letter. This could be relevant on the issue of gift-vs.-exchange.
	iii. We also don't know if A otherwise could in fact have afforded to attend NYC (although we may suspect not?). If she had ample resources, perhaps less likely to be regarded as an action-inducing promise—and also a less appealing case overall, perhaps.
Rules on moral obligation as a basis for enforcement are explicated and then applied to facts.	**II. *Moral Obligation:*** Can this serve as a basis for enforcement?
	A. Generally, things done in the past by the promisee for the promisor will not constitute sufficient consideration to make a promise binding. ("Past consideration is no consideration.")
	1. One exception is the case where a past legal obligation existed, rendered unenforceable by the Statute of Limitations; such an obligation may be revived by a fresh promise without new consideration (although Statute may require a writing).
Systematic decoding of this issue as others.	2. Thus, where past services were performed with reasonable expectation of completion, so that at least *quantum meruit* obligation existed, a later promise could both liquidate and revive it.
	a. Here, facts do not indicate that A's parents when they performed services for W (room and board) reasonably expected to be paid.
	b. Even if they did, and new promise could therefore be regarded as reviving that obligation, liability would probably be limited under this theory to the reasonable value of those services.
Minority rule stated, explained, and applied to facts.	B. Only a minority of courts will enforce a promise on "moral obligation" alone.
	1. Even there, the moral obligation must be more than comes simply from the making of the promise at issue.
Gerke is distinguished from these facts.	2. In *Gerke*, gratitude for past services performed was held to make the later promise binding, even though no obligation originally existed.
	a. But there the *promisee* had rendered the promise—unlike here.
	b. And there the recovery was limited to the reasonable value of the services performed. (This may have been because of the absence of any writing; in A's case, there is one.)
Restatement 2d rule stated.	3. Restatement 2d also takes the view that promise can be binding if based on recognition of past benefit received, at least

	if "necessary to prevent injustice." Several problems in applying that rule to this case:
Restatement 2d position applied to facts.	a. Rule as stated requires that the benefit has been received by the promisor "from the promisee." Here it was received from her parents. Should that matter? The R.2d rule is said *not* to call for a change in the result of *Mills*, apparently because there the benefit was not received "by the promisor."
Some unknown facts that add to indeterminacy of problem and response are mentioned.	It might be similarly strictly construed on this point. (Incidentally, we don't know if performance to A would indirectly benefit her parents, by relieving them of an expense they would otherwise have been willing and able to bear. Indeed, we don't even know if they are still alive—although those who remember the original "Little Orphan Annie" may have reason to doubt it.)
Question of Restatement and "gift" raised.	b. The R.2d rule also is said not to apply if the benefit was conferred "as a gift."
A's parents were altruistic.	i) The facts seemingly suggest that A's parents did what they did for W as a pure gratuity, with no thought or hope of payment in return.
	ii) We don't know whether A's parents were financially well off or not; this might be relevant here.
Additional requirement of Restatement 2d rule stated.	c. Also, the R.2d rule applies its terms only where there has been "unjust enrichment" of the promisor.
Notice that response here too goes beyond facts and engages in speculation. See this practice as restricted only to professors who invite it.	i) It is possible that while in the McA household W did perform various household chores, which come close to being a reasonable exchange for her room and board, in which case little or no enrichment of W resulted.
More speculation from specified facts.	ii) It is also possible that W was taken into the McA home in return for kindness previously shown to the McA family by W's family—in which case the services to W did not create a moral obligation, but rather *discharged* one.
Yet another issue that is difficult to resolve.	d. Finally, the R.2d rule applies only to the extent that the promised performance is not "disproportionate" to the value of the benefit previously received. Again, it is difficult on the facts to make this comparison.
	III. *"Promissory Estoppel"*: Can A's reliance on W's promise serve as a basis for enforcing that promise?
Another arguable basis for enforcing W's promise is systematically discussed.	A. Acts done by the promisee in reliance on the performance of a promise, if bargained for as the price of that promise, will make the promise binding, not on just a promissory estoppel basis, but as consideration, in the classical sense.
	B. Where acts done in reliance on a promise are not bargained for, they may nevertheless serve to make the promise binding, under case law and Restatement §90.

141

Statement of rules again detailed in lawyerly fashion.	C. The elements of this "promissory estoppel" as they might apply to this case are as follows:
	1. Did A in fact *rely* on W's promise, by doing something she would not otherwise have done, or by not doing something she otherwise would have done?
Application of elements of rules to uncertain facts.	a. Did she attend NYC when she would have not otherwise done so? (It might be the only school she *could* attend, or in any case the only one she *would* have attended.)
Again, speculation from sparse facts.	b. Even if not, did she forebear financing her education in some way that she would have otherwise used, and which is now not open to her? (This seems problematic: if she had worked or gotten loans for the first three semesters, is she worse off now—assuming she can still do that for the remaining three semesters—as a result of W's promise and subsequent payment of her first three semesters' tuition? Possibly it is now too late for her to finance her tuition for next spring, in which case the R.2d suggestion of partial enforcement might seem appropriate.)
	2. Was her reliance reasonable?
	a. Seemingly it was, since W's promise was plausible in the circumstances.
Good interweaving of elements and key facts.	b. Moreover, the promise was in fact performed for three semesters, making continued reliance increasingly reasonable.
	3. Did the promisor have reason to *foresee* the reliance?
	a. We have already seen that the promise may even have been made to induce such reliance.
	b. Even if it was not, there appears no question but that the promisor could foresee it. (This should not beg the question, however, of whether there was in fact real reliance, as discussed above.)
Resolution of issue on injustice depends on facts that are not supplied in the problem.	4. Will *injustice* result if the promise is not enforced? Here substantial discussion could be directed to the question which appears to be central to this issue: Will A in fact be worse off if the promise is *not* enforced—and she is therefore left with three and only three semesters of free tuition courtesy of W—than she would have been if the promise had never been made (and therefore never relied on) in the first place?
	This might involve various questions of fact—not supplied—such as whether she can now finance her education from any other source, whether she can practicably transfer to another, less expensive school, etc.

The last basis for enforcement is raised and discussed. Statement of rule.	IV. ***Form*** as a reason for enforcement. A. Writing alone, even if signed, does not ordinarily constitute sufficient grounds for enforcing a promise.
W's letter was not a will.	1. If under seal it might, in a small number of jurisdictions, but W's letter does not appear to have been sealed. 2. There is no showing that the letter was executed with the formality usually required of a will; even in a state which recognized the "holographic" will, this seems unlikely to be viewed as such.
Quick noting of exception.	3. Only a small number of jurisdictions have a statute making written promises enforceable *per se*.

Statute-of-Frauds issue is set forth and applied to available facts.	B. The Statute of Frauds cannot serve as a basis for enforcing the promise.
	
	1. W's promise may come within the one-year clause of the traditional Statute of Frauds.
	   a. It is not clear whether the promise necessarily contemplated a full three years' attendance by A.
	   b. If not, the Statute might not apply.
	
	2. If it does, the Statute is probably satisfied by the letter.

Impressive focus at end.	3. But the Statute of Frauds does not supply a reason for enforcement, where one is otherwise lacking. Satisfaction of the Statute merely removes a bar to enforcement that the Statute would otherwise erect. An affirmative reason for enforcing the promise must be found in some other rule of law.

Additional Comments

This problem is designed by a very experienced contract professor (and co-author of a popular contract casebook) and is designed to raise a multitude of issues. Many, even most, of these issues *cannot be resolved:* the facts, together with the applicable rules, do not permit resolution. Pervasive pro and con discussion is absolutely essential here, and in some parts it is relevant to point out that resolution depends on facts that are not supplied.

Again, this type of problem is sometimes called a "kitchen sink" problem: it requires that you quickly raise a host of issues of various kinds with quite brief responses to each issue. But in other contract problems as follows, the different detailing of the facts, together with applicable rules, lead to more spelled-out, back-and-forth arguments—and resolution of them. You may also have fewer issues and, therefore, more time to detail each response.

BOOKS, BOOKS, BOOKS PROBLEM[7]

Books-R-Books Publishing (BP) advertises its wares in "Wordy," a publisher's trade magazine. Jane, the owner of an independent bookstore, is disappointed by her poor sales. She has a flash of brilliance when she sees BP's latest ad: "Our Newest Title—'Learn to Read!' $100 per 10 copies. Supply limited." If her customers know how to read, Jane figures, they'll buy more books.

Jane faxes to BP a copy of her standard order sheet, listing 30 copies, for a total $300, to be delivered within the month. Written in small type on the front is the statement, "Buyer reserves the right to return any book within one month." BP responds that day by mailing Jane 10 books and a "Bill of Sale" charging $100 due immediately, with a pending balance of $200 for "future shipments."

The books sell out in the first week, and Jane is eagerly awaiting the next shipment. Brad, BP's representative, calls with bad news: "Our factory has flooded, and we won't be able to print any more books for at least three weeks."

"But I'm on the verge of going under, and my current sales are all coming from customers who first read your book!" exclaims Jane. "If I don't get your shipment in the next two weeks, I won't be able to pay the store rent, and I'll have to fold," Jane states truthfully. "Gee," replies Brad, "we do have 50 copies left, but our policy is first order - first ship, and you're just too far down the list. Maybe for more money…"

"If I paid $120 per 10 books, could you move me up the list?" asks Jane.

"Yeah, I think I can do that!" Brad says.

The next morning, Jane discovers that the chain bookstores in town are selling "Learn to Read" for $11 a book; she buys 20 copies. When she returns to the bookstore that afternoon, she finds an express shipment from Brad of 20 books, with another "Bill of Sale." This bill charges $240, due immediately, and has the words "All Express Sales Final" printed boldly across the top.

Jane believes she should be able to return the 20 books, but Brad refuses. At most, Jane believes she owes BP $200, not $240.

When the case comes to court, the judge you clerk for asks you to analyze the arguments for and against Jane's two claims. While your judge does ask you to come to a conclusion, she is interested primarily in understanding each side's best arguments.

---

[7] This is another Type-Two, multi-issue problem from an open-book exam with a given overall issue that requires unfolding into a group of other issues—and here with conclusions. It also illustrates a common "battle-of-the-forms" problem whose significance must be decoded in light of the forms, other behavior, and the relevant rules from both the common law, the Restatement Second ("RSC") and the Uniform Commercial Code. It's step-by-step argument also illustrates a CIRI(P) THREE(b) writing format (pp. 104-105).

STRONG STUDENT ARGUMENT TO BOOKS, BOOKS, BOOKS

Comments	Issue One: Is Jane able to return the additional 20 books that were shipped "Express"?
Please note that this impressive [though not edited] argument was written in an open-book exam. That explains the references to UCC sections by number, which is usually not expected in closed-book exams. Yes, this first overall issue is hostage to the existence or nonexistence of a contract, the initial layer of derivative issues. Discussion of contract terms follows an argument spelling out that a contract exists. Both overall issues are explicit givens in the problem.	In order to determine whether Jane is able to return the additional 120 books we must examine two issues: (1) did Jane have a contract with BP and (2) what were the terms of the contract? Before we examine the terms of a potential contract, we must examine whether Jane had a contract with BP. To see if she had a contract we must find that she had a bargained-for exchange with BP, evidenced by mutual assent and supported by consideration. The Restatement (Second) of Contracts ("RSC") Sec. 17 defines a contract as a bargain in which parties express a manifestation of mutual assent to an exchange supported by consideration.
In classic argument making, the student defines the elements of a valid offer in the first sentence. As you know, the words ("in this case" or "here") signal the end of the relevant rule statement and the interweaving of its elements with the key facts. In the next step, the argument is then buttressed by reference to a similar case studied in the course relating to the offer element. Lastly, the sale of goods (books here) means that the UCC is relevant in addition to common law contract rules. The student details the particular UCC section and its flexible language regarding acceptance. The final sentence in the argument also intimates the next argument spelling out the acceptance of Jane's offer. Do you understand how a sub-issue is posed as to whether or not there is a valid offer that is essential for a contract?	**Mutual Assent—Offer** The first element in a contract is an offer. An offer is an expression of a promise, undertaking or commitment to enter into a bargain made by one party, containing clear and definite terms, that is communicated to the offeree in such a manner that invites a manifestation of assent consisting of a return promise or act. In this case, Jane's faxing of her standard order sheet to BP was an offer. It was her promise to buy books from BP and it contained specific terms that apply to how Jane's bookstore does business. It was specific as to subject matter and price and contained additional terms, namely that Jane reserved the right to return any books purchased in the last month. This communication was similar to the communication between parties in the Dataserve case, in which case Technology began the offer process by sending a purchase order to Dataserve. Since the instant case involves the sale of goods, we look to the UCC for guidance. UCC 2-206 notes than an offer to make a contract shall be construed as inviting acceptance in any manner and by any medium reasonable in the circumstances. That is what we have here in Jane's faxed purchase order.
The next sub-issue in the argument is posed: is there an acceptance of Jane's offer by BP? This argument also begins	**Mutual Assent—Acceptance** In order to prove mutual assent, the offer must be

by defining the relevant UCC requirements for an acceptance, which is then applied to the facts and supported by a relevant case discussed in class.

What's illustrated here, too, is that a challenging problem can include straightforward sub-issues such as the initial clear issue here about an offer by Jane and the acceptance.

This problem and response also illustrate that such issues in exam problems typically herald more challenging issues down the road.

Do you understand how both these sub-issues are raised by the higher-level issue as to whether or not a contract exists?

Note the professor's comment that consideration is "not an issue here," written right on the exam paper. What she means is that the facts are perfectly clear on this element, and no plausible argument can be made to the contrary. Thus, treating this non-issue as an issue is a modest mistake in exam judgment.

Ideally, the student should have pointed out quickly, in a sentence or two at most, why the instant facts are so clear that no issue can be plausibly raised here.

So now that a contract is established between Jane and BP, it's lawyerly to address directly the overall issue explicitly posed by the professor in her problem: can Jane return her books within 30 days?

In responding, the student pinpoints the relevant UCC rules that apply (different from common-law rules).

This argument in a closed-book exam rings with the reality of legal practice. With its detailing of UCC sections and its cogent, step-by-step approach, it could be part of a memorandum of law prepared in an actual case. It is therefore very different from many closed-book

accepted by the other party. UCC 2-206(2) notes that the beginning of requested performance is a reasonable mode of acceptance. This is what happens in the instance case. BP accepts Jane's offer by beginning to ship the books that she requested. Courts have found that beginning performance indicates acceptance of an offer, as in the case of Ever-Tile Roofing when the contractor accepted the family's offer by loading a truck and driving to their house to begin the job.

In accepting Jane's offer, not all the terms of the contract were settled, particularly the question involving Jane's right to return books. Although they may not have agreed on this point, the UCC in Sec 2-204(3) recognizes the existence of a contract even though some terms may be left open. How we deal with those terms will be dealt with later on.

The facts are sufficient to indicate that there was mutual assent between the parties.

Consideration [Professor comments: "not an issue here."]

A contract must be supported by consideration or by a substitute for consideration. The common law provides guidance as to what will or won't serve as consideration. RSC Sec. 71 notes that consideration must be a performance or return promise that is bargained for. It is said that evidence of a detriment experienced by the parties shows that there was consideration. Jane promised to pay for the books that she ordered. BP responded by shipping books and promising more books to fulfill her order. Jane promises payment, BP promises (and delivers) product. It has been shown that this contract is supported by valid consideration.

The above elements are sufficient to show that there existed a valid contract between Jane and BP. So what about the terms and Jane's right to return the unused books? Clearly each party entered into the K with different terms in mind. Jane's terms allow her to return books within 30 days. BP indicated that they will not accept returned books that were ordered "express" as Jane requested.

So who's right? UCC 2-207 provides guidance. Under common law a contract is normally not enforced if both parties don't agree to the same terms. The appearance of new or additional terms in an offeree's acceptance serves as a counter offer (RSC Sec. 39).

exam arguments.

Note the vivid language of the "knock-out" rule below. Like all apt and vivid language, it seizes your attention right away.

Again, the UCC statutory argument is buttressed by explicit and cogent reference to relevant case law studied in the professor's course. Note the simple and illuminating sentence below: "Case law gives us some examples of 2-207 in operation." And not only here.

It might aid clarity to outline the steps in the scaffolding of issues that are spelled out and resolved in this initial cogent argument.

    1. The first given overall issue: is Jane able to return the additional 20 books that were shipped "Express"?
    2. The derivative issue: whether Jane had a contract with BP?
    3. The sub-issues necessary to resolve the derivative issue: are there a valid offer, acceptance, and consideration necessary to form a contract?

A general point: case law explicates, of course, the scope and meaning of statutory language as it is applied to concrete and varied fact situations.

The scope and meaning are then sometimes extended or limited by the judges who decide the parade of cases that come before them. (See *Learning Legal Reasoning*, p. 72-76.)

Such extension or limitation of statutory meaning is inevitable over time because application is inherently interpretive. And such interpretation is always a particular value-laden choice.

In addition, legislative intention and statutory language are not always clear, and thus gaps are sometimes posed by the statutes and cases. Since the judges are obligated, however, to decide these cases, too, they must "fill in the gaps" as best they can—for example, by analogy to

But when dealing with the sale of goods under UCC the provisions are more forgiving. Under UCC 2-207 additional terms do not automatically serve as a rejection of the original offer and parties may even perform while the terms are in conflict. There is a simple test to see whose terms govern this K. Under UCC 2-207(1) we see that an acceptance may contain terms new or additional to the offer. This is what happens when Jane receives the additional 20 books with the note that all express orders are final.

Clearly, this term is different from Jane's original offer that stated she had a right to return the books. Is this a conditional acceptance under 2-207?

An acceptance is conditional if the party who proposed the term would not have moved forward without the term. It is likely that BP would not have shipped the books express without its term in place, which makes this a conditional term. Yet both parties have now performed with different terms and a conditional acceptance. We now look to UCC 2-207(3) that deals with situations like these.

If parties perform and their terms are different, 2-207(3) serves as a knock-out rule, essentially canceling out each term. The operative term will be supplied by UCC "Gap Filler" terms. In the instant case Jane's term and the "no return" policy are cancelled. Since the UCC now governs the terms it's likely that the gap filling terms will allow Jane to return her books.

One note: if BP's term was not considered conditional then UCC 2-207(2) would apply. Between merchants, new or additional terms are incorporated into the K UNLESS the party proposing the new terms knows that the other party has already rejected them (as was the case here, when Jane already rejected them in her original offer) or if the party rejects them in a reasonable amount of time. If 2-207(2) governed, then Jane's terms would apply.

Case law gives us some examples of 2-207 in operation. In the case of Hill v. Gateway 2000 a family received new terms when it received a computer it bought online or by telephone. The new terms were ultimately included in the K since Hill did not object to them in a reasonable time. In another case, Step Saver, gives us a good example of 2-207(3) in action.

Either way, it appears that the parties had a *contract* and the terms of the contract will likely allow Jane to *return*

other rules, by summoning arguably relevant underlying principles, etc.	*the books.*
Such application/interpretation not only determines the scope of coverage of the statutory rule, but also its boundaries with other rules. Should the legislature disagree it can, of course, change most decisions by new legislation. Generally, however, such changes are infrequent. Thus, the dichotomy between law-in-the-books and law-in-action is misleading. Law in action is not exclusively the simple spelling out of legislative intention embodied in statutes. It's more creative.	**The second issue: What price must Jane pay for the second set of books?** Having already determined that the parties started with a contract to buy books at $10, we examine the question of whether Jane must pay $12 per book as she later agreed to do. We must determine whether or not the contract modification is enforceable. A modification of an existing contract is somewhat like finding a new contract. Was there a manifestation of mutual assent between the parties, and if necessary, was this bargained-for exchange supported by consideration?
This student argument also illustrates the usefulness of **COCOA** plus **TBR** (pp.13-14), the mnemonic for basic contract issue analysis.	**Mutual Manifestation—Offer** Jane's offer to pay $120 per 10 books is her offer to BP. She is bargaining for the speedy delivery of books priced at $120/10 units. Her promise to pay $120 invites acceptance to her terms.
Once it is seen that the contract exam problem poses a given issue about a contract term, a glance at the mnemonic reminds the student that an issue about a term presupposes the existence of a contract, and a contract requires a valid, offer, acceptance, and consideration (or substitute). Of course, that's the student's framing sequence here for his two arguments. After the irrelevant C̄ on these facts (capacity), the Ō follows (offer and acceptance), the C̄ (consideration), Ō (objective: no policy violation), Ā (the mutual assent of the parties). This framing also then focuses on the remaining T̄ (term), B̄ (breach) and R̄ (remedies).	**Mutual Manifestation—Acceptance** An acceptance must be clear and it must be objectively understood to be a manifestation of assent to the offeror's invitation to form a contract. UCC 2-204(2) tells us that a contract for sale of goods may be made in any manner sufficient to show agreement, including conduct by both parties that recognizes the existence of such a contract. Although his response is somewhat wanting in terms of clarity ("I think we can" versus "I accept your offer"), this statement could be construed by an objective person as a reasonable acceptance of Jane's offer. However, even if this potential moment of acceptance was not clear enough to constitute acceptance, then BP surely accepted Jane's offer by delivering her an express shipment of 20 books at the price of $240. That the exact moment of acceptance is unclear is not a problem: UCC 2-204(2) notes that an agreement sufficient to constitute a contract for sale may be found even though the moment of its making is undetermined.
To be sure, this skeletal framing needs to be fleshed out in sequential argument making, but the framing directs it. Though much more is needed, knowing the framing is the essential beginning.	**Consideration or a substitute for consideration** Unlike the common law that states that modifications of contracts must be supported by consideration, the UCC notes 2-209(1) that a modification of a K for the sale of goods "needs no consideration to be binding."

As noted, argument about the existence of consideration is unnecessary for the reason mentioned.

The general point is that professors vary in how extensively they expect students to argue on their exams. They may be clear in class or on their exam as to what they expect. If not, follow their actual practice from class.

It's typical in contract argument-making to apply and compare both the common-law case-based rules and the Restatement (Second) ("RSC") rules. In addition, where there is a sale of goods, you also add the rules from the UCC. Indeed, once you see a sale of goods in an exam problem, hypothesize that all three sources of rules are relevant in this popular contract pattern.

Did consideration exist anyhow? BP was under a pre-existing duty to ship books to Jane at $12/book. So can the new price of $12 be enforced when it should have shipped at $10? Although UCC 2-209 does not require additional consideration for the modification, it exists nevertheless. Jane's original K was simply to buy books at $100/10. It did not include the ability of Jane to receive her books before other buyers ahead of her in line. Although she offered a higher price ($120) for the same *product* that she originally contracted for, the fact that she was being moved ahead in line of other buyers serves as new return consideration on the part of BP. Jane gets her books delivered faster, BP gets more money.

This is unlike the case of *Alaska Packers v. Domenico*, in which parties attempted to modify a contract and receive more money, but offered nothing additional in return.

The modification reflecting a higher price in return for speedier shipment is valid, and will be enforced.

Additional Comments

In the earlier problems, both "Mary Lee" and "The Speluncean Explorers," there are singular and vivid harm-producing events that rivet attention and shout out for issue spotting and argument making. Witness the various bodily harms in "Mary Lee" and the different killings in "The Speluncean Explorers." In compelling contrast, in "Books, Books, Books," the issue spotting and argument making do not spring from such riveting events, but rather from the exchange of forms ("the battle of forms"), related conversations and actions of both Jane and BP over days. This exchange of forms, conversations, and related actions is the nexus for issue spotting in this popular type of contract exam (and in practice).

BLOWING IN THE WIND PROBLEM[8]

Dastardly, Inc. (D) is a municipally owned utility incorporated in Ohio that was established to provide electric energy to customers in a major Ohio city. In 1998, it decided to switch from oil as its principal energy source to a new product called syn-oil, a synthetic fuel produced from specially processed coal. The switch took place in December 1998. D has no offices or plants anywhere outside of Ohio, though it does sometimes sell electricity to industrial users in Ohio and neighboring states. Further, its agents occasionally go to Pennsylvania to negotiate fuel purchase contracts with SynFuel, Inc. (S.I.) a major supplier of syn-oil. S.I. is incorporated in Ohio and has had its principal place of business in Pennsylvania. It also owns a large farm in New York State on which is grown substantial quantities of corn, a key ingredient in syn-oil.

Dr. Purair (P) is a distinguished ecologist and chemical researcher who lives (as she has for all of her adult life) in northern New York. In 1999, she learned of D's plan to use syn-oil and undertook a study of its chemical properties. She concluded that syn-oil emissions would be carcinogenic for persons who inhaled them. Further study indicated that because of basic normal weather patterns, prevailing winds would bring large amounts of syn-oil emissions into the area of New York in which P lived and worked. She calculated that she and other persons in that area would, as a result of D's use of syn-fuels, have a substantially greater likelihood of getting cancer over the course of their lifetime than if syn-oil were not used. Symptoms would probably not appear, however, for about ten years from the date inhalation began.

Upon consulting her attorney, P learned that under the New York statute of limitations an action for damages based on pollution-caused disease must be brought within three years from the date of the first inhalation. She thereupon decided to sue D immediately, although she had not yet suffered any physical damage. The action was commenced in 2000 in the Federal District Court for the Southern District of New York. The summons was served on the President of D at his office in Ohio. The complaint sought a declaratory judgment (pursuant to the Federal Declaratory Judgment Act) declaring that D was acting in violation of P's common-law right against nuisance and further declaring that D's acts would increase the danger that P would get cancer at some time during her life.

What procedural defenses are available to D? Briefly describe how each objection should be raised. For each procedural defense that D would raise, present any arguments that would appropriately be made for and against the defenses, then state how the court should resolve each defense. If there are unknown factors that would affect your analysis, please specify them, indicating their relevance.

Note to Students: The preceding question raises many issues. For this exercise, please focus on one of these issues: would it be constitutional for New York Courts to assert *in personam* jurisdiction over D (assuming that New York's long-arm statute applied to D)?

(50 minutes)

---

[8] Another Type-Two multi-issue problem (Civil Procedure) that poses only one overall issue that requires a complex unfolding argument, here with conclusions required. That complexity also illustrates the CIRI(P) THREE(a) writing format (p. 102).

A STUDENT'S STANDOUT ARGUMENT TO BLOWING IN THE WIND

If the court finds D's act falls within New York's long-arm statute, C should argue that §302 is an unconstitutional denial of *Due Process* as applied to D since it permits jurisdiction to be exercised over D without the requisite *"minimum contacts"* with the forum. *Asahi, World Wide Volkswagen* and related cases made clear that the mere foreseeability of tortuous consequences within the forum state was not sufficient to meet the minimum contacts test. If introducing a product into the "stream of commerce," even with some degree of foreseeability that the product will find its way into the forum state, is sufficient contact without some purposeful effort to serve the forum market directly or indirectly (*World Wide VW*), then the mere introduction of a pollutant into the wind stream, even with some degree of foreseeability that it will be carried into the forum state, should be an equally inadequate "contact" on which to base jurisdiction.

P's counter-argument should be that the court's concern in *World Wide VW* was that an isolated fortuity over which defendants had no control should not be enough to expose defendants to suit in a forum in which it has no reasonable expectation of being sued. However, the instant case involves neither an isolated occurrence not a fortuity over which defendants had no control. P's suit involves large amounts of emissions, carried into New York (presumably over a long, continuous period of time) not by a sudden, erratic gust, but by prevailing winds of a basic, normal weather pattern. If a polluter pours wastes into a river, he does so with a knowledge bordering on purposeful action that persons and property in states downstream are likely to be harmed; he should reasonably expect to be called into court in downstream states (the case of some aberration sending the pollutant upstream would be more closely analogous to that in *World Wide VW*). Similarly, if D knew or should have known it was sending pollutants into the air, it could reasonably expect to be called into court anywhere normal wind patterns might carry the pollutants. See *Gray v. American Radiator.*

Moreover, the court in *World Wide VW* was concerned that the events leading to defendant's exposure to jurisdiction should to some degree be within defendant's, and not be exclusively within plaintiff's, control; defendant should have clear notice that it is subject to suit in the forum state so that it can insure itself against the risk or discontinue contact with the state. In this case, D had ample opportunity to avoid litigation in N.Y.; D could have chosen a different fuel or installed pollution-control devices. Conversely, P had no control over the introduction of the pollutant into the forum state. For all these reasons, the court should rule that D's act met the "minimum contacts" standard of *World Wide VW*.

Even if the *World Wide VW* standard was not met, P could argue that the very nature of the interstate pollution problem should move the court to adopt a lower standard such as that employed in *McGee v. Int'l Life Insurance.* Just as the state's heightened interest in providing its citizens with a local forum in which to adjudicate their claims against out-of-state life insurance companies permitted the court to exercise jurisdiction despite a negligible degree of "contact" with the forum, so the state's heightened interest in providing a local forum to its citizens who are victims of pollution-related injuries when the pollution originates out of state, should militate in favor of a reduced "contact" standard. The victim's home state is interested in applying its law to protect citizen-victims, whereas the defendant's state may have relaxed laws in order to promote industrialization. The outcome of this argument is uncertain, however, since it is not clear whether the holding of *McGee* survived that of *World Wide VW*.

Even if the "minimum contacts" are found to be present, C could object that the *fairness standards* of *Asahi and International Shoe* have not been met. They require the court to balance the burden on the defendant in defending the suit in the forum state, the forum state's interest in adjudicating the dispute, the plaintiff's interest in adjudicating the dispute, the plaintiff's interest in obtaining convenient and effective relief, the judicial system's interest in economy, and the interest of the states in furthering certain social policies (see *Kulko*). Here, the burden on defendant, a municipal utility with primarily local functions, may be presumed to be great. New York's interest in asserting jurisdiction (and the interstate social policy interest) may also be great because of the nature of the pollution issue discussed above. Tipping the balance may be P's interest in a local forum and the question of judicial economy. It seems unusual that P who has always lived in northern N.Y. would be bringing suit in the southern, as opposed to the northern district, especially since the facts indicate the pollution was brought into the area in which P "lived and worked." Unless there is some compelling reason why suit in the southern district seemed more reasonable, P has little legitimate interest in this choice of forum. Similarly, judicial economy would argue against asserting jurisdiction, since the trend seems to be to transfer cases out of the southern district whenever possible. Thus, without more information about P's interest in this choice of forum, I would have to conclude that this issue should be resolved in favor of D and the court should dismiss for lack of personal jurisdiction. The same arguments would be raised for and against an objection by D on grounds of *forum nonconveniens*, and although this issue is one of discretion on the part of the court (as opposed to a mandatory issue such as personal jurisdiction), the court should again rule in D's favor.

LET THEM EAT CAKE PROBLEM[9]

It is April of the year 2010. Atlantica has the highest proportion of foreign-born to US-born residents of any state in the United States. It counts some 200 hospitals, private as well as public. These employ a large number of foreign-born nurses. Over the last year, some 50 fatal medical errors were made in the emergency units of these hospitals, half of which were traceable to miscommunication problems involving foreign-born nurses who, when tested later, failed to pass an English proficiency test.

Alarmed, the legislature enacts a law, effective August 1, requiring that emergency-room personnel in all hospitals in the state be composed of persons born in the U.S., or in one of these English-speaking countries: Ireland, the U.K., Canada, Australia, or New Zealand. Hospitals not in compliance will be fined $1,000 for each day of non-compliance, and also lose state funding.

Ivan (born in the former U.S.S.R.), Maria (born in Cuba), and Pierre (born in Senegal) are emergency-unit nurses working in a private hospital in the state. The Emergency Unit Chief rates them as among the best nurses. She so reports to the hospital's Administrator, emphasizing that they speak good English and that she can ill afford to lose them. The Administrator replies that the hospital can ill afford to pay fines or lose state subsidies. He nevertheless asks you, the hospital's in-house lawyer, whether he must comply with the new law. You tell him that it depends on whether the law is valid or not under the U.S. Constitution. You promise to research this subject and send him a written report of your analysis and conclusion. Write that report.

(45 minutes)

---

[9] Yet another Type-Two multi-issue problem that poses only one overall issue that requires complex step-by-step argument, here with a conclusion. It also illustrates the CIRI(P) THREE(b) writing format (pp. 104-105).

A STANDOUT STUDENT ARGUMENT TO LET THEM EAT CAKE[10]

The initial conclusion and implicit issue pinpoint what is at stake: a national origin classification that requires application of the strict scrutiny test.	The new law initiated by the legislature of the state of Atlantica, requiring that emergency room personnel in all hospitals in the state be composed of persons born in the U.S., or in the English-speaking countries of Ireland, the U.K., Canada, Australia, or New Zealand, is a classification based on national origin that violates the 14th Amendment equal protection guarantee.
The relevant constitutional provision is briefly identified and explained.	The relevant law is the Fourteenth-Amendment equal-protection clause that prevents a state from denying to any person within its jurisdiction the equal protection of the laws. The equal protection clause guarantees that similarly situated persons must receive similar treatment under the law.
The first requirement of state action is specified and applied. Note that the reference to the state action requirement is repetitious. State action is easily proved.	The equal protection clause of the Fourteenth Amendment addresses state action only (*Civil Rights Cases*). The *Civil Rights Cases* held that the Fourteenth-Amendment equal-protection clause regulates only actions of the state, not those of private individuals. Congressional authority to enforce the equal protection clause, provided by Sec. 5 of the Fourteenth Amendment, limits authority to regulate state action only.
The next step is the identification of the national origin classification as "suspect" and the specification of the relevant test.	In order for a statute to be judged under Fourteenth-Amendment equal-protection clause, there must be state action. Here, that test is clearly shown. With the legislature's enactment of the very law that is at issue, and the legislature being an arm of the state, state action is clearly met.
The two-part test is then applied to the key facts in two paragraphs. The word "arguably" should be "clearly."	Classifications based on national origin are "suspect" and must be justified by a compelling governmental interest (a pressing public interest) and must also be necessary to the accomplishment of a legitimate interest. Strict scrutiny consists of a two-prong test: the statute must serve a compelling state interest, and it must be narrowly tailored. To be narrowly tailored, the statute must not be over-inclusive or under-inclusive.
The end intended is entirely proper. The difficulty, instead, is in the means chosen.	Under strict scrutiny, the statute must serve a compelling state interest. Here, there is arguably a compelling governmental interest in the state's safety objective of trying to make sure that everyone in the state receives the best emergency care possible.
The invidious discrimination here is spelled out in a persuasive manner. Imagine yourself as Ivan, Maria, or Pierre. This is not what America is supposed to be.	Nevertheless, the means chosen are discriminatory and are not necessary to achieve its objective.
In one cogent sentence, over-inclusiveness of the statute is pinpointed.	The statute must be narrowly tailored to meet that objective. Here, the facts show that all emergency personnel in the hospitals in the state must be composed of persons born in the U.S., or in the English-speaking countries of Ireland, the U.K., Canada, Australia, or New Zealand. The facts further show that Ivan, Maria, and Pierre (born in the former USSR, Cuba, and Senegal, respectively) are thoroughly qualified, speak good English, and are ranked as among the best nurses in a private hospital in the state.

---

[10] This exceptional problem (and argument) emerged from a take-home exam, but it could also appear in a closed-book exam.

The contradiction between the legitimate statutory objective and the illegitimate means provides a concise conclusion.	Thus, the statute is over-inclusive because even though Ivan, Maria, and Pierre satisfy the concerns of the legislation, they would still be excluded from employment based on the broad scope of the impending legislation.
	Based on the facts presented, it appears likely that the statute will fail strict scrutiny because the state's objective in increasing the safety of its citizenry is not met by excluding the likes of all foreign born nationals, save for a few select countries. A justifiable objective must be accompanied by a justifiable means.

Additional Comments

Note how the complicated multi-step argument is simply and fluidly unfolded. From the fundamental framework of the Fourteenth-Amendment's Equal Protection clause, the first requirement of state action is satisfied. The next steps are the identification of the statute as creating a "suspect classification," and the definition and application of the compelling interest test. The final steps in this sophisticated argument are the characterization of the statute as unfairly over-inclusive, and the apt conclusion: "A justifiable objective must be accompanied by justifiable means."

Please note that both this very strong student argument and the prior "Blowing in the Wind" argument illustrate a different architecture for framing and argument. These principle-based arguments are not element centered; instead they emphasize standards and tests or factors as elaborated in relevant case law. Thus, there is a sharp contrast with the typical element-centered argument-making characteristic of, for example, intentional torts and much of criminal law. Instead, here the fundamental and very broad Constitutional principles of Due Process and Equal Protection of the Laws are unfolded in multi-step arguments with the aid of tests and standards, and varying degrees of elaboration of both. Beware the understandable but completely wrongheaded urge to adopt any one form of exam architecture as definitive (e.g., IRAC or even my foundational CIRI(P) ONE format) for all exam arguments. It's a blunder.

ON LOOKING BACK

1. These problems illustrate the types of problems and challenges that you will likely confront, as well as the varied issue-spotting and argument-making skills you'll need to resolve problems with concise, cogent responses—all while faced with intense time pressure. It isn't enough, however, to be aware. As you now know, you must identify each professor's signature pattern of problems and argument-making early in the semester, and then practice it weekly. As you also know, old exams, and especially any available model or strong student arguments, are your best guide for such practice.

2. The prior suggestion to incrementally practice issue-spotting and argument-making, with particular issues in the old exams as each professor teaches the "relevant doctrine" (p. 21), also applies to the exam problems in this Chapter. Old exams take priority, of course, but these problems add additional practice. For students whose professors do not make old exams available, these exam problems could be the priority practice—but use each professor's language if it varies from what is presented here.

Avoiding Common Pitfalls

Keep your emotional balance: don't let resentments seize you

Resentments against your professor, your law school, and life in general cannot be simply forgotten. Contra psychologism, you may not be a "grievance collector" at all, and your resentments, at least some of them, may be well justified. In any event, it is naive to believe that they are forgettable (not after Shakespeare, Freud, and Eugene O'Neill). But they may be temporarily deferrable until after the exams, and it is important to do so—if you can. After years of experience as a member of the Executive Committee at the New York University Law School, dealing with students with academic difficulty, it is plain to me that academic complications are usually a product of what I call eruptions of the human condition: divorces, split-ups in relationships, family crises, emotional upsets including depression, young life crises, and physical illness. Of course, these crises drain your energy and preoccupy your thinking and attention.

If it is impossible to defer the crisis, confront that reality and consider seeking a furlough from school or possibly from the exams. Do not, however, proceed while you are devastated with the expectation that if the exams do not work out well, you can, after the results come out, seek relief *nunc pro tunc*. You will likely meet a frosty reception, and questions as to why you did not raise the matter before the exams. In contrast, requesting relief earlier because of a genuine crisis may well invoke a compassionate response.

Your physical strength and emotional balance are a presupposition of successful exam taking. Guard them carefully.

Keep your intellectual balance: don't become preoccupied with what is secondary, tangential, unclear, or evolving

Keep your eye on the ball. As you now know, most exams are predominantly about basics and various exceptions. Even more challenging issues presuppose the basics. Knowing and applying all the relevant basics and the exceptions emphasized by your professor does more than get you into the ballpark. It can get you a respectable grade, even a very good one, if it empowers your issue spotting and CIRI(P) writing skills. Stress basics and exceptions at every stage: studying, reviewing, outlining courses, and on old exams. Don't ignore any issue because it's too basic.

Avoid the reaction that "she couldn't have meant that we raise this issue: it's too obvious." As noted, she does mean that, and you should quickly demonstrate that you recognize the issue and can resolve it.

It's a beginner's blunder—out of unfamiliarity, insecurity, and frustration—to miss basic issues, often because of a preoccupation with secondary, tangential and irrelevant facts, issues, rules and arguments.

In addition, avoid tendencies to become obsessed with what is unclear, unsettled or evolving. Contrary to naive ideas of the law, each branch has areas that are unclear, unsettled or worse. Lawyers, judges, and commentators in law reviews and elsewhere have typically struggled with these issues for decades, sometimes for centuries. Don't try in your first year in law school to solve this uncertainty. Abandon any expectation that all rules are clear and certain and that you should only learn and apply such rules.

Instead, focus on exactly what is unclear, unsettled, or evolving, and the reasons for this uncertainty. There are always such reasons, and they are often compelling, arising out of competing interests and conflicting policies. Be able to explain these interests and policies, and the different rules that emerge from them. Practice with hypotheticals that illustrate such conflict.

Remember that the grader has a human psychology

Psychology works for you or against you. Make it work for you. Do not underestimate the subliminal power of a neat, attractive, legible exam paper. If it also begins in a clear, cogent manner, you create a positive psychological disposition: the exam looks like an excellent paper. Your professor—all professors—likes to see such exams. Rightly or wrongly, professors feel they are accomplices in an excellent paper: they have contributed by their teaching to the lawyerly excellence of this student. Then an initial series of strong CIRI(P) arguments can sustain this positive tide.

Your professor's positive initial reaction is likely to be accompanied by the expectation that more equally impressive argument will follow. This does not mean that your professor will ignore subsequent deterioration in the quality of your paper. She won't. Nevertheless, the psychological tide, in assumption and expectation, is flowing to your advantage. The value of this positive tide can be appreciated by examining its opposite.

In contrast, do not underestimate the negative, subliminal power of a sloppy, barely legible exam paper that your professor must struggle to understand. If, in addition, it begins in a confused, ill-focused manner, you exacerbate the situation, creating a negative expectation (supported by years of grading experience). The tide is flowing against you, and it is difficult to overcome.

Psychology is important in all grading. Consider its special importance with that segment of professors (including this writer) who grade "subjectively." For example, I read an exam problem carefully, look for issues that I expect to see raised, evaluate how they are framed, and assess the arguments. I do not assign points to particular aspects of the argument, as some other professors do, because I find that so-called "objective" approach not helpful, and even misleading. The quality of each part of the exam and the overall paper are not fully expressible, I believe, in a neat number of points.

As I do this first reading, I form an initial judgment about a grade. Of course, I am influenced by positive and negative psychological reactions about the paper. I then carefully read at least part of the paper a second time. I change my initial grade only in a modest percentage of the papers. The empirical reality is that initial judgments tend to become final. I then proceed to grade the next problem, and so on. If the overall grade is on a borderline, say between a C and a B, I will read again all arguments in that paper and sometimes change the tentative grade. My approach to grading is not universal, but it is not unique, nor even unusual.

For most, use a laptop to write your exams. Many schools permit you to do so, but often with attached conditions. If you write an exam, be sure to write legibly. Ask yourself: do I compose more quickly, without any sacrifice in analytical power, by using a laptop? Do you tend to make changes as you write? Changes are a cinch with a laptop. If you have a learning difference, perhaps a laptop might help you. Don't be shy. I read that David Boies, the remarkable civil trial lawyer, has a severe learning

156

difference and has trouble reading. If you need more time because of a fundamental learning difference, ask for it, and be prepared to carefully document your application.

If you do write your exam, be sure to write legibly. Write on one side of the page and on every other line. It's easier for your professors and if you discover a point or two you want to add after you have written your response, you have space to add the point(s) where it belongs rather than at the end of your argument. Don't abuse this technique, however, with numerous such additions. Follow all exam instructions of your professor, e.g., write only on every other line. Use a decent pen with a fine point. One exceptionally strong student at the New York University Law School (who became the editor-in-chief of the Law Review and later a law professor) told me she used a good pen with a fine point and black ink so that her "arguments would stand out." Have the psychology of grading work in your favor.

An important final recommendation: continue to practice issue spotting and writing exam arguments

Many students, after studying my *Learning Legal Reasoning*, briefing its cases and studying its related materials, tell me that they feel prepared to deal with the dialectics of the law-school classroom. Yes, they are ready to begin doing so. In contrast, after completing this *Exam* book, you are definitely not ready for the formidable law exams. Rather, you are ready to *begin* to prepare for them on paths that will enable you to prepare smart, so that after semester-long practice you are then ready to actually confront the exams with the understanding, performance skills and confidence you need. You will likely avoid all the wrong paths, misconceptions and blunders that afflict and divert so many law students, many of whom are prisoners of their entrenched habits. They prepare vigorously but often for a college rather than a law school exam.

To repeat the mantra a final time: the performance of varied exam issue-spotting and argument-making requires much more than foundational knowledge and understanding. So practice the required performance with hypotheticals each day after class with the rules taught in class and from assigned reading. And include weekly incremental writing of cogent arguments in response to serial issues from old exams and Chapter Six. This dual performance also enables you to learn and understand the required doctrine (rules, principles, policies) with a direct exam focus. To help you with this dual practice, I invite you to contact me at our website if you have a comment or a specific question about it as you proceed [www.JohnDelaneyPub.com]. I will do my best to respond promptly. In addition, there are FAQ and short memoranda that reprise certain parts of the Book. Our website also features a two-page memorandum that could help all students: "A Meta-Framework for Mastery Learning of Law." Over time, student comments have improved this memorandum so that it is now also incorporated in my *Learning Legal Reasoning* as Appendix 'A'.

The website also includes short step-by-step memoranda for "Preparing Before Law School," for "Beginning Law School," and for "Exam Day." They may help you to respond to the really important question that may now be in your mind: HOW SHOULD I PROCEED NOW THAT I HAVE STUDIED THIS BOOK? HOW DO I MAKE ALL THIS DIRECTION REAL FOR ME?

If you have insights from your own preparation, you could share them with others by adding them to my FaceBook page at www.facebook.com/johndelaneypublications.

I am committed to continuing to help students realize their professional dream of becoming a lawyer. Keep at it and prepare smart.

Always seek justice and defend the Constitution.

Professor John Delaney (retired)

APPENDIX A

"HATRI" PRACTICE

Earlier I specified an "Introduction to HATRI" with some easy facts that gave rise to straight-up issues. The purposes of this Appendix, however, are (1) to show you how to practice HATRI during the semester with old exams and other materials, and (2) to demonstrate that HATRI can also unpack more complex legal conflicts with their red-hot facts and resulting issues. As you know, HATRI is an acronym that stands for (1) Harm, (2) Acts and parties, (3) Topics, (4) Rules, and (5) Issues. This presentation presupposes you understand and can apply the five HATRI steps to simple fact illustrations. If you do not understand or cannot perform any of what follows, please check the earlier introductory presentation (pp. 54-56) and write out the exercises there to imprint them in your layered mind.

Do you need to practice HATRI?

First, it's possible that you do not need HATRI. If you have cultivated and convincingly *demonstrated* your own very effective blend of the issue-spotting methods previously detailed, you may not need to practice with HATRI. Sure. But we all deceive ourselves, so to be safe most students should practice HATRI during the semester. It is a safety net you may need on the exam.

For some, learning to practice issue spotting effectively with HATRI is relatively easy. Your mind easily extracts the patterns you need: the necessary responses, the broad and specific categorizations (from Harm, Act and Parties to Topic and Rule), and the resulting extraction of the issue. Indeed, there are some students who find they are natural issue-spotters in applying HATRI (and even without applying it): their minds quickly leap from step-to-step culminating in the articulation of the issues, or their minds skip steps and go directly to the issue. Such leaping and skipping is an extraordinary gift.

For others, it is more difficult—your mind operates in other grooves—and you must practice HATRI a great deal and struggle to overcome weakness. I suggest again that you begin with the basic, more straightforward, issue-spotting examples from simple hypotheticals and only then struggle with the more complicated issue spotting after you have mastered HATRI with the basics. This suggestion merely reiterates the basics-to-complexities model of learning that is essential for so many learners.

As you may have discerned already, this HATRI decoding method works easiest when there are fact patterns that feature *riveting* harms. It therefore may initially work best for you in such areas as torts, criminal law and other subjects in which there are such harms. But the HATRI method may work less well for you in such subjects as civil procedure, evidence, and constitutional law where harms *definitely* exist but may be less riveting, at least when you first begin to study these subjects. An example is "battle-of-the-forms" fact patterns in a contract exam where there may be no single galvanizing event that sparks issue spotting. Instead, the issue(s) emerges from the exchange of forms and other communications and acts.

You might experiment with the HATRI method, ideally using your professors' old exams as the measure of how well HATRI works for you in different subjects. This application of the HATRI method using the old exams offers a subject-by-subject verification procedure for you to determine how effective this method is for you in developing and perfecting your issue-spotting skills. You might initially practice in closed-book fashion, imitating the typical closed-book exam characteristic of most first-year exams. You should begin this practice within a few weeks of starting the semester. If at first the issues do not emerge from your practice of the HATRI method utilizing the closed-book approach, then open your casebook and other materials and practice with an open-book approach until your emerging skill and confidence permit you to close them—and also time yourself in completing your arguments.

You are looking for facts that that are similar to the facts that raised the issues you have already covered in class and in the cases and other materials. Patently, many of the essay issues will be unrecognizable since you have not yet studied the required materials. Don't be discouraged: you are *not* expected to spot issues you have not yet studied. Throughout the semester, you regularly, at least every week or so, practice the HATRI search for additional issues in the old exams. By the end of the semester, you should have spotted all the issues in these old exam problems (and made lawyerly arguments to resolve them). Even better, you have honed your intuitive and related issue-spotting skills, and you have learned much about the fundamental testable doctrine in the course, including the core issue patterns favored by each of your professors in all their exams. You have avoided the classic beginner's blunder of waiting until you "know the materials well" before practicing spotting issues with the old exams.

STEP ONE: "H" (harm) Identify exactly the harm(s) revealed in each paragraph including more sophisticated legal harms

STEP TWO: 'A' (act and parties) Identify who has harmed whom and how

Earlier, you were asked to separately consider these first two steps. Now, you should be able to combine them with the *who-has-harmed-whom* question and the *how-was-this-harm-caused* question. As long as you remember that you are identifying (1) the harm, (2) the parties to the harm, and (3) the act that caused the harm, you can avoid confusion. On exams, it's always one or more of the parties who cause the harm by harm-producing behavior in a unified process. Hence, it's helpful to recognize that interdependence and linking the two questions accomplishes that.

The prior examples earlier in this Book (pp. 55-56) introduced HATRI with straightforward and familiar facts. But harm, as noted, is also used in a more sophisticated legal sense. To illustrate, in Constitutional Criminal Procedure, when the facts spell out a violation by the police of a constitutionally guaranteed right of a defendant (e.g., the failure to administer the *Miranda* warnings properly), that procedural failure by the police is a harm. In First Amendment law, when a protest is squelched in front of City Hall by a police pretext, that spells out harms by the police in the sense of *breach* of their duty to respect the protesters' First Amendment rights (including the right to free expression and the right of assembly). In evidence, when testimony is admitted into evidence by a judge that should be barred by the hearsay or other rule, the admission of such testimony is also a harm. In civil procedure, when an out-of-state corporation pollutes a stream that damages the irrigation of certain farmers in another state, there is a possible procedural harm unless the farmers can get access to the courts to seek damages through their state's long-arm statute that enables them to obtain jurisdiction over the non-resident corporation. As this last example illustrates, the concept of harm includes arguable claims of harm, i.e., a harm that a competent lawyer can argue in a plausible way. In learning each subject, you learn about the set of harms peculiar to that subject. Focusing on these different sets of harms can enable your issue spotting skills.

STEP THREE: "T" (topic) Identify which broad doctrinal topic from your professor's course seems applicable to each harm and behavior.

STEP FOUR: "R" (rule) Hypothesize which rule(s) seems most applicable

As steps one and two can be combined, so too can steps three and four. Conceptually, they can be separated, of course, and it is probably useful to separate them in early practice. But after that, the two steps are so closely related that they can be considered together. After all, once you have the right doctrinal topic, your mind should ordinarily go smoothly to the right rule within that topic. In fact, the right rule is often just the core rule announced by the category, viz., from the topic of negligence to its core rule, from the topic of trespass to its core rule. Of course, if you are experiencing difficulty in selecting the right topics, concentrate on that alone until you feel comfortable with combining steps three and four. If you still encounter difficulty, return to the "Introduction to HATRI" (p. 55). Always individualize general suggestions throughout this book to match your degree of progress in internalizing and demonstrating those skills.

As noted, when the police on a pretext squelch a protest in front of the Mayor's office, you know that the First Amendment *topic* of your professor's course is relevant, and, at the least, the *rules* mandating free speech and assembly are applicable. You might write out in abbreviated form this *topic* and these *rules* on scrap paper or in the margin of your exam paper next to the relevant cluster of red-hot facts: 1st Amend & free speech & assembly. Of course, in selecting one or more topics as relevant to the harm and behavior, you are also zeroing in by excluding as irrelevant the diverse other topics covered in your professor's course.

As you practice this "Step-Three "T" (topic)" selection along with your Step Four "R" (Rule) selection with your professors' old exams and other problems, you'll see more complex legal conflicts, i.e., clusters of facts about harms and behaviors, that trigger the application of more than one doctrinal topic and more than one rule. To illustrate, if A, a driver, carelessly hits and injures B, and the new car's wheel then flies off and injures D because of a manufacturer's defect by M, the doctrinal topics and related rules of negligence, product liability, and breach of warranty are all relevant. Another complex example: If A shoots and kills B, an enemy of theirs, to further an ongoing narcotic venture of A, X, and Z, then the doctrinal topics of murder, conspiracy, and narcotic violation are all relevant. The lesson is clear: as previously stressed, do *not* assume that a single legal conflict involves only two parties, one harm, one act, one topic, and one rule. In the margin of the essay problem or on scrap paper, you might quickly note the relevant topics (Neg., Prod. l., B. of W.; or Hom., Consp., Narc.).

Plainly, it is only those rules within the selected doctrinal topic(s) that are candidates for application. Even more narrowly, it is *only* those rules, within these topics covered in your professors' classes or in the assigned materials that are candidates for selection. Except for the bizarre, professors do not test on rules not covered in class or in assigned materials. Even on bar exams, there are embedded areas of great priority contrasted to others of either marginal or of no significance.

In selecting relevant topics and then the correct rule that applies, you are applying common-law legal argument: i.e., arguing by comparison (analogy) in a search for concrete similarities and differences between the harm(s) and harm-producing behavior(s) detailed in each identified legal conflict and similar harm(s) and behavior(s) detailed in the rules, hypotheticals and other materials you have studied. This search for similarities and differences is roughly akin to what you do in class in reconciling and distinguishing cases by comparing facts from different cases. It is also akin to what you do in practice in seeking relevant authority from appellate cases whose facts are materially similar to the facts in your case.

Your Checklist helps you again

The facts about the abortive First Amendment protest illustrate how your Checklist helps once again. Recall the protest in front of the Mayor's office that is squelched on a police pretext, and the selection of the First Amendment as the relevant topic category. If you studied the First Amendment, the rules mandating free expression and assembly are plainly evident and you should quickly note those two issues. But your Checklist sublistings under this category might well contain abbreviations for additional issue-raising arising from other specified First-Amendment entitlements: rights of association and petition, all of which could also be raised on these facts. Indeed, if the protest contained any religious element, then the facts additionally raise an issue about the right of free exercise of religion. While it's true that a number of these issues could be argued together, it is important to note in your issue-spotting all of the First Amendment issues that are triggered. Without a Checklist, it would be easy to overlook some of these issues. The lesson again: some facts explode with issues, and your Checklist enables quick rolodex scanning of the complete set of relevant issues.

Step Five: "I" (issue) Formulate the issue and verify

Your fifth and final step in mastering HATRI issue spotting is to develop skill in formulating the issue. As you know, you specify the issue in a single sentence in question form, incorporating at least some of the red-hot facts and pointing to the applicable rule. Thus, you formulate the issue in the hypothetical above about the killing in furtherance of a narcotic conspiracy as follows:

> Are A, X, and Z liab. f/ intent. murd. when A sh. & kills B to remove an enem. of the nar. consp. of A, X, and Z?

You verify your intent-to-kill murder hypothesis by matching, either mentally or by quickly outlining, the red-hot facts in this legal conflict with the elements of the two relevant rules, which are the following:

Elements of intent. M. rule	*Red-hot facts*
a) intent to kill	(an inference from) A shooting & killing B
b) manifested in a	(also from) A shooting & killing B
c) criminal-law act that	A shooting
d) causes, both actually and legally,	shooting & killing B
e) the death of another.	killing B

Elements of relevant conspir. rule		*Red-hot facts*
a)	Act by co-conspirator	A sh. & kills B
b)	in further. of consp.	to aid nar. consp.
c)	is act of all co-conspirators[1]	A, Y & Z are co-consp.

You have verified your issue-raising hypothesis about A, Y and Z. First, the red-hot facts prove the elements of the rule of intent-to-kill murder by A of B. Then, the facts also spell out that A intended to kill B to aid the narcotic conspiracy of A, Y and X. The facts also prove this rule, element by element. Your verification of the issue is comparable to what a lawyer does in court when she establishes a *prima facie* case by proving the elements of the crime by, for example, introducing witnesses, whose testimony is the court equivalent of the red-hot facts in the exam essay. (Note that what you are applying here is the legal and fact diagramming previously set forth for learning rules. See pp. 15-17).

A final question to ask yourself in issue verification: Are there facts in the particular legal conflict that raise an arguable question about the application of a relevant affirmative defense? Again, the possibilities do not include all the defenses in the penal code, or even all the defenses you have studied in your professor's course. Rather, they are limited to the restricted set of defenses applicable to a killing and also covered in your professor's course. Typically, these might be the following:

> self-defense
>
> defense-of-another
>
> defense of habitation
>
> prevention of a felony
>
> apprehension of a fleeing felon

A moment's reflection should enable you to reject out of hand the relevance of all these defenses here because there are absolutely no facts contained in the cluster of facts comprising the legal conflict that

---

[1] Have you noticed that the existence of a conspiracy is a *given* in the facts. Thus, there is no issue about it to be raised. Instead, you simply note in your argument that the existence of the conspiracy is a given in the facts.

raise a question about the arguable application of any of these defenses. No facts mean no issue. Remember always that spotting issues is fact driven, not speculation driven. Avoid the common beginner's blunder of raising issues when there is no factual basis for doing so, issues about which your professor is not inquiring in her fact pattern, what some professors call "red herrings." You have now completed the verification of your issue hypothesis. Below are examples of what your HATRI practice sheet might look like. Remember that abbreviations are personal and yours should eventually be much briefer.

HATRI SHEET FOR PRACTICING

Basic examples:

Harm & Parties	Act	Topic	Rule	Issue
Killing of B by A	A shoots B	Hom.	i-k M	Is A, who shoots and k. B, l. [liable] f/ I-k M?
Injury of B by A	A's car hits B	Neg.	basic	Is A, whose car hits B, l. to B f/ neg?
A's intr. v. B	A walks on B's land	Trespass	basic	Is A, who intrudes on B's land l. to B f/ tres?

More complicated examples:

Harm & Parties	Act	Topic	Rule	Issue
Injury by M of B	wheel hits D	Neg.[2]	basic	Is M l. to B f/ neg when wheel flies off & hurts D?
	M's defect	Prod./L	basic	Is M also l. to B f/ P.L when…?
		Br/War	basic	Is M also l. to B f/ B/W when…?
Death of B by A	A sh.B.f/nar. conspiracy	Hom.	i-k m.	Is A l. f/ i-k. m when …?
Death of B by A		Consp.	Act in fur. of consp. is act of all conspir.	Are X & Z also l. f/ i-k. m./ when A sh. B to further consp?
Freed. of expres. denied	Protest squel. on pretext	1st Amen.	Rts. of free assem., speech print, assoc., pet.	Are pol. l f/ denying rights of assembly, etc.

2 Though facts spelling out negligence are scant, the rule of *res ipsa locquitur* enables B in his negligence claim to establish a *prima facie* case at trial.

Exam Checklists[1]

Criminal Law Exam Checklist

1. Cons. Frame. X-post-facto Attainder. Vague. Overbr.	**2. Core Prin.** Mens Rea (Int., reck., Cr. Neg., know.) Concurr. Act Caus. Harm
3. Parties Prin. Accom. & Facilitators	**4. Cr. Hom.** Murd.: In-K M Ex.Reck.M Fel.M Cap.Pun. Mans.: In.-Infl.-Ser-Bod.-Inj Man.[2] Vol-Heat-of-Pass.Mansl/Ex.-Emot.- Dist.Mans. Reck. Mans. Cr.- Neg Mans
5. Inchoate cr. Solic. Attemp. – C.L & MPC Consp. - 3 C.L. types plus RICO Consp.	**6. Just & Exc.** S/D Def. of Anoth. Def. of Prop., Habit. Preven. of Fel. Ignor. or mistake of Fact & Law Entrap.; Necess. - publ & priv. Dur. & Neces.
7. Presuppos. for criml liabil missing if: Legal Insan. Immat. Intox ?	**8. Other crimes** C/L larc. Embez. Larcen. by Fals. Pret., or Trick Robb.& rape

---

[1] Use of your own abbreviations enables you quickly to compile your Checklist at the beginning of each exam. This criminal law example almost certainly includes more topics than would be covered in a typical 3-hour, one-semester criminal-law course. Coverage in scope and hours in any course varies extensively depending on professorial priorities and resulting choices.

[2] Murder in some states.

Tort Exam Checklist[3]

1. <u>Neg.</u>
   Elements of *prima facie* case:
   Duty owed?
   Duty of reas. care or other stand.
   Breach
   Causation, legal & fact.
   Harm
   Respondeat Superior
   Orig. Tortfeas.
   Med. Malprac.
   Fail. to Super.
   Gross negl.
   Punit. Dam.
	2. <u>Defen. To Neg.</u>
	   Contrib.
	   Compar.
	   Assump. of risk
	   No duty

3 <u>Intent. Ts.</u>
   Assaul.
   Batt.
   False Impris.
   In. Infl. Emot. Stress.
   Trespass v. land or chattel
   Conver.
	4. <u>Other defens.</u>
	   Consent
	   Public & Private Necess.
	   Self def. & def. of anoth.

5. Vicar. Liabil.	6. Strict Prod Liabil.
7. Wrongful Death & compensat. & pun. Dam.	8. Defamation: slander & libel

[3] Again, this tort example of a Checklist could be greatly abbreviated and almost certainly includes more topics than would be covered in a typical one-semester tort course. And again, coverage in any course also varies extensively depending on professorial priorities and resulting choices.

OTHER BOOKS BY PROFESSOR JOHN DELANEY

Learning Legal Reasoning, Briefing, Analysis and Theory, 1983, 1987, 2006, 2011

This widely used book in many printings begins with responses to over forty commonly asked questions of first-year law students. It then specifies a six-step approach to briefing a case with specific guidelines for accomplishing each step. The process of briefing cases is then demonstrated with excellent and poor briefs of increasing complexity. Emphasis is placed initially on the techniques of briefing as an introduction to the learning of legal reasoning, the first priority of the first year of law school. In addition, the book also demonstrates the relevance of more advanced modes of legal reasoning, the different architectures, including positivist, pragmatic, policy-oriented, natural-law and other perspectives in decoding and understanding cases. In its introduction of jurisprudential perspectives, *Learning Legal Reasoning* transcends the typical and insufficient legal-positivist orientation of most first-year materials.

Learning Criminal Law As Advocacy Argument: Complete With Exam Problems & Answers, 2004

The theme of this book springs from a comment made to Professor John Delaney by the late Kellis Parker, a brilliant professor (and musician) at the Columbia University Law School. Kellis said: "Students should know the issues that will be raised before they go into the exam room." What he meant was that the set of issues that your teacher typically raises on her exam can be identified before the exam. Decoding and answering these issues with lawyerly arguments can then be practiced and perfected throughout the semester. This book shows you, step-by-step and from basics to complexities with building-block problems, how, over the course of the semester, to decode and resolve the set of commonly raised issues in each topic presented by criminal law professors.

Available from the publisher

John Delaney Publications
119 Green Point Road
Catskill, NY 12414
518-943-9507
www.johndelaneypub.com
www.facebook.com/johndelaneypublications

Other memoranda and FAQ at our website to guide your preparation

Preparing for the Law School Classroom

Preparing for Law School Exams

Suggestions for Preparing Before Law School and Advice for Students Beginning Law School

Suggestions for the Day of the Exam

CIRI(P) Essay Writing Formats Compared to the Reductive IRAC Formats

Essential Differences Between College and Law School Exams

A Meta-Framework for Mastery Learning of Law

THE END